TOM BLASS studied anthropolc _____ politics, and has earned his living as a journalist and editor specialising in issues relating to business, law, human rights and foreign policy. He lives with his family in Hastings. His first book, *The Naked Shore*, was published in 2016.

BY THE SAME AUTHOR

The Naked Shore

SWAMP SONGS

Journeys through Marsh, Meadow and Other Wetlands

TOM BLASS

BLOOMSBURY PUBLISHING
LONDON • OXFORD • NEW YORK • NEW DELHI • SYDNEY

BLOOMSBURY PUBLISHING
Bloomsbury Publishing Plc
50 Bedford Square, London, WC1B 3DP, UK
29 Earlsfort Terrace, Dublin 2, Ireland

BLOOMSBURY, BLOOMSBURY PUBLISHING and the Diana logo are trademarks of
Bloomsbury Publishing Plc

First published in Great Britain 2022
This edition published 2023

Copyright © Tom Blass, 2022

Tom Blass has asserted his right under the Copyright, Designs and Patents Act, 1988, to be
identified as Author of this work

Extract from *Letters from Iceland* by W. H. Auden and Louis MacNeice, published
by Faber and Faber © W. H. Auden and Louis MacNeice, 1937
Extract from *Wintering Out* by Seamus Heaney, published by Faber and Faber
© Seamus Heaney, 1972

All images Copyright © Tom Blass, apart from the below:

Dismal Swamp © DeAgostini/Getty Images
Dymchurch Sea Wall © Getty Images/OzziesImages
'The Owlers Chase the Customs Officers into Rye', illustrated by Paul Hardy, from
The *Smugglers* by Charles G. Harper
Tollund man © Werner Forman/Universal Images Group/Getty Images

All rights reserved. No part of this publication may be reproduced or transmitted
in any form or by any means, electronic or mechanical, including photocopying,
recording, or any information storage or retrieval system, without prior permission
in writing from the publishers

A catalogue record for this book is available from the British Library

ISBN: HB: 978-1-4088-8435-5; PB: 978-1-40888-434-8;
EBOOK: 978-1-4088-8433-1; EPDF: 978-1-5266-5249-2

2 4 6 8 10 9 7 5 3 1

Typeset by Newgen KnowledgeWorks Pvt. Ltd., Chennai, India
Printed and bound in Great Britain by CPI Group (UK) Ltd, Croydon CR0 4YY

To find out more about our authors and books visit www.bloomsbury.com
and sign up for our newsletters

For Marie, Zoë, Daisy and Ludo

Contents

Introduction
Its Strange Mystery

I have an immoderate passion for water ... especially for marshes, teeming with all that mysterious life of the creatures that haunt them. A marsh is a whole world within a world, a different world, with a life of its own, with its own permanent denizens, its passing visitors, its voices, its sounds, its strange mystery.

From 'Love – Three Pages From a Sportsman's Book',
Guy de Maupassant, *Complete Short Stories*, 1903

Here was a nice little irony to ponder on, whiling away the drive around the edge of the Great Dismal Swamp, a few weeks away from the presidential election of 2016, that among the other slogans such as 'Lock Her Up' and 'Make America Great Again', pasted onto placards outside white-owned, white-fenced, white-porched homes around the suburb of Suffolk, Virginia, was the exhortation to 'Drain the Swamp'.

This was the promise that one of the candidates said he would deliver upon in the event of his being elected to the White House.

The swamp in question was not the seething, breathing morass of tangled trees, vines and squelching ooze a few hundred yards from the road. The local community had long ago given up trying – or even wanting much – to drain *that* swamp, although George

Washington, the first elected president of the United States, had given much of his life in the endeavour, harnessing the power of slaves to suck dry the real-life quagmire, felling swamp oak and cypress trees, digging irrigation canals, desiccating ponds. But he never succeeded, albeit the effort was financially rewarding and presented no hindrance to his presidential career.

In the city to which he had given his name, 'swamp' has its own connotations.

A grotesque image by the cartoonist Ben Garrison depicts presidential candidate Donald Trump pulling a giant bath plug, sending his rival Hillary Clinton, her husband Bill and other 'enemies of the people' spiralling into a vortex of dark waters, crime, corruption, lies and war.

Trump would have 'approved the message', as candidates invariably say of campaign initiatives that endorse them. But he wasn't the first to use the slogan, long understood as shorthand for ridding American politics of backroom dealing and pocket-lining by unelected, vested interests.

In another neat irony, the analogy was a favourite with early twentieth-century left-wing thinkers like Winfield R. Gaylord, who wrote, 'Socialists are not satisfied with killing a few of the mosquitoes which come from the capittalist [sic] swamp; they want to drain the swamp.'

In other words, the swamp is in the eye of the beholder. In its murk, bad things thrive. Boggarts and monsters, disease and disorder.

It was from the 'moor-fen, marsh and fastness' that hideous Grendel, son of Cain, inflamed by jealousy stoked by the hearty laughter of Beowulf and the Scyldings, sloped towards the mead-hall to wreak havoc. And back to it he slunk. And if he is the worst of them, almost every bog, marsh and fen has its own cast of spooky inhabitants, from the Bunyip of Aboriginal legend to Jenny Greenteeth, the slime-covered child-killer residing in cattle-ponds and other wet places in the north-west of England, and the Honey Island Monster, which stalks the inaccessible fastnesses of Louisiana's Pearl River.

In the lavatory at the car park at the beginning of a walking trail through the Great Dismal Swamp, I found a chilling graffito: 'Swamp Thing was here.'

Bog, marsh and swamp are night-places illumined only by twilight or by the will-o'-the-wisp, harbinger of ghastly things, performing its *danse macabre* upon their ink-black surface, spectral and taunting like a lost love.[1]

A swamp is unnavigable and typically described as 'treacherous', each step taken within it leading deeper into danger.

In his book *Swamplands of the Soul*, the popular Jungian psychoanalyst James Hollis describes middle age as a time for facing up to life's bogeymen of despair, fading prowess, anxiety, neurosis and mortality. By encompassing both the bright meadow and the bog, he says, 'the goal of life is not happiness but meaning. And meaning, though it may not be all sunlight and blossoms, is nonetheless real.'

And Rod Giblett, author of a book called *Cities and Wetlands*, makes the psychological link with wetlands explicit. Like subconscious desires that we find troubling, we push them beneath the surface or resort to complex denials of their existence.

But as with the suppression of such thoughts, they never entirely disappear.

His book, he says,

> is located within a psychoanalytic ecology that not only
> reads the symptoms and engages in a talking cure of the
> psychogeography of the will to fill and the drive to drain
> wetlands inscribed on the surface of the body of the earth in
> the foundation and development of the city, but also nurtures
> gratitude for the generosity of the earth exemplified in wetlands
> and so tries to prevent the manifestation of those symptoms
> in the first place by developing health through bio- and
> psychosymbiotic lives and livelihoods with it and its wetlands.

[1] In fact, that phenomenon is thought to be caused by self-igniting emissions of the gas phosphene, a product of rotting vegetation.

Good bogs can have that effect.

Long considered dark, subversive, foetid and odorous, our most 'civilising' instincts demand that such places be tamed, drained and defeated, their monsters dragged from obscene and stinking lairs.

Where there are reeds, frogs, eels and fish, birds, leeches and salamanders, impenetrable labyrinths of gnarled-knuckled swamp trees, snakes, bugs and alligators, let there be sweet grasses, wheat fields, potato patches and shopping malls.

One of the largest of the latter in the United Kingdom, the Bluewater Shopping Centre in the county of Kent, is named after the curiously limpid and blue ponds that once sparkled where it now stands. Such is progress.

Their fertile vulnerability is, no doubt, the reason that wetlands make such easy prey for despots and dictators: Julius Caesar had designs on the Pontine Marshes, seeing the potential for job creation by rerouting the Tiber and draining off the wetlands. But Benito Mussolini delivered the goods. What once was interminably bug-blighted and uncultivable is an expanse of featureless arable fields, a 'victory' for Il Duce's 'Battle of the Swamps', the execution of which was undertaken from the 1920s by workers housed in internment camps surrounded by barbed wire. Many would contract malaria in the process. Now, at the heart of the regional town of Latina, among other oddities of municipal architecture, sits a fountain from which emerges a sphere. New land forged from water. Light from dark.

If land reclamation was among the more benign elements of the Fascist experiment, in the Middle East, a dictator's pet project took a darker turn.

Firelight on a half-turned face, the crying of geese, duck flighting in to feed, a boy's voice singing somewhere in the dark, canoes moving in procession down a waterway, the setting sun seen crimson through the smoke of burning reedbeds, narrow waterways that wound still deeper into the Marshes. A naked man in a canoe with a trident in his hand, reed houses built upon water, black dripping buffaloes that

looked as if they had calved from the swamp with the first
dry land.

Such were the explorer Wilfred Thesiger's memories of his first
visit, in 1950, to the marshes of Southern Iraq at the confluence of
the rivers Euphrates and Tigris, where the Marsh Arabs, the Ma'dān,
lived on artificial islands made of reeds, patrolling the channels in
their sleek-as-dagger war canoes, fishing for catfish the size of boar,
and boar the size of horses…

Only a few decades later, Saddam Hussein, seeking revenge
for the Ma'dān's role in the insurrection after the first Gulf War,
sought to destroy the marshes, obliterating a way of life with its
origins some indeterminable time ago, long, even, before the birth
of Muhammad.

Where there is a marsh or swamp, the rule is that someone has
a scheme to drain it, pluck from it its riches and return it to the
world settled, compliant, well ordered (or non-existent).

It is misleading to overplay the opposition between the agencies
of 'Man' and 'Nature'. Wetlands are malleable landscapes shaped
by numerous forces.

What the hand of Man taketh away, sometimes it giveth back.

In East Anglia there is a scheme in place to reproduce, in
some form, the majesty of the Great Fen, which from the 1630s
onwards had been assiduously drained to create 'useful' arable
fields.

'Lusty sweating pioneers', as one contemporary chronicler
described the mostly Dutch labourers, used long-perfected
techniques to transform the Fen from wild fecundity to tame
productivity, waging their war not only against the land, but the lives
of its inhabitants, who had made peace with their aqueous world, but
were seen by outsiders as less than human, subsisting on a 'stinking
diet' of eels, waterfowl and amphibians.

'The rugged condition & debauch'd manners of the people give
but little, all alike neither sweet, clean, nor good … I know not
what to make of them, I think they be half fish, half flesh, for they
drink like fishes, & sleep like hogs, & if the men be such creatures,

judge what their women are…' observed a nose-holding visitor from London.

While the Great Fen project may bring back the booming bittern, the newt and the crane, its human inhabitants, if it is to have any, will enjoy lives as sweet-smelling and banal as the rest of us.

But in Iraq, the rewilding of the marshes of the Euphrates and Tigris is encouraging a return to a life lived on islands of reeds, to the hunting of boar, wildfowling, building of canoes and other apogees of marshland artfulness and ingenuity. The old traditions and underpinning social structures that Thesiger and his acolyte Gavin Maxwell described are remembered, sweetly, painfully, and with the return of the waters may flourish in new forms.[2]

Wetlands can come about quite incidentally to the grand scheme of things. Walking with a friend in the rolling lake district of the north-eastern corner of Poland, I came upon a handful of acres of land within a deciduous forest that had turned to swamp. Trunks of birch and alder lay across each other in a lattice of their own making, semi-submerged in a murky stew of duckweed and fallen leaves. On higher ground, a riot of froglets bounced and crawled across every nearby path, their parents hooting in the margins. There were other such flaws in the forest, which, though only a hundred miles or so from the Baltic, in appearance were something akin to the Atchafalaya Basin of Louisiana, which I had yet to visit.

---

[2]Perhaps Rod Giblett should be indulged when he gushes forth thus: 'Wetlands as womb are the source of life and wetlands as living waters are the first source of nourishment, the first object of love and the first object to be lost in modernisation, colonisation, drainage and "progress".' But I'd suggest he could have been reined in before continuing: 'The living waters of wetlands thus enact, more so than others, a sense of the loss of the breast as a loved object … The loved object, which is lost for the melancholic, is the breast of the mother and the water that is specifically breast milk is the water of the wetland, the first water that nourished life, the breast of mother earth…'

Their existence, said a taxi driver whom we asked about these jade-green jewels, was owed to the efficiency of one national character, or the fecklessness of another, depending on how you looked at it.

Before the First World War, he explained, the area was a part of Prussia, and inhabited almost exclusively by ethnic Germans. Under the terms of the Treaty of Versailles, the Mazury region was absorbed by Poland. The Germanophones stayed until the end of the next war, after which they were pushed out, leaving their houses, fields and carefully tended estates. The new, Soviet-installed Polish government resettled the locality with ethnic Ukrainians, who, while they were grateful for houses, had little interest in managing the land left behind by the Germans. Fields reverted to forest and grassland, and in the forests, trees fell, as it were, of their own accord, or flattened by the wind and lightning, leaving craters where they had once stood. Nature flourished. Swamps ensued.

And the 'wetland' that forms the touchstone of this book, Romney Marsh, would scarcely exist at all, were it not for having been 'inned' – reclaimed, patch by patch, through the careful application of embankments and sewers (that term referring not to anything sordid or unpleasant in their content but on account of their 'sewing together' the land).

None of which is by way of presenting an apologist's argument on behalf of humanity, but only to ask whether and how a 'good' intervention can, in each case, be distinguished from a poor one.

The contemporary generic term for the kind of terrain through which this book wades is 'wetland', a good, clean, healthful, post-superstitious word. But a more archaic taxonomy, using marsh, bog, fen, fenny and quagmire, says more about our experience of such places before ready access to insect repellent, boardwalks and nature trails robbed them of their mystery.

A marsh, typically, is a wet area, permanently or seasonally saturated, 'characterized by herbaceous (non-woody) vegetation', according to the United States Environmental Protection Agency. It may be coastal, and if that's the case, it is, in all probability, salt marsh. Or it may occur inland, at the fringes of a river or a lake.

Swamps are mostly characterised by forest or mangroves, and bogs by peat deposits.[3] And there are deltas, fens and water meadows, science-speak creating a new word for every soggy place. It would be verging on the absurd to overly attribute common characteristics to wetlands. Parallels between the France-sized Sudd of South Sudan and a repurposed sewage works on the edge of metropolitan London, or between the glacier-fed river meadows of Iceland and the Florida Everglades, are tenuous at best. The view afforded by standing upon a bench or hummock on Romney Marsh stretches thirty miles, absence of mist or other vapour permitting. In the Great Dismal Swamp of the American South, the gaze is quickly baffled by a screen of trees. Or met by that of a terrapin.

But look harder, and points of convergence come into focus. Such places, 'fen-sucked', frustrating, boggy, buggy, bedevilled by fever and agues (and of course, the *mal aria* or 'bad air'), rebuff and are rebuffed by 'normal' society and its plodding agglomerations, and thus become attractive to, or last resorts for, outcasts, misfits and escapees. And, or, safe spaces for smuggling, banditry or insurrection.

Not all wetland dwellers were born to their environments. Nor do they possess the fabled and apocryphal webbed feet of the inhabitants of the Venetian lagoon. Many were hounded, literally, to where baying dogs could no longer find their scent, their destinies entwined with lianas and creeping vines only because their fellow men made it so.

I can make no claim to swampy origins, mine being a London childhood of the 1970s. But two pictorial recollections from that time come to mind.

---

[3]You might like this little song that I wrote to remind myself of the differences between types of wetland:

> A marsh is like a swamp without the trees.
> A swamp is only marsh with trees and 'gators
> And a bog is just a bog, a plain, bog-standard bog
> From whence dig your peat and your potaters…'

Or you might not.

The first was that of the quiet repose and soft-wrinkled eyelids of Tollund Man, whom I found in *The Bog People*, by P. V. Glob, a favourite book on my father's shelves.

Tollund's remains had been pulled from a Jutish meadow in Denmark, and I should have been frightened by his photograph, but looked upon it as strangely peaceable, despite the ligature that had strangled him some two millennia past, and from which he has yet to be freed. Tollund has been accorded, if not eternity, extraordinary longevity, by the dark and preserving power of the peat.

Less dramatic, but still affecting, was a picture card from a box of tea I found in the drawer of my great-aunt's kitchen table, with a picture of a Stone Age Man evading unseen pursuers by submersing himself in a lake and breathing through a reed, impossible to see among the bulrushes.

Both impressed upon me, though I scarcely knew it, the antiquity of human acquaintance with such places, for if the world's humours have been tipped towards the dry, it wasn't always the case. Where there are swamps and marshes, there was good living to be had. And it has been had, by, among innumerable others, the fen-dwellers of East Anglia, the swamp-living Seminole of Florida, the Ma'dān of the Euphrates, the Lipovan of Romania, the Cajuns of Louisiana. And the Marshmen of Romney Marsh.

I

The Fifth Continent

The World, according to the best geographers, is divided into Europe, Asia, Africa, America, and Romney Marsh. In this, and fifth, quarter of the globe, a Witch may still be occasionally discovered in favourable, i.e., stormy, seasons, weathering Dungeness Point in an eggshell, or careering on her broomstick over Dymchurch wall. A cow may yet be sometimes seen galloping like mad, with tail erect, and an old pair of breeches on her horns, an unerring guide to the door of the crone whose magic arts have drained her udder...

From *The Ingoldsby Legends*, Thomas Ingoldsby (*nom de plume* of the Reverend Richard Barham), 1837

So commonplace has it become among the tribe of those that have written about Romney Marsh to repeat the observation made of it, almost five centuries past, by William Lambarde in his *A Perambulation of Kent*, that it is, '*Hyeme malus, Aestate molestus, Nunquam bonus*' ('Evil in Winter, grievous in Summer, and never good') that I can scarcely refrain from doing so too.

The phrase tickles even those that love the Marsh and find it always good, not least in winter, when the skies are strafed with rain, and birds fly in from the north and the east for shelter, and summer, which sees the sheep fattening beneath the clouds they almost resemble, because it speaks of its dramas, human and otherwise, and its floods.

Romney Marsh, an easy eastward journey from Hastings, where I live on the south coast of England, is a favourite place for long and contemplative walks, for sounding things out in one's head, undisturbed by superfluous features such as hills or trees, or many, or any, of the conventional accoutrements of scenic beauty. It is unforgivingly flat and harsh, and by its strangeness turned me towards writing this book.

But there are days that I find myself agreeing with Lambarde, when one strains to write about Romney Marsh, its dull, wet fields and ditches, and villages that he described as 'not thicke set, nor much inhabited'. For it boasts no quick-beating heart and few vital organs, and even fails against an (unscientific) suite of criteria by which one may measure 'marshiness'.

A marsh, one might presume, should give way underfoot, or be wholly unsuited to walking. Fit only for sliding and wading. Stilts, perhaps, or a canoe. But Romney crackles in the summer when the hay stalks, and the sheep turds and the cowpats, are done to a turn. In winter it yields little more, plough-pillaged acres stiff or frozen. Should it not be, in short, wetter than this deadpan plain with no punchline and little squelch?

And yet.

The marsh frogs chirruping in the ditches, the breeze in the reeds, the marsh warblers clutching their stems, in their wiry claws, and even the presence of the greater water parsnip, denizen of 'watery places', though kissing cousin of the carrot, cry out that Romney has a place in the marshy tribe.

The expanse that is generally referred to as Romney Marsh is more properly three marshes. Walland Marsh makes up, roughly, the western corner, and is separated from Romney Marsh *proper* by the near-mythic Rhee Wall, now for the most part a stretch of the A259 road, but in medieval times a watercourse for carrying silt back to the sea, until it too fell prey to its burden.

Romney Marsh, closer to the sea than Walland, was reclaimed later than its neighbour. Denge Marsh, in the south-east corner, is, for the most part, a tough, calloused heel of wild, shingled near-desert jutting into the English Channel. And while the strange thrill of seeing France is seldom afforded from the Marsh itself, it is, not infrequently, from cliffs close by, at Fairlight and Hythe, on the scant occasions that a particular species of fog sprawls across La Manche and serves up the Côte d'Opale as a hovering, wobbling mirage.

Inland, the marsh is bounded by the Weald of Kent, an arc of woods and hills described by G. K. Chesterton in 'The Old Song' as 'the place where London ends, and England can begin', and which, though it's now peaceable and pretty, was, in the early nineteenth century, seized with the fury of the 'Captain Swing rioters', farm workers who feared obsolescence in the face of threshing machines and drought.

Between Weald and Marsh, a lazy, sometimes sharply zagging line is drawn by the course of the Royal Military Canal, built at the order of that precocious prime minister, William Pitt the Younger – hence its slangy original moniker, 'Pitt's Ditch'. The intention was to foil Napoleonic invasion, combining a canal with a parapet from which dragoons could shoot the French as they marched across the Marsh.

It is, despite its pompously upright proper name, the gentlest of waterways, mostly untroubled by boats, but beloved by dragonflies and kingfishers.

Where the Marsh meets the sea, its yawning flatness is held together by shingle, and by the rolling dunes of Camber Sands, before curving towards Dungeness, which, in summer, is overrun by sea kale, psycho-geographers, and, dammit, by people like me, drawn by the boxy power stations, by the sloping shingle plunging violently into the sea, and by the promise of a quite excellent crab sandwich.

Running north to Dymchurch, the artificial sea wall, built and rebuilt like a tale told over and over, bounds and binds the three marshes. Were the wall ever to give way, or when it does, in the space of two tides, the Marsh would, or will, become a huge expanse of mire. The fingerless hands of the sea, having raked out the guts and sewers, ditches and hedges, would wipe the slate clean, drown the sheep, smother their bleats, sluice the ancient churches and the farms-turned-B&Bs, the Sainsbury's in New Romney, the weekend homes, and the pleasant opportunities for bicycle touring in the more clement months.

Molluscs would then reign in a kingdom of mud. In spring and autumn, even greater numbers of birds would spend the season here than the thousands that do already. Silt would block rivers and change their course. The shingle beaches would be all over the place, sweeping up and down the coast like windscreen wipers. Sometimes, the sea-turned soil would burst into meadowed splendour.

Of sheep, there would be fewer.

All this may yet come to be.

Were it to, William Dugdale would thunder from his grave at the negligence that permitted it.

Dugdale, historian, fellow of the College of Arms and witness to the Battle of Edgehill, is the author of *The History of Imbanking and Drayning of Divers Fenns and Marshes*, a tome which, though published in 1662, remains the definitive work on Romney Marsh.

It was of this 'spacious tract', he wrote, that the absence of written records, 'left from any historian', does 'strongly prove', that 'the first gaining [of land from the sea]' is a work of great antiquity.

But this is not an achievement that could ever be credited to the ancient Britons, for they were too 'rude and barbarous', just as the Saxons were too 'illiterate'.

Thus, by a process of elimination, nudged along, perhaps, by his age's adulation of the classical, he points the finger at the Romans, and notes by way of proof that Tacitus said they were always being moaned at by the natives for wearing them out with clearing woods and building roads – and 'banking the fens'.

Venerable and learned as Dugdale was, he may have underestimated the Saxons and stood, in this particular, in undeserved awe of the Romans, who, though they built modestly fancy saltworks where the shifting sands allowed, harboured no great hopes of more extensive reclamation.

By the close of the Roman era, floods across the Marsh brought sufficient sediment that the landscape they had left behind began to wear its modern clothes: mostly dry, even at high tide.

The Saxons helped by 'inning', draining out parcels of land by digging ditches and sewers, creating embankments that also served as way-paths. Far from being illiterate, they were prone, if anything, to a prolixity that would wed the transformation of the Marsh to the law, and helps us read in it the evolving relationship between Church and State, especially through land grants of the following kind:

> In the name of Our Lord Jesus Christ, I, Whitred, king of the men of Kent, having my future in mind, have decided to give away something of all that has been given to me. After taking counsel, it has seemed good to give to the church of the Blessed Mary, the Mother of God, which is situated in a place called Lyminge, the land of four ploughs which is called Pleghelmestun ... Also I grant to be possessed for ever by the same mother of God, Blessed Mary, a little land called Ruminging seta, for the pasture of 300 sheep. This is on the south side of the river Limenea but we do not set down the boundaries because they are well known to the countryfolk all around.

In 1287 the Marsh was hit by a great storm (it is, indeed, referred to in texts as 'The Great Storm'), which not only redrew the map, destroying the town of old Winchelsea and flooding Walland Marsh, but brought far-reaching political changes, the vestiges of which remain, at least in ceremonial guise, today.

And yet there is much about the Marsh that must look little changed from the time of Whitred's gift. Sheep still graze on its pastures as they ever did. The Church remains the owner of much of the land. Nobody is quite sure where or what the river Limenea was or where it ran, but boundaries are 'well known to the countryfolk all around'. And now as ever, there is need for vigilance against the 'inundations of the sea'.

But it has recovered from a reputation for sickliness. Lambarde held that parts of Kent were healthy, others were wealthy, some healthy and wealthy, but the Marsh had the curious distinction of being wealthy, on account of its rich grazing, but unhealthy, the air full of mists and mortal miasmas.

He noted the absence of homes fit for gentry, who spent their fleece-money on houses in the pleasant uplands and maternal folds of the Weald, where the air was wholesome, anemones and bluebells flourished among sylvan hills, lichened woodland lent lingering shade, and from the not-dizzying but refreshing heights of which you might gaze upon your grazing assets masticating on the almost tessellated pastures, with half an eye on lucrative markets across the Channel.

The ague was long waved away by steam trains, modernity and other balms. The players have come and gone, but the soft boards, though well-trod, bear and are marked by the weight of the years. As it must have always, the sea-mist imparts a salty tang to a joint of lamb, and the sense not only of apartness, but ephemerality, contingency, as though it may all yet slip away, endures.

All that, and the Marsh still isn't posh.

Everything, by which I mean to say, the very little, that I might now *know* about the Marsh, as distinct from what I've read about it, has been by way of excursion from Hastings, following the road northward via the nondescript suburb of Ore, and then along the coast as it rises and falls with the line of cliffs, down beyond Fairlight. ('Strange goings on in Fairlight,' an antiques shop owner in nearby St Leonards once told me. '*Swinging* and so forth.' His wife had left him for a policeman.)

It heads east, to Pett Level, past the former coastguards' houses, which, though tiny, have become desirable and expensive, and underneath the sea wall, with, to the north, the beginning of the Royal Military Canal, where, depending on the season, any number of twitchers park up by the side of the road in the hope of seeing the voluminous flocks of lapwings or curlews, a rare bean goose among the ubiquitous greylags, the harrier on its daily rounds, or even a snow bunting.

In keeping with the rule about the gentry living on the hill, the silhouette of Paul McCartney's windmill-turned-recording studio up at Peasmarsh is just visible on the skyline.

The road passes on, through Winchelsea Beach, keeping the rough-looking pub beside the Co-op on the left, and further along on the right, the posh-but-odd Ship Inn with its 'high-class butcher' strangely affixed, before slowing as it heads into the environs of Rye, a prim and doughty town of tidy streets and tea shops that keeps its eye on the Marsh but its mind on other things. It curves around the bend, where silver-haired bikers like to meet on Sunday afternoons, past the cricket pitch and the skate park and the rugby club and the hut selling fish on the quayside, and across the Rother on the quick and narrow bridge, and finally on to the Marsh...

Romney Marsh is a hard taskmaster. You could drive across it in distracted mood and notice only that you'd noticed nothing. Its points of interest are spread wide apart and unsung. The little huts, in which shepherds, or 'lookers', sheltered from sweeping winds and pitiless rain, are mostly dissolved in those elements – and the 'lookers' themselves, likewise, are a vanished feature.

Perhaps, that way, the dykes are kept safe from cagoul-igans, and smugglers' secrets and relics of war can stay largely uninterred. And, partly for lack of a vicar (there is one, but she must service them in turn, week by week), the old churches retain their dignity and their quirks.

One, built upon the site of a longship burial, was repainted on the inside by the Disney Corporation in an effort to make it a more 'authentic' setting for a film scene. And so it remains. Another was rumoured to have reeked so strongly of smugglers' tobacco that its rich odour served better as a landmark than its steeple, especially in fog.

In the ends-of-the-Earth barracks town of Lydd, the church is the size of a small cathedral (but isn't one). Its internal structures are very much less (or more?) than perpendicular, and charmingly so. The upright church, by contrast, which calls itself the Cathedral of the Marsh, in the village of Ivychurch beside the Bell Inn, is, strangely enough, quite ordinarily proportioned.

And at Dungeness, another place of worship: a small, black, timber-framed cottage sitting in a garden of driftwood and stones, withstands troops of quietly adoring photographers, poets, artists.

'That's it,' they say. 'That's Derek Jarman's house.' And they move on, because really, there isn't a great deal to see.

At Camber, the rolling dunes, and their lush sprouting of marram grass, and behind them the knick-knack shops, induce a kind of intoxicating happiness in day trippers and the temporary residents of the resplendently purple-fronted Pontin's holiday camp. Across the road, a convenience store revels in the name of BJ's on the Beach.

Sewn into copses, ditches and remote corners of lonely farms, bunkers, war graves and untold war stories have turned back to the soil, the sky and the sea, affecting a kind of invisibility, as if hurrying to be forgotten.

The Marsh doesn't shout about itself.

I have yet to come up close to the fabled concrete 'listening ears', precursors to radar, screened behind a thin line of semi-detached houses running north from Lydd, parallel to the sea, each attempt stymied by an encampment of holiday chalets determined, it seems, to prevent the ears from being seen.

Some preliminary exploring days proved so generally unproductive that it was impossible not to feel that one had returned empty-pocketed, especially in the interstices between the seasons when the Marsh holds its breath. But something always turned up, even if, perversely, its significance was magnified by its smallness beneath the dome-like sky.

An early foray in early March, walking in the company of friends, began in the ancient town of Dymchurch, generously endowed with fish-and-chip and bucket-and-spade shops and which, though it boasts by way of a billboard of being 'Paradise for Children', also trades on a darker reputation.

Across a little bridge and into a grazing pasture. Deceptively fine weather had induced the ewes to lamb early, and the fruits of their loins gambolled and wobbled beneath the sooty-bottomed clouds and a collective maternal gaze. Soon we were surrounded by a babble of *baas* through which we strode bravely, continuing over a broken stile into an arable field, scratched and stubby and parched.

The rain having held off in recent days, the dark soil was firm enough to walk upon. Not clagging or cloying as it can be. But there were few birds to see beyond the rooks and crows, the gulls and wood pigeons. The dour, bare-banked ditches were lifeless and sullen, and when we stumbled upon a badger latrine, we made much of it, for there was little else.

We took lunch at the Star Inn, in St Mary in the Marsh where, at the bar, a Jack Russell sat on a stool at his master's side. Or vice versa.

A young, pre-celebrity Noël Coward had once lived at the pub. And in the churchyard across the road, beneath a simple wooden marker carved from oak by her last husband, one Thomas Terry Tucker, lies the body of Edith Nesbit, Fabian Society stalwart, and author of *The Railway Children*. She'd lived nearby in St Mary's Bay, and smoked 'incessantly', according to a biographer, before she died in 1924. But long-dead literati left few other signs of their presence. I drank lime soda, ate a beef pie, and praised the landlady for the excellence of her peas, their crunch and freshness.

'They're not peas, my love,' she said, 'They're *petty pwah*.'

As noted, on a not-so-clear day you can see France from the cliffs at not-so-far Hythe.

Heading out into a cruel March breeze, we spotted a brightly coloured object apparently attached to a hawthorn hedge.

In medieval times, before the Marsh had fully emerged from its inchoate muddle of sandbanks and islands, harsh penalties such as the loss of an ear or worse could be levied for not growing hawthorn.

There, in the hedge, was the thing.

'What is it?' I asked my friend Mark, who knows the Marsh well.

'I don't know,' he said.

We drew closer.

'It's a little man,' he said.

Indeed, it was. A tiny figurine of the celebrity wrestler Hulk Hogan meticulously bound with thread to the tangle of spur-armed branches.

I remembered something that someone had told me he'd been told by a Marsh vicar: 'You wouldn't believe the number of deliverances I have to do,' she had said, with an other-world-weary sigh. 'There's just *so much* evil on the Marsh.'

'What does it mean?' I asked Mark.

'No idea,' he said.

'Numquam bonus,' I said.

Hogan said nothing at all. And we left him there, being loath to interfere with the ancient ways…

2

Drawing a Line

Tis remarquable that, towards the heart of this horrible desart, no beast or bird approaches, nor so much as an insect or a reptile. This must happen, not so much from the moisture of the soil, as from the everlasting shade occationd by the thick shrubbs and bushes, so that the friendly beams of the sun can never penetrate them to warm the earth. Nor indeed do any birds care to fly over it, any more than they are said to do over the lake Avernus, for fear of the noisome exhalations that rise from this vast body of dirt and nastiness.

Colonel William Byrd of Westover, *Description of the Dismal Swamp, With A Proposal To Drain It*, written between 1728 and 1738 – first published 1922

The Great Dismal Swamp straddles the boundary between and shared by the states of Virginia and North Carolina. The swamp's current perimeter is, in places, as straight as a plumb line but in others mischievously meandering. For the most part it is densely forested with red maple, loblolly pine, swamp oak and musclewood, hornbeam, poplar, cedar, cypress, sassafras, sourwood, and at least a dozen kinds of oak beyond the swamp oak. There are few alligators. But you'd hesitate before spending the night among those trees.

The Dismal, as it's known locally, isn't the size that it once was. But still, it makes for a formidable splodge of wildness, an oasis amid tidy fields and townships. It is a different kind of watery place to Romney Marsh, but like its Kentish cousin bears the cross-hatching, of sorts, of the inevitable efforts to make it 'useful'. How could I not visit a swamp called Dismal?

The end of a six-mile stretch of gravel road, flanked by a canal and hemmed in on both sides by, variously, tapered-trunk swamp trees thrusting out of the mire, or just their stumps, dead and obscenely stalagmitic perches for egrets and oversized herons, gives way to the revelation of Lake Drummond, a roughly circular body of water ringed with more trees, and to a small wooden promontory or jetty, marking the furthest point at which one can be most intimate with the lake without imperilment. It was upon this little structure, jutting modestly into the lake, that I found myself, shortly after arriving in the nearby town of Suffolk, on the Virginian side of the state line.

There were three other men on the promontory beside me. A father and his nearly grown-up son, and an older man, seemingly in his anecdotage, and certainly in shorts and sandals.

I had seen him at the refuge headquarters – a low, box-like building amid the trees, its interior walls hung with posters warning of swamp dangers, desks cluttered with papers and permits, all rather harshly lit by fluorescent tubes. Apropos of nothing at all, he had collared a park ranger at the entrance and, resting his hand on the head of a small stuffed bear, told her where Barack Obama had gone right, and where Lyndon B. Johnson had gone wrong, and why the Germans, 'Why, they never bad-mouth Hitler. No sir. You betcha.'

The lake was placid, and the temperature was cooling. But the air was still humid as I joined them on the jetty.

Now the older man was in full flow. It seemed that the two other men had enjoyed only five, or at the most ten, minutes' greater prior acquaintance with Mr You Betcha than I had at that moment.

'Yes sir. You gotta take care of your health. That's something I've learned over my seventy-three years. I made a stack of money in my time, but you can't take it with you. I mean, my sister, she's younger than me, but she nearly ate herself to death,' he was telling them.

Before Governor William Drummond found it and named it after himself, the Chesapeake Indians, after whom someone else, but not themselves, named a river and a bay, would come here to fish and hunt. But they gradually dispersed, as though the naming of the lake made it less special or more dangerous to them.

The older of the two younger men was reaching into a plastic pot of what looked like chicken livers, manoeuvring the slippery mess onto a large fish-hook connected to a nylon filament by a wire trace. I moved a little closer to see. Whatever he was fishing for was carnivorous and possessed very sharp teeth.

'Darn. I forgot what I was saying. What was I saying?' said the older man in sandals.

'You was saying as how your sister nearly ate herself to death. Or something,' said the youngest man in our ad hoc party.

'Oh yes. Nearly ate herself to death with her anorexia and the bulimia. And the diabetes. But she had one of those bands put on.'

The middle-aged man, clearly father of the younger, languidly swung his rod, landing the baited hook some few score yards away, where it plunked into the dark water leaving only short-lived ripples.

'Strange to say it,' said the brother of the woman unfortunately well-endowed with an appetite, 'but you know, some years ago, I headed back to the town where I was born and brought up… I graduated in sixty-five, first time I'd been back since then. And Don, my old friend Don from way back, he said, "You remember Annie's Diner?" I said, "Sure I do. Who doesn't remember Annie's? That's where we used to hang out with everybody. Chuck and Lisa and those guys."'

He said it in such a way as to suggest if the rest of the world was not as familiar with Chuck and Lisa and those guys as he was, well that was a shame.

'We've been here for more than an hour, and scarce a bite,' said the middle-aged man, more to himself than anyone.

'Don said, "Let's head over to Annie's. That's where the gang still hangs out – what's left of 'em."'

'Uh-huh,' said the boy politely.

'So Don and I headed over to Annie's. She's long gone, rest her bones, but the place still bears her name. And the first man that

I saw was Joe Peaky. "Peaky Joe". He used to play quarterback back in the day. Yessir!'

A giant grasshopper flew into my head and whirred off into the rosy sky, annoyed.

'I said, "Hell, Joe, you're looking mighty well!" and do you know what he said?'

'What did he say?' said somebody. It might even have been me.

'He said, "So I darned should, amount a money my triple bypass cost me!"'

He laughed hard at his own story, and said, 'Anyways, nice to meet you all. Gotta get going.'

'Sure thing,' said the youth. 'Have a blessed day.' And the older man bade us farewell.

I had never been in the South before, and I was afraid of everybody. The state slogan, 'Virginia is for Lovers', hadn't take the edge off its guns'n'Bible Belt reputation.

Now there were just the three of us on the pontoon. Over the lake a pair of ospreys scouted for fish. I watched them through a pair of binoculars that was permanently fixed to a pedestal, kindly donated by the County of Suffolk.

'That man was a talker,' said the older man.

'He sure was,' said his son. 'He sure had some things to say.'

'Yup.'

Silence reigned for a few minutes as, I suppose, all of us contemplated how to make an introduction.

'Where *you* from, anyways?' asked the son, obliging.

I replied, conscious of my accent and its out-of-placeness.

'The United Kingdom,' said the son. He nodded reflectively. 'That's awesome. We get people visiting from everywhere, it seems. Had some folks here from Iran one time,' he said.

'… and those history professors from New York,' said his dad. 'My, how they carried on, talking about this country they'd been to, and that country, and what their kids were doing now…'

'Yeah,' I said, not sure as to why…

'People sure say some stuff,' said the son.

'*That's* true,' I said.

I was coming into my own now, minutes after arriving in a corner of the planet that I could scarcely have contemplated as existing only weeks before.

The ospreys were having no luck, sizing up their chances then dropping on the lake, not just dipping a claw, but going all the way in up to their shoulders before hoisting themselves out again empty-taloned, flapping wearily towards the bare boughs of a shoreside tree to recuperate and repeating the exercise.

I asked the men what fish they were trying to catch.

'Crappie, bowfin, bullheads,' said the elder. I said I'd never heard of any of those.

'Bullhead's a catfish,' he said.

'Oh yeah. We've got those too,' I said, uncertain as to whether that was actually true.

We watched nothing happening for a while. The boy said, 'Looks pretty deep, don't it? No more than six feet, though. Dad, isn't it true you was once out in the middle in a boat and as you could touch the bottom with your oar?'

'Yup,' he said. 'Bottom of the lake's all peat. That's as accounts for the colour.'

I had read that its high tannic content once made water from Lake Drummond uniquely desirable for its extended keeping qualities aboard ship.

'They say,' said the son, 'as how maybe the lake was formed by a meteorite landing here and blowing a whole chunk out of the forest.'

I knew there were other theories. One was that 'the ol' de'il himself' had made the lake. Another postulated that slipping tectonic plates had been responsible for its creation. But I liked the meteorite idea best. It made a splash, and more neatly accounted for the lake's almost perfectly disc-like perimeter, as if the meteor were a Giotto, commanded by some greater power to scribe a circle on the surface of the Earth.

It turned out that the older man had moved nearby to be closer to his grown-up children. Prior to that, he had been living in Missouri since breaking up with their mother.

I didn't enquire about the circumstances that had cleaved the
family so far apart, both in distance and in accent. He said that the
fields in Missouri were much bigger than those in Virginia, though
whether he thought that bigger meant better was unclear. But he
liked the fishing here, quite unambiguously, even if today he hadn't
been particularly successful.

'Why are *you* here?' asked the boy. And I said why.

'You written a book before?' he asked. I affirmed that I had, and
I told him about it.

'That's awesome,' he said. 'I'm going to look that up.'

And he cast his line into the peaty, chromium-plated waters of
the lake.

They were a nice pair. Sure, the backs of their necks had caught
the sun, but whose wouldn't, down here in the swamp? I hung
around for a while to see if the crappies and the bullheads were
up for biting, but then I thought, it's time to head back, to leave
the pontoon to father and son. And I had begun to have thoughts.
Perhaps they would consider me to be memorable, like the Iranians.
But worse, I thought, they might have me down as a 'talker' with
all my annoying questions. As bad in my own way as the boastful
history professor.

'Good to meet you,' I said.

'And you sir. You have a blessed day,' said the younger.

'Take it easy now,' said his dad.

There wasn't a great deal of it left to be blessed, but the sun
was sufficient to throw bough-broken shadows of a turkey vulture
cruising above the canopy, and silver the plumage of an over-
extended wader, picking an imperious path through the roots,
gnarled, wet and arthritic, of trees blasted by long-spent storms.

It was entirely possible, given that it was the weekend, and
that the park rangers had, by now, no doubt knocked off for the
day, that we four had been the only people in the swamp during
the time that we lingered on that pontoon exchanging pleasant
banalities. Which meant that we had been outnumbered, maybe
ten to one, by the black bears that slink and mosey in the dense
forests of cedar and cypress and liana-like vines, and which

even now, as dusk loomed large, were quite probably becoming hungry, egged on by croaking amphibians and crickets with their cricketing…

To my outsider's eyes, the trappings of history around the Dismal are confused and confusing. Suffolk, the largest town in proximity to the swamp, at least on the Virginian side of the border, defies easy equivalence with any European counterpart. A spread of low-rise activity ripples across a huge square mileage of malls and fast-food joints: Papa John's, Chick-fil-A restaurants, Cazadores Mexican *restaurantes*, Panera Bread marts, Dollar Tree supermarkets and Walgreens. In that it is neither small, nor obviously a 'town', it could be said to embody small-town America.

The British burned Suffolk down during the War of Independence in 1812. In the Civil War it played an important strategic role, not a dramatic one, but significant enough to impact on the local cemetery, which remains, with its family plots to Dukes, Lukes, Hickoxes and Parkers, and tombstones lamenting the men who had fought for a South free to enslave ('To My Husband, A Confederate Soldier'), is about the only place of interest in which to take, say, a preprandial stroll.

For over a hundred years, Suffolk lived largely on peanuts, and in places around the edges, when the breeze is just so, a sweet, cloying, nutty odour wraps itself around the abandoned or ill-maintained industrial buildings, railway sheds and overgrown yards. The tourist board explains all on its website: 'In 1912: Suffolk becomes famous around the world when Italian immigrant Amedeo Obici moves here with his Planters Nut and Chocolate Company.'

But for the most part, it serves as a dormitory for the navy and port complex of Chesapeake to the north-east, and in so doing sustains a modicum of outwardly urbane facilities, such as coffee shops and a farmer's market.

The swamp itself is reached by driving south along Main Street, past the strip malls, the Hilton Waterfront Hotel and the Civil War cemetery, and taking a left turn onto East Washington Street, where you see immediately that you're in an area that is predominantly black, the weatherboarded houses with their verandas and broken bug screens variously folksy or merely miserable, according to the state of employment of their inhabitants.

In this part of Suffolk, riding a bicycle represents a means of transport; it is not primarily a leisure pursuit.

In the white areas, the picket fences and the weatherboarding are literally whiter, the lawns trimmer, greener and larger. The car of choice is a pickup truck. Some houses have genuine pretensions to grandeur, with their white-columned porticoes and three- or even four-storey construction. The grandest of all are set back from the road, some at the end of a tree-lined drive from which you could almost hear the crunch of gravel beneath ghostly antebellum carriage wheels.

It is quite ordinary, here, to possess a flagpole in your front yard. The Stars and Stripes is run up most often. Less common, but not infrequent, is the Confederate flag. Some fly both, and it seems that one would have to be fastidiously pedantic to read into those drooping articles of faith any contradiction in terms.

The boundary of the swamp itself is marked by a dark wall of trees beyond an acre's strip of agricultural land, buffering the safe, ordered world of the road from the squelching chaos of snakes, bears and butterflies beyond, and vice versa.

At the rangers' office, deputy ranger Lynn had told me about the dangers awaiting me in the Dismal, such as three species of poisonous snakes – water moccasin, copperhead and rattle – and the 'chiggers', minuscule trombiculid mites, also known as berry bugs, which 'if they git you, is so itchy you wants to scratch off your own skin', not to mention, though she did, the ticks and the attendant joys they bring with them.[1]

I asked about the bears. A very English question. But if I were to see one, what would I do?

Ranger Lynn said she'd been working in the Dismal Swamp for a year, and only seen one bear, and it had run away. If that was her

---

[1] Having been infected with Lyme's disease while snoozing on a bed of heather in Jutland, by way of researching *The Naked Shore*, I was all ears.

track record, it was unlikely that I'd have better luck. Of course, she conceded, there was always that possibility.

'What we like to say here in the Park Service is, "If you see a bear today, treat it as the gift that it is."'

I joked about not looking at its teeth, and she returned a weak and toothless smile in return, no doubt mentally summoning bears to do their worst.

She advised that, by way of acclimatisation, I walk the course of the Washington Ditch. After five miles or so, I'd be back at Lake Drummond, albeit at a different point on its 'clock face' than the day before. Thus, armed with leaflets and pluck, I headed back into the Dismal. In my light pink, almost white, shirt I must have stood out a mile.

'I saw you comin' way off in that white shirt,' said the only other person that I met on my walk along the Washington Ditch. 'You stood out a mile.'

'Yes,' I said, 'I saw you too.'

'Close your eyes, and hold still,' he ordered. And I obeyed.

Hitherto, the foray into the heart of the Dismal had begun to err on the side of the *ho-hum*. It was true that I had been jerkily, disarmingly chaperoned by a Palamedes swallowtail butterfly, the size of a man's two hands, and equally charmed by profusions of clouded sulphurs. And that every five or ten yards an arpeggio of plops and splashes signalled that my presence had so impinged upon the collective consciousness of a sleepy family of terrapins as to send them lurching reluctantly into the ribbon of dark water that is the ditch American history celebrates as having been dug by George Washington and his brother, but was actually hewn and hefted from the swamp by an army of men stolen from the west coast of Africa (or their children, or their children's children).

Had I encountered a flock of prothonotary warblers, reputedly like walking into a swarm of flying lemons, that might have taken the edge off my sense of being underwhelmed. But the trouble with a swamp of the Dismal's nature is that, if you walk along a trail blazed through it, whatever lurks behind the surrounding foliage is almost totally obscured. Even its miserable history.

There is an element of tautology in the swamp's name: in the seventeenth century the word 'dismal' was a catch-all term for a swamp, a morass, a quagmire or bog. In other words, all swamps were dismal by dint of being swampy.

But only one was *Great*. Great not only in scale, but also in its potential, which, though eyed for almost four centuries, has never, blessedly, been fully realised. Had it been, the Dismal might have only survived to the present as a name wedded cynically to a shopping centre or referred only to a (dismal) pocket or two of remaining wetland, certainly too small for bears.

That is how Colonel William Byrd of Westover would have had it, as would have George Washington, and generations of successive gentlemen of Virginia, chivalrous, cultivated, scheming and speculative, some waggish, some Whiggish, all inured to, or complicit in, the evils of their age.

Byrd, depicted in a single surviving portrait wearing a black wig, gold-buttoned blue velvet coat and a sardonic smile, was quite prolific as author. In his lifetime, he was best known for his account of his involvement with the demarcation of the boundary between the states of Virginia and North Carolina, the *History of the Dividing Line*.

But he also published a secret, jauntier history of the same episode, which gives a greater insight into Byrd the *man*. More salacious still were his personal diaries, written, like those of his near-contemporary across the Atlantic Samuel Pepys, in a cypher, in which he recorded his daily business affairs, eating habits, paternal anxieties and a volatile relationship with his wife.

'I danced my dance,' he says, referring to self-prescribed calisthenic exercises.

'I flourished my wife on the library couch – and gave her much ecstasy and refreshment.'

'I committed an uncleanness' (usually written when he's in town on business, without his wife there to flourish). 'And I ate dry roast beef for supper.'

'My wife and I walked around the garden, eating cherries.'

'My daughter is recovered from her sickness, praise be to God.'

'In the afternoon I read Italian [or Hebrew, or Greek or French...].'

Byrd and his wife argued frequently, and he was evidently insufferable; their squabbles, inevitably, culminated in her grudging capitulation, or prolonged sulking on the part of each of them.

On one occasion, a 'minor trifle' conflagrates while they're in bed, with the upshot that they get out of it and both refuse to get back in until the ridiculousness of the situation dawns on them. The poor health of his daughter worries him greatly, as indeed does that of not only all his family members and associates, but also his servants.

Always the egomaniac, Byrd knows that the afflictions suffered by those for whom he feels responsible are punishments from God for his own misdeeds. But this is also a man who punishes a bed-wetting domestic by forcing him to drink a pint of his own piss. And Mrs Byrd, though one may feel sympathetic on account of her gripes, her fits of melancholia and her husband, is otherwise little gentler.

'I rose about 8 o'clock, my wife kept me so long in bed where I rogered her. I read nothing because I put my matters in order. I neglected to say my prayers but ate boiled milk for breakfast. My wife caused several of the people to be whipped for their laziness. I ate some boiled beef.'

All of Byrd's traits are reflected in his grandiose scheme to realise the value of the Dismal, which he describes as,

a very large swamp or bogg, extending from north to south near 30 miles in length, and in breadth from east to west, at a medium about ten miles. It lyes partly in Virginia, and partly in North Carolina ... No less than 5 navigable rivers besides creeks rise out of it ... all these hide their heads in the Dismal, there being no signs of them above ground ... The ground of this swamp is a meer quagmire, trembling under the feet of

that walk upon it, and every impression is instantly filled with
water.

This description prefaced Byrd's plan, presented to the British
Crown in 1728, which would, he insisted, bring considerable
benefits both to Crown and colonies, not only generating rental
income from tenant farmers, but making the adjacent countryside
'more wholesome', purifying the air, which, he said, 'is now infected
by the malignant vapours rising continually from that large tract of
mire and filthiness'.

Despite the apparent immensity of the challenge, he said, all
was easily surmountable. Once the financial arrangements had
been made, the first steps would be to procure from England, or
from the Netherlands, 'a man that perfectly understands draining
of land – at a moderate salary' and a 'proper piece of land be chosen
on the skirts of the Dismal, whereon to make the first settlement'.

These accomplishments achieved, the company formed for the
purpose would build houses and provide tools, bedding, clothes
and provisions for the project's labourers, and 'when these are all
ready, let 10 seasoned negroes be purchased, of both sexes, that
their breed may supply the loss'.

If the very fact that, centuries later, I found myself walking
along the towpath of a canal named after George Washington,
heir to Byrd's vision, is testament to its partial realisation, the
still-trembling quagmire through which it inches, and the
brooding, gloaming shadows of the cypress trees, the loblolly and
the swamp oak, and the snakes and vultures, as the Americans
say, speak to its failure.

As I squeezed my eyes shut like a 'seeker' in hide-and-seek, the
man on the towpath enveloped me in a miasma of bug-killing
chemicals. He had been amused, he said, to watch me swatting at
my own neck and face for the past half-hour, the comic element
growing with every nibble and yelp. And it was true that by the
time we stood alongside each other, few were the exposed inches of
my skin that were not bloodied or raised in welts.

I told him I was writing a book, sort of about swamps and marshes.

'Should have known better,' he said. And he told me he lived in Colorado, that he loved coming down here for the birdwatching, that he lectured in sociology, and Donald Trump could never win the presidential election – his stockbroker had already factored that into his portfolio composition.

He had, he said, always wanted to go to England, and was planning to visit Yorkshire with his son in retirement. Some of his family was from there, he thought, possibly Manchester.

I had mostly liked the very few people that I had met in the Dismal so far. Even the presumption of the guy who talked about 'Annie's bar', that anyone in the world should *care* about his bittersweet recollections of an ordinary American life, was illuminating.

And this man too, I liked. I told him about how, close to where I lived in Hastings, there's a marsh – very different from this swamp, mostly inhabited by sheep. And how William Pitt had dug, or had *had* dug, by Irish navvies and soldiers, a canal, with the intention of scuppering Napoleon's plans for invasion. He made a vague noise and moved his head and shoulders in a way that suggested that he thought that that might be very interesting, but it seemed distant and too much to imagine.

Some yards preceding this encounter on the towpath, I had stumbled upon a pile of faeces so generously proportioned, dark, and studded with seeds and berries, that I had an inkling as to the kind of creature that had deposited it. I asked the man who had a long-standing desire to visit Yorkshire whether, based on my description and his superior knowledge and experience of the Dismal, it could be, notwithstanding what the ranger had said about the slim chances of encountering one, a bear?

'Oh yes,' said the man. 'Family of them right ahead, waiting for you. Just keep walking up, you'll see 'em!'

And so I proceeded, feeling lonely and small as one might in a dark swamp, on the way to receiving, as Ranger Lynn had it, one of nature's gifts.

3

The Keys to the Kingdom

See you our little mill that clacks,
So busy by the brook?
She has ground her corn and paid her tax
Ever since the Domesday Book

See you the windy levels spread
About the gates of Rye?
O that was where the Northmen fled
When Alfred's ships came by!
              'Puck's Song', *Puck of Pook's Hill*, Rudyard Kipling, 1906

There are those, including this author, who, as Jim Pilcher, the oldest man on Romney Marsh, would point out, prefer smaller cuts of lean young lamb over mutton, and don't know the meaning of hard work, who decry the death of rural England, believing that only *elsewhere* does the countryside retain bucolic charms: chickens clucking in the yard, merry farmer's wives, brimming pails of milk. Those who imagine that, over the centuries, the land has given too much. The pastoral, we sigh, has been sacrificed for the sake of pasture, old tempi beaten into industrial beats to a bar, the weary earth subjugated to demanding, complex markets and supply chains.

Farming today, we assume, as we drive along roads that cut through small prairies of rape, wheat stubble or sugar beet, is purely business. Rural communities are severed from the lore, dances, songs and rituals that once made country living bearable, by the inexorable, one-way tide of progress.

Disheartened, we hurtle along in our cars, past hay bundles shaped like Weetabix, eyes bruised by bright and jarring rape fields, and we book *agriturismo* holidays in Italy and France, where the promise of being roused at dawn by the crowing of a rooster or the hawing of a donkey has not been wholly consigned to a fading collective memory.

Romney Marsh makes no effort to disabuse us of that muddled notion at first blush, for it has the appearance of having been levelled according to the mantra that 'flatter is fatter', and if there is a sense of 'community', it isn't tangible to the passer-by.

Rob Monje, who works for the Internal Drainage Board and thus knows *everybody* on Romney, introduced me to Larry Cooke, chair of the board, a 'big name' in sheep farming, and who oversees a family business providing hay to local stables.

His farm to which he invited me to breakfast of a Saturday, is reached via a track that comes off the main road to Camber, tucked out of sight of passing glances.

On my way to visiting, I noticed, some distance from the farmhouse gates, half a dozen people, a couple of men, but more women, gathered at a section of hedgerow flanking the road. They had cameras and notebooks, and while one glowered as I drove past, others smiled, as if by way of a wave.

Later, Larry would tell me that that would have been the 'bumblebee woman' and her volunteers.

As I approached the door, a man was just leaving. He said that Larry was expecting me. And then as I entered, scarcely having had a chance to greet Larry, another man knocked on the door and took a seat. Mrs Cooke, who looked friendly and capable, greeted him warmly, asked after several family members, and offered us both mugs of coffee.

A young, glossy-coated sheepdog thrust its muzzle into my hands.

Larry, I saw immediately, liked to hold court, and did so at a round table in a large room adjacent to the kitchen of a farmhouse that had been in no way prettified, which is to say that Larry is a real farmer, and not, to use his own term, a 'slipper farmer'.

A muddle of objects – a pile of wire-mesh dog crates, a sprawling heap of farm-tool catalogues on an oilcloth table, a distinctly farmhouse odour – and a suite of closed-circuit television screens bore witness to that authenticity. As did Larry himself, rolling-timbred of voice. Forthright in presence.

The man who had arrived at about the same time that I had looked to be in possession of youth, but also great responsibility. While I'd hazard a guess that he was no older than thirty, he seemed preternaturally grown-up. Or perhaps he was older, and preternaturally youthful.

That I, having no ordinary connection either with the Marsh or farming, should have taken a seat at the table, appeared not to puzzle either him or Larry, who, though he had been taciturn to the point of brusqueness on the telephone, swiftly allayed concerns about his ability to communicate. For Larry spoke.

The conversation that followed was in part by way of suggestion, by Larry, of areas of interest that he assumed I should be pursuing, and in part a by-the-way chat about the price of heifers, the lack of rain, the deteriorating health of a neighbour, and near-endless gripes about the needling bureaucracy that blights the farmer's working day. ('Natural England?' exclaimed Larry. 'Don't talk to me about Natural England!')

Exposition and conversation made for overlapping discourses about the Marsh, about farming and the world generally. Larry's neighbour had succeeded in selling all his heifers to a mutually known and regarded acquaintance. There'd been no let-up in the drought, and there was no immediate prospect of it ending. 'Most of the time we speak, we talk in millimetres – of rain!' said Larry. And the lambing was late. Or early.

Had I ever underestimated the complexities of farming, I would not from now on. Most of what Ben and Larry had to say to each other was almost incomprehensible to a layperson, which brought home the fact that being a farmer means negotiating a maze of often arbitrary rules, and somehow making the numbers work.

But if there was a recurring, underlying theme, it was repugnance for outsiders' perennial desire to interfere in, or possess, what they don't understand or can never own, and a swarm of characters who had tried both swam in and out of the conversation.

Forty years ago, by way of example, Larry was taking a turn around his farm when he encountered some busy-looking people with theodolites and bits of string, and he discovered that they were designating areas of it as sites of special scientific interest (SSSIs). This, he knew, would impose any number of restrictions as to the way that he was to use his land, without conferring upon it any great environmental benefit. All of which, he said, he pointed out in 'no uncertain terms'.

Towards the 'bumblebee lady', whom I had seen, flanked by her companions, on my way to Larry's, and who was reintroducing a species of her namesake insects, he was sympathetic. But he was less well inclined towards the ecologist who had once told him how he should be managing some ponds he possessed on Pett Level. 'When I asked her whether she knew how the ponds had come about – how the shingle had been dug out just after the war to create the sea wall – she didn't have the foggiest! But there she was, telling me what to do with it!'

Of a former banker trying to buy up huge acreages of the Marsh as his own personal fiefdom, Larry's smile betrayed only amused contempt. The man, he said, had bought up a neighbour's land. 'I said to myself, "A couple of weeks and he'll be knocking at my door." Couple of weeks? It was the very next day. I feigned ignorance as to why he'd come, but I knew all along.

'When he asked, I said, "Buy it? *Buy* it!? Of course, you can't *buy* it, because I'm a farmer, and a farmer doesn't own his land – he just looks after it until it's time to pass it on to the next generation."'

Of course, he can. But what he meant was that what is insufficiently appreciated about farming are the continuities, the linkages holding one generation to another.

Larry's scepticism about environmentalism also made sense, for not a single acre of the English landscape is pristine, and the Marsh is arguably little less the product of human hands and wiles than, say, a tractor. Or a tower block.

It turned out that the man who was just leaving Larry's as I came in was Dave, the water bailiff, someone Rob Monje had also suggested I should meet, and who later offered to show me the Marsh.

And so he did, on a day in mid-June. The rain so craved by the farmers had yet to fall, but still, the Marsh didn't look parched. In fact, everything – crops, fields, sheep, clouds – was taut, swollen and well-nourished. Greens were rich and verdant, whites whiter than white, and the sky of a stamp of blue through which, were it water, you'd push a hand to feel its coolness between your fingers.

How dispirited I had felt some months earlier on the 'Hulk Hogan' expedition, walking from Dymchurch to St Mary across scoured fields. Then the sewers looked raw, wound-like intrusions rent in the soil. Now they were hidden by singing reeds.

Dave had spent his childhood in the village of Pett. His father had worked on a farm, and the family lived in a house in the middle of a field surrounded by trees to climb, rabbits and pigeons to take a pop at, and orchards and woods. In the summer, they'd decamp to Pett's splendid, if muddy beach.

It was, he says, a perfect childhood. He could remember people keddle-fishing at Pett, setting nets on long poles to catch mackerel and herring and taking the catch to sell at Rye fish market.

'Nobody keddle-fishes any more. Which is a pity, really,' he said.

I agreed, especially given the huge shoals of mackerel that roil the inshore waters along the coast. From the beach in Hastings some summers, you can wade into the sea and scoop them out with your hands as they drive the little fish, shooting from the foam like flickering bullets, towards the shore. For £300 you can still buy a licence to keddle (conditions apply). But where you get the keddling kit, I can't imagine.

We met at the offices of the Internal Drainage Board. Tall, deeply tanned and long of neck, he was wearing shorts and boots and a polo shirt, like a safari ranger.

Soon after we hoisted ourselves into the Land Rover, with its water-bailiff clutter of rolling tobacco, widgets and things generally, we abandoned the A259 for a country track, and found ourselves coming alongside a large 4x4 headed in the opposite direction. Dave pulled in to allow it to draw alongside. The driver was in his early sixties, balding but heavily bearded, forearms mottled with oriental tattoos.

'It's Barry,' said Dave, 'who works at the sluice.'

'How's it going, Barry?' Dave asked, and Barry rolled his eyes as if to say, as so many say about whatever it is they do, 'Well. What can you do… What with this. And what with that. And what with everything else.'

The this and the that and the everything else, in Barry's case, was the continuing lack of rain and the farmers, each of whom wanted more water than the system could deliver. Only this morning a locally known personage of consequence had called at the crack of dawn, demanding an explanation for the fact that his land was only receiving a trickle. 'Shouting and swearing! "You effing this and effing that,"' said Barry, and he laughed. Dave grinned.

The weather forecast for the next few months was that the rest of June would be 'as dry as a bastard'. July would be 'chucky' and August most probably a bit chucky too. That's what Barry had heard from one of the potato farmers. But then, they were a funny lot. Sometimes their predictions were way off, and who ever knows, anyway?

The conversation warmed to other characters and their traits, and the retelling of the story of a fight on the bank of the White Kemp Sewer between two landowners, each of whom blamed the other for the inequitable distribution of water to their respective fields. 'And they had their fists up, like proper Victorian boxers, Queensberry Rules and all that!'

He amusingly reconstructed the riverbank bout, wrists and fists curled like ferns, beckoning, inviting, threatening. And he recounted another occasion, many decades past, when a local farmer not only threatened him with a shotgun but fired off a couple of cartridges. Badgers seemed to be the cause of the altercation, though I couldn't tell how.

'He's all right now,' Dave said. 'Mellowed out a lot. You should go and see him and have a chat. Passing good company since him and his wife split up and he got a new one.'

Barry wasn't so sure. He'd seen this man's many moods; for bollock's sake, they'd been at school together and he'd been odd then. He doubted whether he'd changed. A man doesn't.

'Go and see him,' said Dave. 'He really has. A changed man!'

Dave had an accent, not strong, but discernible. It changed the 'a' in 'change' to an 'i' sound, as in 'fine' or 'wine'. When he said 'rain' it sounded like 'rine', and when he said 'place' he said 'plice'.

'Well,' said Barry, 'if I go and see him and he has me bollocks off, I'll be ringing on your bell to get 'em back...'

I smiled through this to-ing and fro-ing, having no prior acquaintance with its subjects, whose qualities, good or bad, I could neither vouch for, concur with nor disclaim. But this was a funny conversation, partly, but not wholly, held for my benefit. And Barry, who exuded a kind of beefy benevolence, was an amusing interlocutor.

But then the mood darkened. Just two days before, the national press had run the story that Brian Bellhouse, a former Oxford professor and creator of a needle-free system of vaccination called PowderJect, had been trampled to death by a herd of cows. I had read this of course, but not made any connection with Romney Marsh, a not inconsiderable amount of which Professor Bellhouse had, it seemed, bought with the proceeds of his invention.

By Dave and Barry's account, Bellhouse was an 'excellent' man who had failed to attract the scorn typically poured upon rich outsiders trying to farm the Marsh. Undoubtedly it was a tragedy, but also a conundrum. What would happen to all that land? Dave and Barry gave each other knowing, slightly squinty smiles. 'There'll be a buzz about that land,' said Barry.

'Oh yes,' said Dave. 'There'll be a buzz.'

As we drove off a little later, Dave said that the farmers on the Marsh 'all ended up swapping partners. And if they can have land under a neighbour's nose, they're like crows on carrion.'

Dave didn't envy the farmers. His own job, he said, was as good as any in the world. It was certainly the best that *he'd* ever had. For a while he'd worked as a farm labourer and then as a sexton. When he started out as the water bailiff, he hadn't been given any training or guidance. He just had to get to grips, from a standing start, with the Marsh, understand its needs, how the fields were fed by the capillary-like ditches and sewers, when to open the sluices, when to close them; how everyone who used the land, whether sheepmen, cattlemen, potato people, arable growers – and nature, each had their own wants and needs. And how things sometimes culminated in demonstrations of petulance, even fisticuffs.

Now, he traipsed across the Marsh in his trusty Land Rover in all seasons, regardless of the weather, responding to calls for assistance, checking water levels, monitoring the vegetation in the ditches. Because he possessed carte blanche to access anyone's land, he probably knew it better than any other single living person.

'You've really got the keys to the kingdom, haven't you?' I said.

'Oh yes,' said Dave.

We had pulled off the road again, and Dave was showing me one of the sluice gates – no more than a simple metal plate that could be raised and lowered, depending on the water in the ditch and what was required on the other side of it – and having a fag.

He had filled his Zippo lighter from a gallon tank of petrol he kept on the back seat.

'Oh yes,' he said again.

In the breeze, the reeds rustled like grass skirts worn at a slow dance. Dave pointed out a marsh frog just bulging out of the ditch and then it had gone.

To hear them sing, he said, you had to be there in May, in the mating season, when they're all clamouring to be heard and their singing rises to a climax so powerful you can feel it in your head…

He drew deep and exhaled slowly.

'I'd say that you have to be a more independent, more resourceful person to be out here on the Marsh, doing what I do.'

'I can imagine that's true.'

'You have to be able to cope, be self-reliant.'

'Of course, it isn't always a beautiful day in June when you're out here…' I added helpfully.

'That's right. It's a completely different story in the middle of winter. Completely different.'

Dave had said when we set out, 'I don't have any idea of where to go really. Thought we'd just follow our noses.'

And that was fine. We carried on, rolling along byways and lanes past meadows and dykes and gates until eventually, not knowing where to go, he took us to the Brack Pumping Station, a concrete hut, which had etched on its façade:

BRACK

PUMPING STATION

1909

Inside the hut sat the original and resplendently moss-green pump, coolly alone save for a little desk and chair, which may also have occupied a corner of that mostly quiet place for over a century. On one side of the sluice, the channel was broad and still, a deep, coppery demi-glace, beneath the surface of which flicked, slowly, the brooding red tails of a dozen rudd, each the size of a man's forearm, give or take a finger or a fin. Pea-green pondweed and the ever-present reeds framed the aqueous mystery around which sheep blithely carried on as they had for a millennium and more.

We moved on, towards a place close by where a man was repairing a tractor in a shed by the side of a farm track. Dave knew him and hopped out of the Land Rover. I got out (less deftly) and Dave introduced us. He gave me a card which, alongside his name and telephone number, advertised his services: 'Tractors repaired.'

He, Dave and I headed into a little Portakabin, on the door of which a sign said, 'No unauthorised coursing for hares or trespassing on this land.'

I asked about the sign. Coursing, trespass and petty theft weren't the only manifestations of criminality on the Marsh, Dave said, reserving his particular disdain for those just passing through, committing acts of lawlessness and moving on, beyond the Marsh. Not so long ago, the tractor repairman said, a local farmer, known to have money hidden in his house, had been tortured to death in a bid to get him to reveal its whereabouts.

'That's right,' said Dave, who shook his head at the memory of it and drew a breath through his teeth.

'When the farmer's daughter arrived at the house in the morning, she couldn't recognise her own dad's body.'

The murderer, or murderers, had poured boiling water down his throat in an arguably counterproductive bid to persuade him to talk, he said. No one local, Dave and the tractor repairman agreed, would ever have done that.

At the end of my day with Dave, he took me to a secret, favourite spot. Three separate structures in varying states of dereliction stood arranged in such a way as to loosely describe a right angle. One, evidently, had been a two-storey, tile-clad farmhouse. Now it possessed neither roof nor ceilings, but strangely, endearingly, cosseted a small oak, which had grown up within and was embraced by the four barely standing walls, on the outside of which the remaining tiles hung, many by a single nail, on horizontal wooden slats fixed upon the old red bricks.

The hanging tiles sang like chimes in the wind – a lullaby for the improbably dandled tree.

A second building was no more than a shed or workshop. Dave said that once, as he entered, stooping to avoid scraping his head upon what is left of the door frame, a barn owl flew out at just the same moment, but without making a sound.

But we startled noisy pigeons, scrambling through a broken window, leaving little eddies of confusion that took some moments to disperse.

On a workbench, rusting and scattered amid the splatters of bird excreta on the concrete floor, were the clues as to what the shed was used for. A veritably geriatric Wolseley shearing machine, circa any year between 1920 and 1960. Coils of orange cord, objects of indeterminate purpose, dry-cell batteries. And scratched into an old window-shutter, a tally of sheep: 1,668 – so many rams, so many ewes and lambs, so many tupped, so many stillborn. The hand was old-fashioned and sloping, and the number quite astronomical, said Dave, who peered at it with me, both of us awed by this *Marie Celeste* in the Marsh.

Dave didn't know when the farm was abandoned. He became the water bailiff in 2003 and stumbled upon this place shortly after and it was as lonely then. I suggested that maybe the buildings fell out of use incrementally. Perhaps the inhabitants of the farmhouse were drawn to the comforts of a nearby village, but the shed remained in use, albeit with dwindling frequency. Dave said, 'Yes, maybe.'

And yet it appeared to have stayed unmolested through its lonely vigil. There were no signs of vandalism, no smashed bottles, syringes or empty cans. Its odour was that of nesting birds and windborne traces of the sea and surrounding fields, not that of piss or ordure.

Perhaps that was because no one had dared to leave their mark, or on account of its almost-remoteness, for it lay only a quarter of an hour's drive from the main road; either is remarkable, more so even than the transformations the house had undergone in the soft, clumsy hands of the wind.

On our way to this place, the sensation of bouncing along the rough track reminded me of the time I had been on a 'desert safari' in the United Arab Emirates, and how miserable it had been to be thrown from side to side, clutching, bracing, hoping the horrible vehicle wouldn't topple as its grinning driver accelerated up sand dunes and tumbled over their crests. I told Dave about it.

'He'd be looking to show off, I'd expect!' he suggested.

'Too right,' I said.

But now, as we headed back, I almost regretted saying it, because Dave, buoyed, perhaps, by my evident and vocal enthusiasm for his discovery and in imaginary competition with the Emirati driver of my short anecdote, gunned the engine hard and boyishly until the point that the track rejoined the main road, with the sun setting over the wind farm, churning the warm air.

While we had been talking in the Portakabin, Ranger Dave and the tractor repairman had mentioned the Hangman's Toll Bridge near Brenzett, the very place where, sometime in the early 1800s, the last known incident of a sheep theft being punished by hanging had taken place – or so they thought. Some weeks after the conversation, I set out to try to find that spot.

The way they spoke about the bridge made the event real in my imagination. Toll took on a double, maybe a triple meaning. A financial toll. For whom the bell tolls. The ultimate toll. And bridge. How fitting to be hanged by a crossing point.

The Hangman's Toll Bridge is marked on the ordnance survey map as being close or adjacent to a minor road that runs almost parallel to the A2070, by Walnut Tree Farm. And so I drove to a spot from where, were the map lettering manifest in the 'real' world, the 'e' in bridge should be close enough to grab.

There was a cottage by the side of the road, with a ramshackle garden. A pair of men, dark-haired and very tanned, were feeding a pair of ponies, baling hay from a hayrick. I said hello and the men said hello, in a way that was heavily accented, and continued talking to each other and the ponies in a language that I think was Romanian. Just beyond the cottage began a footpath, as the map suggested it should, little more than a shadow in the grass, which soon drew close to the ditch, the Abbatridge Sewer.

Looking back, I saw the sewer met the road just at the point that I had parked my car.

The reeds had died back since high summer, but the sewer wasn't dead. My walking close to the bank prompted a tumbling of fat frogs from the edge of the ditch into it, quite rhythmically. As the sound of my feet crushing the tawny grasses reached a scarcely audible climax, *splop* went a frog, like the first seconds of popping corn.

I could see no Hangman's Toll Bridge. Back towards the road there was a little access bridge above the sewer, the first step raised high enough to stop the sheep crossing. But nothing to match the description of the lugubrious construction, semi-formed in my imagination and spelling the deepest melancholy. Those dread last minutes. Hard, fast breaths. Chafing ropes and downcast eyes. Life cut short by the smack of a gavel.

But it was all happening in the skies where whatever confluence of meteorological circumstance had whipped together a towering cloudscape – and a flock of gulls, larger than I had ever seen sucked into the thermal, swirled ecstatically, the ubiquitous birds rendered rarer by their huge number, which dwarfed the only other thing that I could see breaking the monotony of the Marsh, the rectangular façade of a white house on the far horizon.

Only when I returned disappointed did I come to see that the Hangman's Toll Bridge was little more than the spot where I'd parked, a place where the dirt track happened to cross the ditch, which ran through a culvert. Nothing sinister at all, but quite ordinary.

4

In the Soup

The Lipovan ethnonym has generated over time much controversy related to its origin. Numerous researchers, not only historians and linguists but also foreign travellers who passed through settlements with Russian-Lipovan populations have tried, in their published studies, to explain the genesis of this term which gives a name to the Russian ethnics who settled on the territory of our country…

Points of View Regarding the Origin of the Lipovan Ethnonym,
Cerasela Dobrinescu, 2015

It is just before the Romanian port of Tulcea that the Danube, which has stayed intact for the course of a 2,000-mile journey through Vienna and Belgrade, Vukovar, Linz and Novi Sad and everywhere in between, bifurcates into the Chilia branch, which makes for a section of the boundary between Ukraine and Romania, and a lower branch, splitting again, just downstream of Tulcea.

One channel heads due east, towards the port of Sulina, where it dissolves with an ethereal sigh into the Black Sea.

The other hugs the southern edge of the delta, reaching, eventually, the town of Sfântu Gheorge, famed for its natives' skill in fishing for sturgeon, and for an annual avant-garde film festival.

The delta itself is a 2,000-square-mile labyrinth of reeds, islands, rushes, lakes and streams, threaded with willow- and poplar-fringed corridors, which in summer clog with the leaves of lilies and water chestnuts, and in winter with ice.

There are few parts – though some – that are firm enough for human habitation, and none for roads to speak of. This is a wet world for the birds and fish. And it was in the middle of it, in the village of Mila 23, which means 'twenty-three miles' and indicates its distance from Sulina, that I was served the delta on a figurative plate, though in a very real and capacious bowl: fat chunks of carp, pike and zander especially chosen from the head and the tail, simmered in a broth, red with pepper flakes, fragrant with lovage, bulked with potato, tempered with *smetana* sour cream and devilled with tongue-addling garlic. Traditionally, no liquid is used that is not drawn from the Danube, but perhaps that wasn't so in this case, poetic though it may have been to imagine.

'So, first you take some broth…' Adrian, or Adi, who was my interpreter, said, taking his cue from our landlady, Tianu Alexandru's wife, 'Doamna' Maricica,[1] who watched proudly with a Cheshire-cat smile, '… and when you have had enough, a piece of fish… and you put the bones and scraps in *this* bowl, and you eat with your fingers. Or if you like have the fish and then the broth. Actually, I have the feeling that it doesn't matter…'

Beneath surgically bright kitchen lighting, each poached fin, scale and lip lent itself to scrutiny. But the flesh was succulent and richly flavoured, and not muddy, as the English hold coarse fish to be. To dispel any residual plainness of seasoning, of which there was none, pickled peppers were provided alongside.

And at a point that Doamna Maricica deigned that we had proved ourselves worthy of her cooking, she brought fat slices of fried catfish and a bowl of polenta.

Tianu, a huge septuagenarian with the downturned mouth of a grouper, sat at the same table with us, but although I had wanted to ask him about the delta, and the village of Mila 23, and the

---

[1]'Miss' was his translation of 'Doamna', an honorific applied to older women, not as pompous as 'Madam', and not necessarily denoting married status.

Old Believers who inhabited it, he was firmly in the grip of his favourite television show, which saw teams of fit young men and lean, attractive girls competitively engaged in tasks that would have been pointless were it not for their ulterior purpose, of showing off each participant's physical charms.

I had arrived earlier in the day from Tulcea, with Adrian, a kayaking photographer, who, though he swears that Hollywood taught him English, says things such as, 'I have a feeling that it is preferential to lean towards a more diminished price in the negotiation of an acceptable fee in commissioning the services of a faster boat for completion of our journey.'

This he said shortly after we had met in person, after weeks of discussion about this trip via various social media. We were climbing the umpteen steps that lead to the top of the monument that celebrates both Romania's liberation from the Ottoman Empire and the coming together of the western half of the country with the ancient region of Dobrogea, awarded to Russia in 1878, but swapped in a shake for the glories of Southern Bessarabia.

For all that I now stood in one of the most ancient and renowned Dobrogean cities, I had not in truth even heard of the region before that evening.

From the top of the monument, we could see the U-bend of the river, in the crook of which Tulcea sits, and the sun setting in a thousand windows, the long-stilled cranes of the old shipyard, and barely perceptible, like the proboscis of a gnat or some such, the spire of the cathedral in the Ukrainian town of Izmail, a whole alphabet away across the Danube.

Closer sat the churches of a handful of orthodoxies, Russian, Ukrainian and Romanian, and the mosque – a legacy of the Ottoman times. At the fringes of the town one could see little country houses, and beyond them, fields, orchards and marsh.

'And look there,' said Adi. Just to the north of us was what looked like an overgrown, reedy football pitch.

'What is it?'

'This was a stupid, stupid idea, to build a *mini*-delta so that tourists could *experience* it without having to leave Tulcea.'

'What happened to it?'

'Nothing. They never finished it. Stupid Ceauşescu thing.'

Now, he said, it was quite literally a wasteland, a convenient place for the disposal of unwanted goods, dead dogs and household rubbish, a failed vision of an ersatz delta upon which the sun had long since set, as it now did again.

Later that evening we sat in a bar at the quayside with his friends Vlad and Victor, discussing the various ways we might get to Mila. Speedboat fuel is expensive and the 'public' boat service had not yet begun to run, the season being some way off. But there's always someone, a friend of a friend ready to strike a deal, and sometime after lunch we left, throttling through the industrial outskirts of Tulcea, past a quayside where Romanian naval vessels rotted, beneath the moribund cranes of a shipyard. And by and by urbanity thinned into the greens of the delta.

Doamna Maricica was waiting for us beneath a willow tree, apologising for the height of the river, which had submerged her pontoon. 'What can you do?' she asked.

A wrought-iron gate opened into the Alexandrus' yard: a dozen chickens scratching, a herb garden growing, a fuzzball of a dog clamouring for attention, a dead magpie hanging from a post, a satellite dish pointing skyward – all the typical accoutrements of a small Romanian country home. And everywhere the polyphony of frogs, like a massacre of rubber ducks, squashy, urgent and mocking.

Mila is wholly unreachable by road, and even the poorest house possesses or has access to a large freezer, for in winter, when the Delta freezes, a freezer is, by some homeopathic rule of thumb, the only thing that can stave off starvation.

Geography dictates that Mila can only be a few hundred yards deep. But it stretches, ribbon-like, along a riverbank patrolled by impossibly friendly canines, alert to every stranger who might be chaperoned and entreated upon, and equally amiable village people, all friends of Adrian, and all pleased to see him. There were many smiles, and much shaking of hands as we took an evening walk.

De rigueur apparel for any delta male old enough to walk includes combat trousers, woolly hats pulled almost to the brow line, and rubber boots up to the knees, for they are all alpha in the delta. One thus dressed approached us boldly and made a declaration before turning on his heel and striding away. I asked Adrian what he'd said.

'He said, "My name is Mikhail. How are you? I would like to say something. I don't know what I'd like to say. I am only six years old. You are welcome here. Thank you."'

Delta hands are broad and strong. Those parts of the head that are not beneath a woollen hat are tanned to a chestnut turn. 'You always know a delta man at a wedding,' said Adi, 'by their foreheads, which are half white, half brown.'

And if few wear the huge Old Testament beards that they're famous for wearing, that's not to say they belong wholly to the present age.

When, two days later, I heard the story of the Lipovans, the source was a very young Old Believer. Victor was twenty-one. He had worked as a fisherman in Jersey, which, he said, 'was very different, being at sea, to fishing in sweet water', and he had a reputation for sending mischievous text messages, especially to his married friends.

'Like what?'

'Like nothing to speak of.'

'No really, what kind of thing?'

'Oh, you know…'

'No, I don't know…'

'Like sexy noises.'

Victor's many aspirations included that of becoming a professional rap artist and studying the archaic Slavic liturgy of the Old Believers in their spiritual home of Braila, in Moldova, and I came away thinking that in his case both were not only feasible, but compatible.

'It was in the time…' he began, as a group of us sat drinking beer at a bar on the waterfront, squeezed between the squelching of the frogs and the sonic idiocy of a fruit machine, '… of Czar Alexei, in the late sixteen-hundreds…'

Victor broke open a packet of mentholated cigarettes of delicate calibre, lit one with a flame-thrower of a lighter and continued, '… that those that became the Old Believers, or the Lipovans, first left Russia when the changes that Alexei made to the liturgy with the connivance of the Patriarch Nikon were deemed by them to be unacceptable…'

He exhaled a minty miasma of smoke.

Alexei's intention was to bring the liturgy into line with Greek Orthodoxy, he said, but in so doing he alienated many traditional worshippers. When, in 1666, the Great Orthodox Synod of Moscow agreed to endorse Patriarch Nikon's recommendations, which included changes to how many figures should be used to make the sign of the Cross and other blasphemies, it triggered a schism or *raskol* between old and new. The Church had words to describe those who refused to accept the changes, deeming them *raskolniks,* or *starovery*, and harassed and harangued them for the heresy of refusing to adapt.

Expelled from their own Church, the *raskolniks* fled into the sparsely inhabited plains and steppes of Russia, where they could worship as they saw fit. Today, he said, there are communities of *starovery* as far or near to each other as Alaska and Siberia. And in the delta of the Danube.

Those that came to the delta had most likely inhabited similarly marshy environments, such as the delta of the Volga, which flows into the Caspian Sea on the other side of the Caucasus, and developed a way of living based around fish, and coming to be known as the 'Lipovans'.

The traditional way of life, he said, revolved around the men setting out to secret spots in the lakes amid the reeds, setting traps for the constituent ingredients of the broth I tasted at Doamna Maricica's house, and many other species, among them several kinds of sturgeon (the Danube, the starry and the diminutive sterlet are all endemic), and a rare kind of mackerel. These they would take to primitive 'factories' amid the reed islands to be smoked and preserved to barter for grain and hay, which would otherwise be in short supply.

The exhibits in the aquarium-cum-museum in Tulcea include, on the floor above the tanks where a small shoal of sturgeon endlessly follow their knobbly snouts, a diorama of the Old Believers' (old) way of life. It has apparently been constructed from a community of mannequins appropriated from a clothes shop and bundled into sackcloth and rags, which has been frozen in the act of illustrating – to the best of its ability – those traditions: smoothing the planks of a small, carvel-hulled workboat or *lotca*, setting traps for carp and bundling reeds. The dried fish are the real thing, a consummate testimony to the Lipovan art of desiccation.

'They live by vodka, the Bible and the gun,' Adi's rather earnest friend Vlad had said in the bar the night before we set out. 'Arguments they cannot settle with a drinking bout or with their fists end badly.'

But this seemed at odds with the genial men we met on the riverbank, and with a more general reputation that while fond of their drink, the Lipovans are less partial to serious alcoholism, such as the imbibing of 'Mona', the 70 per cent proof *alcool sanitar* (surgical alcohol) that makes for such a public-health menace in much of the country. And the Lipovans, if much in the majority in Mila 23, aren't the only people in the delta: there are Ukrainians, Turks, Greeks and others.

'And then there is Tigaie!' said Adi.

Tigaie, which means 'saucepan', muddled by a day's drinking, stirred at the mention of his name. He, too, had been listening to Victor's account of the history of the Lipovans, despite not understanding it – for Victor spoke in English.

Nor did Tigaie understand why everyone called him Tigaie, and when Adi tried to explain, it wasn't clear to me either.

'Tigaie', said Adi, 'is from Moldovia.' Tigaie gave a confessional shrug.

'He came to the delta', he said, 'for love.'

It reminded me that, over two decades ago, I had *not* come for much the same reason. I had set out with a girlfriend on a trip to Romania that was to culminate in Sfântu Gheorge, but one night, as we shivered in a fog-bound Carpathian cabin, she told me that pelicans, and that kind of thing, held no interest for her, and that in the morning she would be making her own way to see the painted monasteries of Moldovia. And while I was under no obligation to do so, I was perfectly at liberty to accompany her and assure her safety.

It turned out that the painted monasteries, bathed in constant drizzle during our visit, only held the slightest interest for me. And so the delta had become more dream-like and elusively out of reach. I would have liked my first foray into the watery paths of the delta to have been in a *lotca*. Almost as soon as we'd disembarked, Adi had found one propped on the riverbank, and knelt before it reverently as it lay, seemingly exhausted by a long life exchanging notes with a river that had begun its journey in the Black Forest, and had also reached the end of its course.

Even in death, this was a boat worth sighing over.

'Look at how the planks run longitudinally for the entire length of the boat, so that it can retain its elasticity, its strength in the current,' he requested.

The *lotca*, Adi impressed upon me, canoe-sterned, and believed to be the distant and diminutive relative of Viking boats, was once the medium by which men knew the delta: without it, who could have set fish traps, gathered reeds, caught frogs, hunted boar, or fed their beasts their winter hay? Or courted, paid their respects, visited church, or escaped or dispatched justice? The *lotca* was as integral to the Danube as the carp, and almost as serene in aspect.

I could even hear, in my mind's ear, the slow splock (two, three), spluck (two, three) of a *lotca*'s heavy oars as they dipped and pushed, creaking and groaning where they turned and rested on the tar-black gunwale. Each stroke a fateful thing, loaded with promise, or purpose, or peril…

But it's now rare to find a river-worthy *lotca*. They're expensive and difficult to maintain, kept for the most part as reminders of a pre-mechanised past. And not extinct so much as reiterated, in the form of the *canotca*, the hull of which retains the same shape, but is cast in glass fibre, the canoe stern trimmed to a transom upon which can be mounted an outboard engine.

It was in kayaks that, the next day, we paddled across the Sulina branch of the obliging Danube, first into the sheltered backwaters, behind an acre or so of an island of cows, a few dozen resting swans and some cormorants striking poses as they dried their wings, perched upon a log.

The chorus of frogs grew louder, and, pinned against the blue, a boldly rectangular white-tailed eagle, the size of a door, hung above all of us, men, swans and frogs, huge and senatorial.

We paddled through a screen of towering reeds, across a threshold, so it seemed, into the narrow channels and hidden lakes of the delta that I had imagined a quarter of a century past, and that I had forsaken for the blessedly dull painted monasteries.

Though lacking the gravity of the oar of a *lotca*, our paddles still splocked as they broke the surface of the teak-coloured water – like an exquisite French polish – and splickered where they snagged in a tangle of aquatic vegetation. And were silent where we allowed ourselves to be borne along upon the most scarcely perceptible of currents, through avenues of willow and poplar and reeds.

Adrian pointed up at a squadron of pelicans sawing their way through the sky. And here was a squacco heron, a purple heron, a little egret and a pygmy cormorant. And there was a hobby chasing starlings, hoopoes, a flock of glossy ibis and a water rail. The delta, I now discovered, was, or could be, as warm, bright, colourful and paradisical as I had imagined it might be.

Big snows in the Carpathians and subsequent thaws had pushed the water to knee height on the trees. Later in the summer, Adrian said, the water lilies would create a thick and almost impenetrable pelt. 'Everyone says, "Ooh, water lilies." But my God, they're impossible. They choke up everything. It becomes like a jungle.'

Adrian had grown up in Tulcea, studied journalism in Bucharest for a while, and has had every opportunity, as a highly intelligent, English-speaking photographer and citizen of the European Union, to leave his hometown and native soil. But in his early twenties he discovered the joys of kayaking in the delta, a pleasure impossible to exactly replicate anywhere else in the world, as I now understood, conveyed by the merest hint of a current through corridors of reeds, plucking at sprigs of marsh mint, pondering where might lurk the fattest carp, the whiskeriest catfish.

He told me about other journeys he'd made in less clement weather. On one expedition, accompanying a party of holidaying Israeli special forces fighters, the wind whipped a lake into a maelstrom just as the evening light began to fail, and the channel that led out of the open water, which was marked by the merest break in the line of reeds, had become indiscernible.

Each member of the party had a reputation (for fearlessness and general indomitability) to maintain. But when they found the channel that took them to safety, he said, the big strong men shook with delight.

Only weeks before, he and serious Vlad had camped in the delta, melting ice to drink and to make coffee.

But right now, the delta was warm, well-tempered and perfectly poised, a sculpted landscape as intricate as blown Murano glass. Glistening, green, other-worldly and out of time, as the Carpathian meltwater lifted us through and between the straggles of club moss and sword flag, marsh thistles and water hemlock.

Later, turning back against the wind, the paddling became hard work. Adrian's kayak was propelled by a kind of breezy languor. He hummed nonchalantly as I struggled, fretting that I might get pushed into the reeds and lost among them.

'This,' said Adrian, who is incapable of boastfulness, 'really is nothing. Really.'

Presently, we had to stop.

'I have the feeling,' he said, 'that there is a snake in my kayak.'

This, he said, was almost certainly a *şarpele casei*, a grass snake (literally a 'house snake'), and, though it was harmless, one liked to know where such a creature was, in the close confines of a kayak, in the interests of avoiding any misunderstanding, and we nudged the nose of his craft onto a clump of vegetation that he might all the better, but without exiting the kayak himself, locate the serpentine surprise and dispense with it.

Always such a joy to see a snake. A one-line verse upon the superfluity of limbs. It was found, scooped up and juggled back into its element, from which it raised its head and gave a salutary hiss.

We splocked on against the current towards the main channel of the Danube, and across it, to the urbanity of Mila 23.

The footprint of a delta settlement can be measured by its stork nests. If there are none, it's a negligible place. Three, a bustling metropolis. By late April, the pair of storks that descends on the single nest that is its summer residence in Mila has already arrived. Village life wakes from winter slumber, and, though a ban on fishing remains for the next few weeks, men fix their nets in anticipation, and dress in a permanent state of readiness for the water, and in casseroles and frying pans deliciously fresh and finned delights have already begun to be cooked.

No one has much truck with the various authorities charged with the administration of the delta, it being a universally acknowledged truth that bureaucrats are crooked and ignorant, and their rules scarcely worth abiding by. Still, ask what a man is doing in his *canotca* outside of the fishing season with such studied concentration and the answer is likely to be that he's 'catching frogs'.

Victor, now my source on all local ecclesiastical matters, said that the whitewashed, domed church no longer had a permanent priest, and that it was open only when the bishop deigned to visit from Brăila. But we found it so on a Saturday afternoon, the interior an elaborate collation of icons, silk drapery and tapestries. Colours were cool blues and soft yellows, wafts of incense fragrant but not oppressive.

Whether it was the bishop from Brăila visiting, we weren't sure, but a priest, splendidly robed in white and gold, was just visible near the transept behind a screen.

Facing him, an elderly man and woman led the reading of a large Bible written in the archaic Slav script that Victor was so keen to master between rapping and sending sex-noise texts. The priest chanted, his voice plunging into an abyss of rumbling, bone-seizing bass notes, and the man and woman read and sang.

Sometimes there were pauses and everyone moved position. In between verses, the old man and woman, who seemed to have difficulty, in places, agreeing which page they should be reading, had a little giggle together, very quietly.

The man wore the traditional beard of the Old Believers, his tunic bound around his waist with a bright, embroidered cord. Worshippers, for the most part women, their headscarves brilliant and floral, stood on both sides of the church. Several more joined as the proceedings forged on, bowing with urgent and repetitive combinations of crossing and bobbing as they passed from profane daylight into the smoke and shadows of sanctity and prayer.

It felt both vital and ancient, a page from a novel by Lermontov, Turgenev or Gogol, or perhaps a painting by one of the Peredvizhniki artists, the Russian realists like Ilya Repin, who captured, on bright, expansive canvases, scenes such as these. And yet this was also the present, almost exaggeratedly so. No less 'contemporary' than the slim needle of a jet plane stitching the sky together above us, on its way to Batumi, Bucharest or Istanbul.

But no one appeared to see Adrian or me, our presence only affirmed in any meaningful way at all by the mild interest of a small girl, slung over the shoulder of her rapt mother, who let her cool but not unkind gaze rest upon us for a spell. Otherwise, we might have been invisible.

'Who says you have to have a beard to be a Believer?' said one half of a pleasantly drunk double act we stumbled into when we finally left the church. 'Who even says you have to be a believer to be a Believer?'

Mikhail had been asleep, he said, when Sergei woke him with the novel suggestion that they should have a drink. Mikhail was tall and blond, with a day or two's growth on his chin, and Sergei shorter and dark, with the face of a comic tragedian. *Did they know what the service was in celebration of?*

'Some sort of religious thing,' said Mikhail. He said something that didn't sound like anything at all in any language. I asked Adi to translate.

'I'm having the feeling that it is something like "blah blah blah",' he said.

Less irreverently, Sergei told us, 'Tomorrow is the Women's Day. Go in the morning. You'll see some beauties.'

'In my life I have been,' said Mikhail (I had not asked, but I had intended to), 'a fisher. A sailor. A baker. An engineer. A killer.'

He cackled.

Sergei laughed.

'A killer?' Adi asked.

'A baker,' he said.

The words 'Harley Girl' were embroidered on Mikhail's baseball cap.

Sergei shrugged, as if to say, *What can you do with him?* and he showed us an ugly, and not quite healed, laceration in the ball of his hand. It had been unintentionally self-inflicted, he said, during the cutting up of a carp.

He wanted us to look at his hands. Indeed, they were impressive: deeply tanned, lined and muscular.

'Everything I have,' he said, 'I owe to these hands.'

We all talked, about this and that and nothing, and about storks, and hands, and gravely they staggered away.

The next day we found that Sergei was right about Women's Day. A long trestle table had been laid out in the garden by the church, and village women, wearing again their brightest headscarves, had gathered to share food and chat with each other. The sun had somehow opened its hands, and the colours – the green lawn, the white picket fence, the pink-cheeked women, the blue church, the orange Fanta bottles – were, just as they had been the day before, vibrant and ancient and present.

We took a path that led past a jumble of hives in some waste ground, and a mud-walled house, its thatched roof caved in and long emptied of contents, with the single exception of a cheap print of the Virgin Mary, keeping guard among birds' nests and bones, beneath the gaze of the stork installed in its summer residence, amid clucking, barking, hammering, smoke, and the thrum of a generator.

In a place like Mila, there is the sense that its sounds and smells wax and wane in a great band in time and space stretching from Poland to the easternmost edge of Russia. And that as the seasons change, so will all of these: the woodsmoke richer in the autumn, the clucking of hens and mewling of kittens louder in spring, the barking of dogs, hacking at the winter stillness like a log-splitter's axe, regardless of the variant of Slav spoken or other tongue, the shape of the steeple, the liturgy or form of prayer.

We left Mila in the boat in which we had arrived. 'You will like Letea,' said Adrian. 'It is different,' and for half a day we sped along the Danube and various tributaries and channels in search of it.

As a name-word, Letea had me lazily but appropriately thinking both of Lethe, the Hadean river of forgetfulness, and *lyet*, the Russian word for summer.

It consists of an island of sorts, an accumulation of sediment brought down the Danube and prevented from proceeding further by the cold waters of the Black Sea. At its northern end is a lush forest of poplar, ash, alder, oak and lime, the presence of which is attributed to the accidental discharge of seeds by Ottoman trading boats. Access to the forest has been strictly protected since before the Second World War and remained so in the Ceauşescu era. For the most part its residents are wild horses, cooling themselves in its shade when they choose to escape the heat of the nearby dunes.

The village of the same name is inhabited by Hahols, descendants of Ukrainian soldiers who fled the town of Zaporozhye for the sanctuary of the delta, having been defeated in battle by the armies of Catherine the Great.

Like Mila, Letea can only be reached by boat, and the first sight of it is of willow-flanked banks, against which *canotka* sidle, and semi-submerged *lotca* slump like hippopotami. Whereas in Mila 23, houses are built a few yards' distance from the water's edge, in Letea there are fewer constraints of space. Behind the bank are meadows for grazing and growing crops, a buffer zone in the event of flood, protecting the village 'high street', such as it is, and at the southerly end of which sits an incongruously large religious building – not a church, but a monastery, albeit the monks are long gone.

Here begins a broad and unmetalled, unpaved avenue, strung on each side by telegraph poles. Its houses, mostly in a state of decrepitude, are neatly spaced, set in their own patch of land, busy, where inhabited, with hives and vines, pigs, bean rows and chickens. Or with nothing at all, save tall grasses and thrown-away pots, pans and broken plates.

Among the most prosperous of all the village houses was that owned and inhabited by Doamna Viorica and her husband.

A mile of walking from the riverside brought us to a neat ensemble of whitewashed, low-ceilinged buildings set behind a picket fence, which enclosed a courtyard and a canopied area for eating.

A small dog kept guard over a basket of newly hatched chicks. Miss Viorica's family was finishing lunch, and she urged us to share, spreading the trestle table with a new cloth upon which she placed some red and orange tulips in a vase, before replenishing the dishes: rich beef stew, grilled sterlet ('Well, yesterday was my birthday,' she said), babaganoush, two kinds of cheese, identical in appearance, but one sharp and tangy, the other mellow and easy on the tongue, home-pickled cauliflower with snap and bite, and a jar of carps' eggs, a sort of sandy-coloured caviar.

Where had we come from? With whom did we stay there?

She had not met Miss Maricica, she said, but knew of her culinary prowess by a repute which had travelled across the delta.

We gorged beneath a watchful gaze.

'How,' she asked, through narrow eyes, 'does Doamna Maricica's cooking compare to mine?'

I looked at Adrian for guidance.

'Just say, "Really good. But your cooking is fantastic."'

'Really good. But your cooking is fantastic,' I said.

She nodded, seemingly satisfied, stooped down, bundled up a wandering chick, and dropped it back into its basket.

Letea village was pleasantly torpid. Families sat in the evening sun on benches outside their houses, chatting and watching. And on one of our perambulations we were slowly overtaken by a huge red tractor. Tumbling over the rumble of the engine was a wonderful giggle. The driver of the tractor was a girl, perhaps not yet twelve, sitting on her mother's knee. They were fond of each other and smiling, and they jumped from the cabin just by the front garden of their house, with its poppies and sunflowers and sweet peas, both vital and happy. And further along the avenue we watched a man riding on a huge horse, the man without a shirt, the horse without a saddle, pulling a ploughshare through a small plot. There was nothing plodding about the horse, which was scarcely broken, bridling at a task so unsuited to its temperament.

One evening, Adrian winced to hear the strains of a *manele* tune, highly produced gypsy music that has more or less displaced traditional Romany song forms. From around a corner three boys appeared, solemnly dragging a large battery-powered speaker, ventriloquising their adolescent passions through the medium of autotuned pop.

'I hate *manele*,' Adi said. 'It is nothing – just musical bullshit.' But, as it rang out through the quiet village and beyond, over the reed beds and the river, I thought it quite fun. We passed the boys, who looked a little sheepish, as if unsure of the ultimate purpose of their procession.

If it was to impress girls, I wondered whether the greater challenge lay in locating very many. If their collective intent was really to stake their claim in the world, perhaps they had succeeded a little, however much it may have upset Adrian.

But most of the inhabitants were elderly, many widowed, like Doamna Eugenia, who we found sadly ushering her cows into their stalls for milking.

'It is so unfair,' she said. 'I started off with five cows, but now I have my son's cows. And now he is a ship's captain – in Austria – and he didn't tell the government about the cows. Now I don't have any subsidy for the extra cows. And the hay is so expensive. And the vet's bills. And now one cow produces no milk...'

I could tell that Adi was having difficulty translating Eugenia's woes. 'I have the feeling that the challenge is less a question of idiom or dialect,' he said, 'but slightly more related to the use of tenses, and general coherence.' Eugenia leaned heavily on a staff, her cows mooing sympathetically.

'He sent the *mail mail*...' she said.

'What is *mail mail*?' I asked Adi.

'I don't know exactly,' he said. 'Maybe email?'

'… from the embassy… but they didn't translate it in time…'

'When was this?' I asked Adi.

'I don't know exactly,' he said. 'She doesn't remember…'

A lengthier story then unfolded, about some land and a house *'up there* …' (she gestured towards the main street), which were by rights hers, but she had lost them in a dispute, the ins and outs of which she wasn't sure of... And had she mentioned how expensive it was to feed her poor cows, in the winter, when the river freezes and when, for months, Letea cannot even be reached by boat?

'What will become of me?' she asked. And I wondered, guiltily, whether whatever it was that would, already for the most part had.

Up there, in the direction towards which she had nodded, we met another woman of similar age to Eugenia, but of a quite different humour. She, too, had tales of woe involving cows, which in her case had been stolen, though by whom and when it was difficult to understand. When she was a young girl, she said, each winter, she had helped her father row the family *lotca* all the way to Tulcea to buy supplies before the Danube froze over. It was so cold. And if she refused, her father would beat her with an oar. He was a big man, an important man, who had men working for him. She would help her mother make pumpkin pies – huge pumpkin pies, the size of a cartwheel – to feed them all. And cauldrons of broth.

Her poor mother became paralysed in the end.

'How old are you?' I asked.

'I'm not quite sure. Maybe seventy-something. Or eighty. I had two older brothers. Strong men like my father. But one of them died! Can you believe it?'

Her very wrinkled face moistened as tears oozed from the clearest blue eyes… But the tears dried, and she brightened to tell us that things weren't so bad for her. She seemed to have acquired some land in a legal dispute. She wasn't quite sure how. But she remarked that it was interesting how things turn out, and she cackled happily and wished us the best.

That evening, Miss Viorica's husband joined us for a supper of a carp that had first been roasted and then gently boiled in whey with locally gathered herbs. He'd brought some wine, apologising that it wasn't the famed wine of Letea, which induced near-instant narcosis, but some stuff a colleague from Constantia had made in his back garden. The carp was sublime. The wine had bass notes of manure.

I tried to glean anything that I could about the past, but he wasn't terribly interested in talking about it. The village, he said, had been established in 1783 by two families (I presumed to be Hahols), who had an intense rivalry 'like the Montagues and the Capulets'. Each had vied for dominance, competing with evermore generous gifts to the monastery, explaining its disproportionate size. That was what he knew about that part of history.

About the Communist years, what he had to say was by no means in the tragic vein of the stories I had heard when I visited Romania in the mid-1990s, when the country was still reeling from poverty, mismanagement and the Securitate's intrusions into every facet of everyday life.

Miss Viorica's husband's account was more of reorganisation of agriculture and fishing practices – bureaucracy spawning self-defeating idiocies by the dozen. But the deep-veined invidiousness that had characterised the regime, he had either forgotten or not experienced. In some ways, he said, life before, during and after Communism was much the same.

Now the greater blight was corruption and graft. Where, could I tell him, did all the EU development funds disappear to? And how was it that money could magically accelerate the provision of medical services that the state was supposed to provide gratis? No wonder so many younger people left Romania to find opportunities abroad.

But his son, another Adrian, appeared to have no desire to leave Letea, let alone Romania, devoted as he was to helping his parents with the animals and house repairs, and fishing, and being with his girlfriend Maria, who possessed a bewitching degree of almost feline, strikingly urbane attractiveness, watching the world with good humour through gold-framed spectacles. Neither could have been older than eighteen.

Adrian, son of Viorica, said that, for the price of the fuel we'd need, he would take us in the *canotca* to what Adi had referred to as the 'Suez Canal', an almost impossibly straight conduit (*japşă*) between the lakes Merhei and Matita.

His girlfriend came too, sitting beside her beau at the stern of the *canotca*, which he so expertly steered, with the engine at full throttle, through a channel marked by scarcely concealed sandbanks and the occasional tree, apparently orphaned from the ground in which it had grown by the channel.

We carved a white bubbling streak through the silver water. I saw a pair of falcons (Eleanor's? Red-footed? Lanner?) briefly alight on a sandbank before being pushed off it by our wake. And a golden bird, bunting-sized, but which I've still yet to identify.

The channel gave way to a lake, sky and water kept in their own respective elements by the thinnest, darkest line, like a single strand of horsehair, of distant reed beds, which grew fatter as we moved towards it, coots and mallards whirligigging in its wind-shadow.

Then a break appeared in the line that announced the entrance of the 'Suez'. The younger Adrian dropped the outboard engine's revs. His girlfriend looked up from her mobile phone and we nudged forward hushedly, as one might when opening the door to a church or mosque.

The channel, between sinuous tree-lined banks, was a hundred yards or so wide. Semi-hidden behind reeds and branches sat clapperboard cottages, patchy and ramshackle, but neither derelict nor destitute, merely awaiting the return of their owners – fishermen, who, when the season began, would spend their summers setting nets.

And from both banks, an eerie mewing.

'*Pisici*!' said Maria.

A thin phalanx of cats, impatient for the return of the fishermen, for scraps, strokes and easy living, patrolled the riverbank, each narrowing its eyes into slits of pathos with acidic intensity.

'*Mieew, mieew,*' wailed the little sirens. But we stopped our ears, figuratively speaking, as the *canotca* slid further, through the Suez Canal, somewhere at the fringes of the Black Sea.

5

The Ploughing Match

> The practice of ploughing, however, is not general; and the greatest quantity in any one person's hands, hardly exceeds eighty acres; very few have half so much, and most of the tenants none.
>
> *A General View of the Agriculture of the County of Kent*,
> John Boys, 1796

On setting out to write about Romney Marsh, it had been suggested to me that I might speak with Jim Pilcher, then near universally considered to be the 'oldest man living on the Marsh', and author of a self-published memoir, *Pilcher's Progress*.

As Jim was amenable, I visited on a day in early January when *winter* winter had yet to materialise, in so much as that, while torrents of gale-driven rain had unleashed themselves on the turning year, it had neither been cold, nor had it snowed.

He had, he said, lived ninety years on the Marsh, born only a few hundred yards from where he now sat in his chair on the other side of the living room from Mrs Pilcher, in a neat and well-seasoned bungalow built in the early 1960s, at a little turning from the A259 amid a great swathe of flatness, studded with the giant wind turbines which, from the vantage point of his little garden, looked like dandelions gone to seed.

The house was huddled with a few others and some sheds, sheltered by hedges and a handful of trees bent before the wind…

You might drive past and think, 'Who would ever want to live in such a place?'

But Jim wouldn't live anywhere else.

There had been, Jim Pilcher told me, Pilchers on the Marsh for 'hundreds of years'. Some Pilchers, he said, had even been known to live right at the other end of the Marsh up by Dymchurch.

Jim said that, to the best of his knowledge, the original meaning of 'Pilcher' meant 'pilch-maker', a pair of pilches being a pair of trousers. But at the grammar school he attended until he was evacuated in 1940, his teacher told him it derived from a French word meaning 'villain', though whether that was just a piece of villainy itself wasn't clear either.

Either way, his line of Pilchers had nearly reached the end. His own son and his brother's son had both only had daughters, who had married and taken non-Pilcher names.

'So,' he said, 'that's the end of us.'

He had, I sensed, been limbering up his powers of reminiscence in anticipation of our meeting.

'Sit here. You stick that recorder down there. That's right.'

A tall man (I could tell, though he sat) and a distinguished man, Jim reassured me that he and his wife, who melted softly into her easy chair like a snow lady, were comfortable, tended by their son and carers, and fortunate in being able to afford to 'keep warm and feed ourselves'. His wife looked up at him adoringly and looked down at her knitting, also adoringly.

'Tell me what you remember about growing up on the farm, Jim?' I asked.

A mantelpiece clock filled a pause as Jim cleared his throat and ordered his thoughts.

His grandfather, he said, had taken over the tenancy of the Collyers' farm, less than 300 yards from where we now sat, in 1901. The farm was owned by a Miss Hannah Collyer, who lived just across the road.

'When I was a nipper, it was all sheep. Or at least it was mostly. One farmer had some Sussex cattle – single-grazed, mind.

'During the war, that's when we had to pull our socks up and plough up the meadows and go into arable. That broke the sequence of graze land. There's only a small bit of original marshland – as hasn't been ploughed in five hundred years – left. That's the last remaining grass pasture…'

Of course, he said, before the war, there was no electricity or running water. 'The only water we had was rainwater off the farmhouse roof. When you have to carry water in by bucket, you take care of it, I can tell you!'

'Did you have any siblings?' I asked Jim.

'Oh yes. A sister and a brother. My brother and I farmed together for fifty years. I only nearly killed him a couple of times! He was on the sheep. I was on the machines. I always preferred the smell of diesel to that of sheep shit. But do you know, I still came fourth in the England sheep-shearing finals in Wandsworth and Putney in 1984. Of course, no one gets a medal for coming fourth. It still means something, you know.'

I knew. But I felt that the years were passing too quickly. Extraordinary, I thought, that friends of mine a third of Jim's age had spent the past ten years agonising over their first two decades, while Jim glided over his so easily. We'd covered over half a century of his history in the space of a few sips of tea.

I tried to steer him back to the past.

He was, he said, fourteen in 1940, and had been studying at the local grammar school for three years. In that year it was evacuated, and his father said, 'Well, if you're not going to school, you're working on the farm.'

'So that was the end of my education!' said Jim.

'At, least,' I said, 'the end of your formal education.'

'That's right,' he said. 'But I don't regret it! When they bought a tractor, I was landed. I couldn't wait for the horse to be sent off to France, because I hated it. They wanted me to feed it on a Sunday. I was put behind a horse-plough, and my feet ached and ached. It was uncomfortable to sit on and there was no roof. It bit at one end, kicked at the other and the steering was terrible!'

A little giggle rose from where Mrs Pilcher knitted. Clack-clack…

During the war, he said, the Marsh became a 'terrible' place.

'Half a mile from here there was a radar station. They [it scarcely needed to be said who they were] bombed that one Sunday, and they put the fear of God into us. Bombing and the threat of invasion.'

But luckily, he said, he was saved from joining up when he came of age, being a farmer; farming being a reserved occupation because 'we were so short of food'.

In the 'old days', said Jim, farms could employ a good number of people. 'Nowadays,' he said, 'finding the labour's a problem. Can't get local.' So the farmers employ Polish labour to do the heavy lifting, 'Coming up and down the tracks on their tractors like madmen…'

He talked about his father, and his brothers, and their respective travails, and we paused to reflect. And then he said, 'Do you want any light-hearted stories?'

Please, I said. I'd love a light-hearted story.

'Well,' he said, 'I had an uncle – he worked with us. He never told any mucky stories at all. But there was this one looker's hut right out into the middle of the Marsh… Of course, there are no real lookers about now. Original lookers looked after sheep by the acre. They'd check over the animals, see to fly strike, and get extra pay for sheep washing, trimming, clearing out the dead. Extra for shearing… Used to be hundreds of the lookers' huts. But they're all knocked down now.'[1]

Toc. Toc.

'Where was I?'

'You were telling the story about the uncle who never told any mucky stories,' I reminded him.

'That's right. Well, there was one Pilcher that was a shepherd up by Brookland. And he went out for a boozy night and came back into the hut and started to make a fire…'

---

[1] This isn't quite true – there are some, more or less intact, brick built and about the size of a large garden shed. But as there is no obligation to preserve them, many have been demolished or lie atrophying and unused in the fields.

'... mmm?'

'... and the fire wouldn't burn. He couldn't make it out. And he looked up and saw that some local yobbos had stopped the chimney up – just a bit of vandalism, you know.'

'Right.'

'But the other story...'

'Your uncle's story?'

'That's right. He went to a wedding out there on the Marsh. And after the church service, the party went out into the fields with a barrel of beer, I suppose.'

'Yes...'

'But during the celebration, they lost the bridegroom and the bridesmaid.'

'*Yes...*'

'So, someone went to find them... and...'

'*Yeeess?*'

'He was only giving her a portion in the farm wheelbarrow! Well,' he said, 'that was the end of the reception, I can tell you. They all went home quick. In a wheelbarrow! And in those days, a wheelbarrow was a big wooden old thing. The mind boggles.'

It did.

But now, he said, 'A lot of the houses have nothing to do with farming. Just people who like to live in the Marsh. Like that chap in Rye. He's a national expert on antique glass. He's on the television. He's a cheeky devil. He's full of old nonsense. But he's an educated chap.'

For a while we all sat in our chairs. Mrs Pilcher knitted. Jim seemed to be thinking, his eyes young and blue and lucid. '*Giving her a portion!*' I liked that one...

So I went to make the tea.

When I came back with it, he'd collected his thoughts.

'Well,' he said. 'Dungeness, that's a different world out there.' Mrs Pilcher shivered at the thought.

'Camber's being developed. When my mother married, there were half a dozen houses out there. Now they're building houses in the floodplain areas. Lydd, Camber, New Romney, Dymchurch. Hundreds of houses being built.

'All those houses are well below sea level. It's stupid to my mind. If there ever was a flood. But there's two sides to it, you see. Because what it *does* mean is that they're spending money on the sea wall. And that's good because it protects the farming.

'Down at Collyers', when I was a nipper, we were flooded out twice. My mother was expecting her last child. I was sent to an aunt in Rye. I thought it was living in luxury. She had electric lighting. A single bulb hanging from the ceiling. An inside toilet. Street lighting. It was marvellous, I thought, living like that.

'My father said that they sat indoors with furniture up on boxes with rubber boots on and their feet in the water. That year they went to Mrs Collyer to pay the rent. My father said, "Mrs Collyer, I'm afraid we'll have to give up the farm. It's been a terrible year. We've made no money. The floods have ruined everything, and we can't pay the rent." Do you know what she said?'

'What did she say?'

'She said, "Just stick it out. I don't want any rent this year. And I don't want you giving up the farm!" Who'd do that nowadays?'

The clock continued ticking without interference from Mrs Pilcher's knitting, for she had nodded off and the needles and ball of pink wool lay cosily in her lap.

'I remember,' said Jim, slowly, savouring the remembering, 'as how one year we went to see Mrs Collyer, and she was very, very old. And she reached into her purse, and pulled out a coin, and she gave it to me. And it was half a crown!

'Well,' he said, 'I was bloody rich! I can see her now. Very old, she was. But she bought a bit of my memory with that half a crown…'

We continued to spend it.

Jim told me about a nearby sheep farm which was called Lamb Farm, because it was owned by a man called Lamb.

'And of course,' I said, 'there's Sheep Farm down the road towards Guldeford.'

'Oh!' said Jim. 'But that's just because of lack of imagination. Sheep Farm! I bloody ask you…'

And he remembered how in the 1930s things had got so bad that his father had had to make and sell hay to local farms, and to Mrs Wilson nearby who milked all her cows herself and made farm butter, and who cooked with nothing else, though her husband never got fat on it. Because he worked hard.

That's the trouble now, nobody does work hard. Back then it used to be only two-year-old wethers that went to the abattoir.

'We used to send the joints up to the working men in the Midlands. They wanted a big joint with a bit of fat on it. That's where the energy came from. They needed it because they'd work it off. Nowadays people sit on their arse and have little bits of lean meat and "work hard" like you're doing! But in those days, they wanted the bigger joints.'

When men were men.

Before I left, I asked Jim whether he had any regrets about the old ways of farming, despite its hardships, having gone.

'Well,' he said. 'I was the first one to rejoice at the horse leaving the farm. And then we had a local ploughing match nearby, and I said to someone on the committee, "We must have horses ploughing, because that's how it all started." And he said, "Right, well, you want 'em and you can pay for 'em, then." And I'm the mug who – glad to see the back of the horses off the farm – I was the first to sponsor the horses at the ploughing match and the first to see 'em. Glad to see 'em!

'... so, there's a memory thing there, isn't there. Got to be.'

Got to be, I said.

As Jim had said, after the war, when there was a huge push to ensure Britain could produce the food it needed and that it would never again be at the mercy of U-boats cutting supply lines across the Atlantic, more of the Marsh was turned over to the plough, which, in purely calorific terms, is a more efficient way of farming. New artificial fibres started to depress wool prices at around that time, and sheep made less and less sense. Before the war, nine-tenths of the Marsh was given over to pasture, grazing almost a quarter of a million sheep. Now the first statistic is as good as reversed – only one-tenth remains pasture. The sheep are commensurately fewer in number.

Also, as Jim said, there are parts of the Marsh that have never been ploughed, and it's quite evident where that's the case. The pasture is more rough-textured, like the pelt of a friendly farm dog, and the undulations in the land, subtle as they are, represent the culmination of almost a millennium of comings and goings by sheep and sea. 'A carpet of grass covering a fossil medieval landscape,' in the words of Jill Eddison, a famed archaeologist of Romney Marsh.

Much of that old landscape remaining is protected through the designation of a number of areas as Sites of Special Scientific Interest (SSSIs). But they aren't all contiguous; they're more a patchwork of the Marsh's old self.

The soil being fertile, it delivered rich dividends by way of valuable arable yields, for the farmers who had the capital to invest in the machinery needed to reap them. And the temptation to do so must have always been only shallowly buried.

The eponymous heroine of Sheila Kaye-Smith's novel *Joanna Godden*, written in the 1920s but set in the late 1880s and 1990s, a 'headstrong' young woman in the opinion of almost all its other characters, was one who so yielded.

The book begins as Joanna inherits her father's farm, Ansdore, somewhere near Brookland, and decides, against the judgement of the local community, to continue to farm it herself.

Just over a third of the way into the book, Joanna is grieving for her fiancé, Martin, a man of a higher social status but with a weaker constitution, not having been brought up on the Marsh or worked the land as Joanna had. The two had set out in a pony cart, on a day trip to Dungeness, a world away from her corner of the Marsh, closer to Jim Pilcher's house, and there they walked, 'to the end of the Ness – to a strange forsaken country of coastguard stations and lonely taverns and shingle tracks', and stared at where the water drops 'to sinister, glaucous depths'.

She says, 'Well, it ain't too much to see.'

He says, 'It's wonderful. It's terrible.'

And then he teases her with the prospective delights of Venice and their planned honeymoon. They squabble. Martin insists they must marry in early June. But that's too early for Joanna, who says that she 'shan't have got in my hay, and the shearers are coming on the fourteenth – you have to book weeks ahead,' and as she points out, 'It won't make any difference to our marriage, being married three weeks later – but it'll make an unaccountable difference to my wool prices if the shearers don't do their job properly – and then there's the hay!'

Martin concedes that he must wait. But the mood on the way back in the pony trap is more subdued, and the weather worsens such that, 'in half an hour they were both wet through to their shoulders, for the rain came down with all the drench of May', and while he chivalrously expresses concern for his beloved and intended, she assures him as how she is like 'our Romney sheep – I can stand all winds and waters. But you're not used to it like I am…'

Five pages later, Martin succumbs to a cold caught in that dismal shower, and he's dead. ('Lovely Jo' are his last words…)

In her grief, Joanna Godden throws herself into farm work, 'waking the girls, hustling the men, putting her own hand to the milking or the cooking, more sharp-tongued than ever, less tolerant, more terribly alive…' and upsetting her old retainer Stuppeny, who complains that she 'spicks short wud me. And I've told her as she mun look around fur a new head man.'

Worse, her head is turned by the prospect of growing crops.

By autumn, her new ploughs had delivered 'eight bushels to the acre', and she had 'triumphed gloriously over everyone who had foretold her ruin through breaking up pasture; strong-minded farmers could scarcely bear to drive along that lap of the Brodnyx road which ran through Joanna's wheat, springing slim and strong and heavy-eared as from Lothian soil…'

One neighbour, Farmer Vine, is so distressed that (it was rumoured) 'he had once gone by train from Appledore because he couldn't abear the sight of Joanna Godden's ploughs'.

In all likelihood, Vine's descendants, if they're still farming the Marsh, have also now broken up the pasture, and enjoy the early autumn delights of the annual Romney Marsh Ploughing Match (and Family Fun Dog Show), which on the year that I dropped by took place at a far-flung spot between Camber Sands and Lydd, not far from Dungeness, where Joanna's beau had caught his fateful cold.

From a nearby firing range, the army pings shells into the Channel and there are all sorts of other more-or-less secret facilities, including a mocked-up town, a few hundred yards seaward from the road to Lydd, wherein, one presumes, soldiers sometimes pretend to engage in hand-to-hand, street-by-street fighting and counter-insurgency.

Pylons, wind turbines and little else punctuate this plain, which, when viewed from the sea wall, with your back to the kite-surfers, the ships and France, could pass for a diorama, such as you might find in a museum, perhaps of military history.

'To The Ploughing', said a hand-painted sign resting on a stack of tractor tyres, nudging visitors along a rutted track, past a flooded gravel pit and the rusted machinery for conveying its spoils (but to where?), a wind-battered barn and some sheep. A big man in a field jacket asked me for a fiver for admission. I gave him a £20 note and he handed back two £10 notes before a small herd of boy and girl scouts directed me towards the impromptu car park in the wheat stubble.

There was music, popular hits by Abba, Queen and Hot Chocolate, as arranged for and played by a mobile steam organ, a kind of aural beacon to drawing spectators beyond the car park, past hay bales, to the main event.

I had vague expectations of the ploughing match resembling a slow, heavy equestrian meet – perhaps with running commentary delivered by public-address system, and however modest they might be in number, members of the crowd urging on their favourites: 'Go Piers, go!'

But these stalwarts of the share worked unbated and unfeted, arranged by competition classes[2] correlating to the age and size of

---

[2]Of which there are many, including but certainly not limited to: three-furrow conventional, intermediate reversible, vintage furrow, novice reversible, farmerette conventional. Horse. And 'loy digging'.

the tractor, some being diminutive, strange, two-wheel machines, which took as their model their immediate ancestor, the horse, and which in like manner demanded that they be coaxed, goaded and kicked. Many of the tractors dated from the last world war or before. The competitors were neither universally old, nor male. Each was allotted a patch of field to plough, and the day to do it in. For this kind of ploughing is about precision and craftsmanship. Not speed.

'You see, what you're aiming for…'

I had collared a competitor, a man of seventy or so with a squint and a smile crafted around his fieldsman's eyes, who would be taking part in fourteen such competitions this year, even the Nationals in Yorkshire…

'… it isn't just that each furrow is straight…'

He took off his flat cap and drew it against a sweating brow.

'. . . but the depth must be even, and the crown has to be neat, and there shouldn't be any rubbish on it as I have there.' He waved a huge brown hand dismissively at his patch.

It was early autumn, and still warm. For three nights a long-desired storm had yet to break and the ground, he said, '… isn't good for this kind of thing. It's hard. It's difficult to work, not soft enough. Though I suppose, at least, it's the same for all of us.'

The air throbbed with a comforting rumble of old engines. Around us, occupying a football-pitch-sized patch of the Marsh, the tractors and their riders made cautious way, stopping, restarting, rejigging, adjusting the ploughshares to cut through the soil with the clean sweep of a ship's bow racing headlong through surf, albeit more slowly, and with fewer bubbles.

It was work that required meticulousness, punctiliousness, akin to the travails of a calligrapher or a sculptor. Any slips or laxness would quickly, obscenely, declare themselves in the fresh, black churn of soil. The ploughmen sat facing forwards, but always glancing backwards, because to know where they were going it was necessary that they see where they had been. One, I saw, worked with his son, a boy of eleven or twelve, who measured the breadth of the furrow with a tape measure, keeping his father, who was ensconced in the saddle of a battleship-grey Massey Ferguson, in check with low and unintelligible mutterings as he inched along.

On the sidelines, casting their expert eyes, stood country men with roast-beef complexions, huddled in convivial or conspiratorial groups, sharing jokes and winks. One wore a sweatshirt bearing the words: 'The deeper I plough, the louder she grunts.'

But there were other entertainments. Two men from the local hunt arrived to show off their pinks, their mounts and their pack of hounds. One spoke through a loudspeaker and asked the not-very-many people who had gathered around whether they would like to ask any questions. The 'crowd' looked among itself as if to see whether it could collectively muster sufficient curiosity to do so. The man on the horse looked disappointed at the lack of interest in what was probably his favourite subject.

His fine mount's tail twitched, and it did a little dance.

He was put out of at least a little of his misery by a man who asked, 'So, what do you actually hunt, then?'

This seemed to be the question that the huntsman was gagging to answer, and he leapt to it.

'Many of you will recall,' he drawled, 'that among the other great things he did for this nation [sniggering, sarcastic] Tony *Blaar* sat on his sofa and dec*laared* that he was banning fox hunting...'

Hounds jostled around the grey horse upon which sat this paragon of country values.

She, the mare, looked uncomfortable amid the thin throng of pedestrians. The man atop her was rather enjoying himself now, and the hounds were baying adoringly. It was, it couldn't be denied, a stirring and ancient sound.

'These hounds hunt to the trail. But let me assure *you*...' he said, though his audience didn't look in particular need of any kind of assurance, '... that they are *fox* hounds through and through... and whilst we are law-abiding citizens and adhere to the *letter* of the law, we are always...'

There was a pause...

'... more than happy to come to the aid of the farmer when he requests it.'

And to demonstrate the fluidity, the poetry, the God-given grace of Man, Horse and Hound in union, they all cantered up the field for a couple of furlongs and cantered back again.

Impressive though these rough-hewn, good-natured killer beasts were, most people came neither for the ploughing, nor for the diatribe against urban liberals, but for the element of the event that was the Family Fun Dog Show, a motley assemblage of caninity, and though it stood to win no prizes, humanity, promenading around the perimeter of an oblong of neatly arranged hay bales.

All I know about dog shows was gleaned from a conversation with a once highly regarded Crufts judge, who cautioned: 'Always judge the four legs [there's an implied play of words in 'four', homonym of 'fore'] and not the two.'

This, as I had understood it, was a means of saying that a dog shouldn't win on account of the judge's appreciation of the owner.

But I was so much more interested in the two than the four. Dogs are dogs, but opportunities to gaze upon multiple members of the population of Romney Marsh are not extravagantly granted. And in truth, for a country event, the ploughing match attracted a jovial mob.

Curiously, with the exception of the man on the horse in his crimson jacket, no one was obviously 'county'. The only headscarves I saw were worn not by Princess Anne-alikes, but members of the Bruderhof, an Amish-ish Christian community based in Robertsbridge on the Weald, who fund communal living through the export of factory-made furniture.

And if there were trophies or champagne showers, I don't recall them, the day ending easily, as a light loam is broken by a ploughshare, the diesel fug clearing, and a new narrative of the Marsh's utility is etched deeper into its skin.

6

The Bailiff of the Marsh

All the infections that the sun sucks up
From bogs, fens, flats, on Prosper fall and make him
By inch-meal a disease!
The Tempest, Act II Scene ii, William Shakespeare, 1611

On a clement day in May, the year after the Armistice that closed the hostilities of the Great War, a platoon of soldiers, hardened or otherwise altered by fighting at Ypres, Gallipoli and the Somme, and led by a handlebar moustache attached to an army major, spread out on Romney Marsh on a reconnaissance mission.

This 'band of brothers', armed with what appear to have been outsized gardening tools – hoes, rakes and shovels – scoured cottages, sheds, barns, ditches, sewers, rain barrels and watering troughs for the enemy, which was detected in large numbers, and diligently photographed, enumerated, quantified and tabulated.

In the photographs from the official report the platoon members resemble, almost, a troupe of music-hall chimney sweeps, ready to burst into song. Their foe, six-legged and tiny, could scarcely be the cause of mirth.

That malaria was once commonplace in England, and most of Europe and the United States, proves how swiftly the facade of modernity obliterates memories of the past. Malaria is responsible for the deaths of almost half a million people each year, many of whom are children, and is caused by the parasite *Plasmodium*, carried by any one of a number of subspecies of the mosquito *Anopheles*, long regarded as endemic to wetland areas.

For at least four centuries, the ague, confirmed by the late nineteenth century as most probably malaria, was the presumptive cause of mortality in areas of Britain that were boggy, marshy, brackish or swampy, such as Romney Marsh, where it was known as 'the bailiff' for its ability to stop anyone in their figurative, or not so figurative tracks.

From the sixteenth through to the eighteenth centuries, one in three babies born to women living on the Marsh were dead before they were a year old, and life expectancy hovered between twenty-five and thirty for Marsh dwellers, where those that lived on the adjacent Weald could expect to live twice as long. Parish registries from the villages of Appledore, Brenzett, Brookland, Snargate and the (apparently now disappeared) village of Stone show that every year for over two centuries more people were buried than were christened.

'The contours of mortality appeared to parallel those of the landscape. Romney Marsh parishes shared their bleak demographic prospect with other marshland areas of Kent. Low-lying marshland and estuarine areas were unusually mortal, upland areas were refreshingly healthy,' writes the medical historian Mary J. Dobson, diving into registers of births and deaths and the ague-blown mists of time.

So formidable was the Marsh mosquito that it took on the might of the Church, hounding clergymen from their parishes.

'My health would permit me to stay no longer,' wrote an eighteenth-century vicar of Tenterden in his resignation letter to the bishop. '[I am leaving] on account of the disagreeable situation and to avoid the unhealthiness of the marsh air,' wrote a contemporary near-neighbour.

'[The Parish of Aldington is in] so unhealthy a situation as to be absolutely unfit for any curate,' wrote the man who held that post, a survey conducted by the Church in the late 1700s finding that where curates refused to live in their own cures, agues, and the general 'unwholesomeness' of the surroundings, were the cause.

Meanwhile the squirearchy, the gentry farmers who owned the rights to the profitable grazing, gazed down from pleasant situations on the fever-stricken Marsh folk, of whom outsiders generally formed an unsavoury impression:

'Mean quality marsh Lookers … of the lower sort … mostly such as are employed in the occupations and management of the level, or a kind of seafaring men who follow an illicit trade, as well by land as water,' was a typically damning judgement. Indeed, it wouldn't be wholly far-fetched to say that *Anopheles* colluded in shaping the social evolution of the Marsh, chasing out anyone who had the luxury of not living there, and keeping those poor enough and risk-hungry enough to weather the bad air and foetid chequerboard of ditches in their place.

Courtesy of the records of a doctor, Jeremiah Cliff (long deceased), we have a goodish understanding of what did for marsh people.

Cliff's intended life work, in which he was wholly successful, was to make 'a true and perfect and exact list', as far as he was able, 'of all those persons … that have died in Tenterden' (just at the edge of the Marsh, and marshier then than it is now), beginning 18 March 1712, with their names, their ages as near as could be guessed at, their date of death, 'and also what distemper they died of and also who was their doctor that did them in their year of sickness'.

He did so with exemplary thoroughness until the end of his own life in 1742, by which time he had diagnosed apoplexy, asthma, bloody flux with thrush, breast cancer, cancer of the navel, colds and coughs, colic, convulsions, drink, erysipelas, fits, French pox, gangrene, gout in the stomach, gravel, green sickness, harelip, imposthumus, internal bleeding, jaundice, measles, mortification, palsy, pleurisy, rheumatism, scabies, St Anthony's Fire, tumour of the knees, ulcers in the side and bladder, vomiting, whooping cough and worm-fever, alongside the occasional drowning, suicide or cudgelling, and noting en route, the remarkable proclivity shown by the natives to lunacy, insanity and dying distracted, frenzied or melancholic.

But 'fever' was given as the greatest single cause, in most years accounting for more than a quarter of deaths, and in some years more than half of them. Plague, by contrast, which had in previous centuries scoured the Marsh and nearby towns, didn't even make it to the top ten.

Should the blame be laid fully at the door of *Anopheles*?

'Fever' is a portmanteau for any number of fatal pre-'scientific' malaises, but the association between those of its variants that were prevalent where there was proximity to areas of marshiness and still-water areas was understood, even if the means of transmission was not, and some parts of the Marsh were commonly regarded as 'ague-ier' than others.

Of Appledore, now well kept and well heeled (and well healed), it was said by the Kentish historian Edward Hasted that 'the vast quantity of marshes which lie contiguous and come close up to it, make it very unhealthy, and this is rendered much more so, by a large tract of swamp, called the Dowles, lying about a mile south eastward from the village, within the marsh'.

Snargate, late parish of the author of *The Ingoldsby Legends*, was regarded as 'a very forlorn and unhealthy place ... of the same bad qualities of both air and water as the neighbouring parishes in the Marsh and if possible to a greater degree, for the whole is an entire flat of marshes', such as made 'dreadful havoc on the health of the inhabitants of this sickly and contagious country, a character sufficiently corroborated by their pallid countenances and short lives'.

But later sufferers of the ague 'enjoyed' at least some chance of alleviation, even if it was expensive and hard to access, where those struck with, say, most of the other horrors on Dr Cliff's list would make do with quackery and prayer.

This they owed to a man from Cambridge who had dropped out of an apothecary's apprenticeship in the late 1600s and would become one of the world's first pharma tycoons, winning royal patronage, and overturning a whole basket of silly and long-held prejudices on the way.

The bark of the cinchona plant, or 'fever tree' (*Cinchona officinalis*), a small flowering shrub, is the only natural source of an alkaloid substance better known to the world as quinine. Native to South America, in the seventeenth century it was, like the potato and the tomato, an import from the western hemisphere which, though known about, met with mild disdain in England and was mostly ignored.

Several obstacles stood in the path of the bark's adoption in the shires.[1]

First was the fact that it appeared nowhere in the works of the great physician and natural philosopher of the classical age, Galen, born in 129 CE, and whose works on the workings of the body and its malaises still towered, despite their antiquity, over medical thinking. Galen (who, it needs to be said, was an early champion of empirical learning, especially vivisection) attributed the ague, as he attributed the cause of most illnesses, to an imbalance of humours.

That cinchona bark was hot and bitter suggested to his disciples that it was at odds with what that rationale suggested a cure for the ague ought to be: *ergo*, to those steeped in the Galenic method it shouldn't, and thus it didn't, work.

Worst still, cinchona, used by the (malaria-free) native South American Quechua peoples to treat myriad illnesses for centuries, had been 'discovered' by Spanish Conquistadores, appropriated by Jesuits, and was thus tainted, in the eyes of the English, by its Papist associations.

Compounding those crimes, nobody really knew, nor had they taken the time or expended the energy to discover, the correct method of administering cinchona or appropriate dosages before Robert Talbor, the afore-mentioned former apothecary's apprentice, worked them out.

Seizing the day, and a large quantity of the bark, Talbor 'planted [himself] in Essex near the sea side, in a place where agues are the epidemical diseases, where you will find but few persons but either are, or have been afflicted with a tedious quartan', and began to experiment with different dosages, the local population happy to

---

[1]Given the popularity of chips and tomato sauce, and general enthusiasm for a gin and tonic, all three Latin imports can be said to have thrived.

be figurative 'guinea pigs', given the promise of being rid of fever, diarrhoea and other discomforts without paying.

All the while, he was mindful of the need to protect the identity of his cure – for twofold reasons: on the one hand, he saw that cinchona should be insulated from the inevitable bias against it on politico-religious grounds. More prosaically, he understood that his own profits would be lessened were he not to. To those ends, not only did he disguise its distinctive and bitter taste with opium and wine, describing it only as a 'secret remedy', but he himself propagated slurs against 'Jesuit's Bark', 'Fever Bark', 'Princesses' Bark' and cinchona in all its other guises, maintaining the fiction that whatever his cure-all consisted of, it bore no relation to any of those.

From Essex, where he had established himself, he met a French officer, 'late returned from Flanders' and serving with the court of Charles II, who was suffering from an intermittent fever that his own physician had been unable to cure. A first-person account of what happened has been left by the officer, who neglected to reveal his name but described how he was introduced to 'a very poor man' who had already cured a number of his servants, and how, 'there being nothing of the charlatan about him, I had no hesitation whatever in taking his remedy, although both it and he were quite unknown to me at that time'.

The anonymous officer took three doses of the bark in powdered form steeped in wine before heading to Sheerness on the Thames Estuary ('the most fever-ridden place in the whole of England') with the king. Talbor, he said, gave him permission not only to swim, for amusement's sake, but also to indulge 'in debauchery if I felt so inclined'.

The man told the king about his 'little doctor', who 'at length … ordered me to bring the man to him and he made many experiments with the powder'. Since the physicians could not guess what it was, the king gave him a pension of 300 pieces of gold and a knighthood, and made him one of his personal physicians, 'solely in order to find out and eventually to publish a secret of such importance for the health of all mankind'.

The royal doctors maintained a professional distrust of Talbor, the king's regard for whom they viewed as an affront. For one thing, they perceived the calling of the apothecary as lesser than their own; that Talbor had failed to complete his years at Cambridge suggested he was clearly unqualified to treat the royal person. And yet his medicine worked.

Talbor became rich from the king's patronage but died before he was forty (not, it scarce needs to be said, of the ague), having isolated and promoted one of the few seventeenth-century medicines that would survive into the twenty-first century as an effective remedy for a potentially fatal disorder.

It is good that the ague's hosts no longer reproduce in the shallow waters of the ditches and sewers, in water troughs and rain-settled furrows in the wet ploughed fields. But its ghost, if it is to be allowed one, is harder to expel.

How many cadavers beneath the buckled turf and lichen-clad stones of Romney's numerous parishes were its victims? Was it any worse a death than any other? Not that to suffer it was always to die of it. But even where not fatal, it impressed upon its victims, individual and collective, a morbid pallor, jaundiced air, liverish demeanour and enervating deflation of spirit.

In 1812 French chemists isolated the active agent in cinchona and created the modern-day quinine, ever since used effectively, frequently alcoholically and deliciously, to treat the ague. On Romney Marsh it was becoming less prevalent anyway.

In a way, this can also be credited to the French.

William Pitt completed the construction of the Royal Military Canal in 1809, five years after the threat of invasion by Napoleon (which the canal was intended to repulse[2]) had passed. Building the canal had cost almost a quarter of a million pounds, the largest ever government-funded infrastructure project of its time, and Pitt's government looked to stave off the inevitable criticisms

[2]William Cobbett doubted it would have repulsed the French: 'Here is a canal made for the length of thirty miles to keep out the French; for those armies who had so often crossed the Rhine and the Danube were to be kept back by a canal thirty feet wide at most!' he wrote in his *Rural Rides* (1822–6).

of overspend by recouping money through leases, navigation rights and the sale of parts of it to farmers and landowners.

None of this would ever rescue the canal's reputation as a cash-pit. But it did at least reinvigorate the still and stagnant waterways of the Marsh, easing drainage, facilitating the regulation of water levels and generally rendering the Marsh less aguey, if not wholly absent of it.

In 1884 the Chief Medical Officer of Great Britain noted of the marshy areas of Kent:

> the heat of the weather in the summer months developed
> a large amount of Malaria with the effect that Malarious
> Fever became very prevalent. In olden times these fevers were
> designated 'low fever' both by the public and by the profession
> … but mostly in this locality [they] derive their origin from
> Marsh Malaria and spread by contagion when suitable cases
> come in contact with persons suffering from the contagion.

Earlier in the century, by contrast, Edward Hasted described the inhabitants of the Kent marshes as 'very rarely' *not* suffering from 'severe agues', their complexions thus rendered 'dingy yellow'. If the sufferers survive, he said, 'They are generally afflicted with them till summer, and often for several years, so that it is not unusual to see a poor man, his wife, and whole family of five or six children, hovering over their fire in their hovel, shaking with an ague all at the same time.'

And yet when, in 1919, Major Angus MacDonald led a detachment of the Royal Army Medical Corps into the fields of Kent, he found that the people of the Marsh attributed their better health to almost everything other than the actual cause of it. One suggested it had something to do with the felling of elm trees, and another to the arrival of the steam engine, yet another to the war, and another to the king.

MacDonald and his troops were on the Marsh because, in the penultimate year of the First World War, an outbreak of malaria had particularly affected troops barracked at Lydd and Sandwich: only through epidemiological investigation and comparison with the symptoms of untravelled local people could he be certain that it was a Romney-specific strain that presented itself in his troops, though his greater fear was that local mosquitoes might carry parasites borne by soldiers convalescing in northern Kent, who had contracted the disease elsewhere – such as India and Greece – and feed a resurgence of the 'bad air'.

Armed with science and, as previously mentioned, gardening equipment, the Corps was empowered to take measures such as lime-washing farm buildings, unblocking drains and checking watercourses for larvae, to consign the Kentish ague to obscurity at the very least, if not the dustbin of history.

And yet.

'There is no work more wanted in medical statistics, than a geography of malaria,' wrote John MacCulloch, a geologist and physician, in 1827, 'a work which ... seems of pressing urgency from the increase of travelling as well as of migrating residents abroad, and from the mass of misery, added to the considerable mortality, which results from this ignorance.' Two centuries later, the need still stands.

There is a cruel irony attendant on quinine's otherwise benignity. South America provided the cure for malaria, a disease which that continent's own inhabitants were untroubled by. Those who stood to benefit most significantly from the cure, the ever-more curious and avaricious Europeans, burst that bubble, introducing *Anopheles* to the continent alongside a Pandora's box of other diseases, along with bridges, roads and all the other appurtenances and arrogances of empire.

What's more, the bark from the jungles of Peru equipped colony-hungry Europe with the armour it needed to foray deeper, and for longer, into sub-Saharan Africa in search of ivory and slaves. Unlike the native peoples of America, Africa's inhabitants, if they survived to adulthood, did so with a considerable measure of childhood exposure and thus greater protection. So, it would seem, quinine allowed Western colonialists to replace the native labour they had lost in the Americas to the malaria they introduced, with African slaves...

Malaria was regularly, if not frequently, recorded on Romney Marsh until the 1950s, and though Europe was declared free of malaria in 1975 (and the United Kingdom earlier still) the 'rollback' isn't irreversible.

As late as the 1970s, local councils in Kent sprayed waterways with DDT as a preventative for a feared outbreak. In 2016 several cases of indigenous malaria were reported in France and Spain... and I've heard rumours of rumours of incidences on the Marsh – which may be untrue or premature and yet, in 2004, an article in the *British Medical Journal* prophesied thus:

> Return of indigenous malaria in the UK has not yet occurred. The greater availability of cheap tropical and subtropical travel will result in more *primary* infections of humans with blood that could infect home grown mosquitoes.
>
> With increased global warming, occasional cases of *secondary* malaria will occur in UK residents who have not been abroad, but the average *tertiary* spread will be to less than one other human and thus malaria will not establish itself (for malaria to persist, on average a patient with malaria would have to transmit infection to at least one other human, otherwise the infection would die out). Within the next few decades tertiary spread of infection may occur in the UK, with spread to at least one other person. Indigenous malaria will then be with us again...

7

In Europolis: A Danube Coda

As a final evidence of the personality of the joint agent of the Danube, one may note that after fifteen years of existence the commission was allowed to have its own insignia and flag. Such is the history, and such the achievement of the European Commission of the Danube, the most ambitious and the most successful experiment in international administration. It remains to consider what light this experiment throws on the problem of bridging the gap between sovereign states.

The European Commission of the Danube: An Experiment in International Administration, Edward Krehbiel, 1918

As we left Letea for Sulina in the *canotca*, we passed another *canotca,* in the stern of which sat the priest who had led the service at the church in Mila. He, like Doamna Viorica's son's girlfriend, was taking photographs of himself, and was most probably headed, thought Adrian, to the near-deserted but ecclesiastically important town of Sfiștofca. And he looked very nice. He had changed his white-and-gold robes for red ones.

And as our *canotca* came alongside the quayside at Sulina, we saw yet another *canotca*, in which sat, aside from a man at the stern evidently in charge of its navigation, three bearded men wearing military fatigues. The *canotca* was towing a long, inflatable kayak, its name, *Tirpitz*, carefully painted in naval Gothic on its bows.

'I think they're Germans,' said Adrian. 'Anything strange floating on the Danube always turns out to be German.'

'But are they actually *military*?' I asked. 'Some sort of training exercise?'

'Don't know,' he said.

It is possible, though not advised, to travel the length of the Romanian Danube without becoming waylaid by the glittering delights of the delta, its island forests, axe-wielding carp choppers, snakes and pelicans.

The passenger boats steam directly from Tulcea in no more than a morning to Sulina, the last town on the river before it fades into the Black Sea and a port that perhaps no longer deserves the epithet Europolis, given it by the writer Jean Bart in the novel of that name.

I would like to think of Bart (who was not at all as French as he sounds[1]), resting his eyes on the silvery Danube between composing paragraphs, perhaps from a window of one among many of the once imposing, now charmingly derelict riverside mansions, of which there are many in Sulina, and of which one, now a hotel, bears his name.

But it was a different kind of place when he wrote, as he did, one sultry day in 1930,

> Day and night, we worked to load the boats. Only at the heart
> of the day was the port ever still. Under the rays of the summer
> sun, nature, numb, was all asleep. No sign of life. Not the
> slightest puff of wind. Earth, water. Men and animals, all fell
> suddenly into a kind of deep tiredness. When the sun reached
> its zenith, the port resembled a kind of enchanted, slumbering
> necropolis. Petrified by the centuries. A phantom town.

Once Sulina was an obscure Ottoman entrepot, 'a collection of adventurers … from the entire Orient … in a very humid

[1]And whose real name was Eugeniu Botez.

environment, full of mosquitoes, waiting to find an opportunity to make money, even at the risk of their own life, which they do not cherish much,' as a Romanian traveller described it in 1856. Another visitor noted that its between 2,000 and 5,000 itinerant inhabitants were mostly involved in 'navigation', and when they weren't, in heavy drinking.

But in that same year it had geopolitical importance stamped upon it by the Treaty of Paris of 1856, which drew a close to the Crimean War, and established the European Commission of the Danube as an international body that would be responsible for riparian issues, like pilotage, collection of customs and harbour fees, navigation rights, maintenance of docks and channels – and, especially after a cholera epidemic brought by an Ottoman transport steamer in 1865, public health issues – which would in some form endure for almost eight decades.

So successful did it become that a strong argument would be made that Sulina should be elevated to the League of Nations as a quasi-state in its own right; and so essential was it to the management of the river that two years into the First World War its members, including Austro-Hungary, France, the United Kingdom, Prussia, Italy and Turkey, continued to meet to discuss its affairs.

By 1904 Sulina's inhabitants included Greeks, Romanians, Russians, Armenians, Turks, Austro-Hungarians, Italians, Bulgarians, English, Montenegrins, French, Tatars and Indians, with places of worship to suit all tastes. It was a heady efflorescence of tea dances, spices, headwear and general cosmopolitanism, with a reputation for costume balls, intrigues and scandal. The great musicians of the day would play sell-out concerts; diplomats schemed and plotted; love affairs, boats and adventurers came and went.

Of all that, the evidence is mostly in its architecture which, to one arriving fresh from the backwaters of the Delta in a *canotca,* is grand in scale, almost to the point of being intimidating.

Pale villas on the left bank, carefully spaced and kept at arm's length from each other by the judicious planting of poplars, smack of the Ottoman influence. Larger, later buildings, including the

Jean Bart Hotel, and mid-rise apartment blocks, and of course the headquarters of the original European Commission of the Danube and all its successors, tell of its international standing. A long-abandoned factory on the right side of the river presents a monolith of Socialist rectangularity.

But for all these booming architectural voices, Sulina is a friendly sort of place, and the little wooden houses in backstreets are brightly painted and full of interesting things wrought from iron or pine.

'I can't wait for you to meet Christie,' said Adrian, adding, 'We also call him *Morrison*, like Jim Morrison from the Doors.'

'Why?' I asked.

'Because he has a leather jacket. With tassels.'

We met Christie, or Morrison, who was an artist, in the garden of the Jean Bart Hotel, just after breakfast time. He was drinking beer with a man who had had a head start on him and was very drunk. Christie had spent a lot of time in England, and we shared some observations on High Wycombe, where he had once worked as a cook. Neither of us had much to say about it.

His friend had also been a cook, but on ships in the Red Sea, and at Christie's urging, he told how on one of his trips, the vessel had been hijacked by pirates, and he had been held captive for several months before there was a kind of prisoner rebellion over the quality of food and the lack of clean, drinkable water. He stood up and pulled down his trousers to below the hip, revealing a long, ugly scar. The pirates had taken umbrage.

'That's where a machine-gun bullet went in. They were just firing off rounds…'

He was woefully in his cups. But he became more animated showing what happened next, how he had grabbed a gun, and shot first one, and then another, and then another, and then another of the pirates.

It wasn't clear whether this had happened, or if it was a kind of re-enactment of what he would have liked to have done, a kind of *esprit de l'escalier*, the thought armed with an automatic weapon…

'Nothing like that ever happened to me in High Wycombe,' said Morrison.

Adrian shook his head.

'I don't think I've ever seen a real bullet wound before,' I said.

'I've been drinking ever since,' said Morrison's friend.

There was a lot of urging by Morrison and the cook to spend the day with them, but neither I nor Adi were inclined to. I wanted to visit the famous lighthouse built by the Danube Commission and which had once guided ships into the river mouth from Batumi and Sebastopol and Constantinople to unload their wares in the heart of Central Europe, before, as happens so often, the course of the river changed, and with it the usefulness of the lighthouse, from helpmate to treacherous distraction.

It is a stalwart lighthouse, middling in height and girth, and robust, surrounded by a wall in which is set a door that leads into a rather magical courtyard garden, with sweet peas and runner beans and snapdragons. It no longer possesses a keeper, in the sense of a person responsible for keeping it alight and throwing its beam across the mouth of the Danube, but it does in the form of a lady called Maria, who boasts hair magnificently and interestingly dyed in shades of orange and pink, and a master's degree in history from the University of Bucharest, the knowledge gleaned from which, and from elsewhere, she readily imparts to all comers, blithely unconcerned by any intimation on their part that they'd prefer to skip the lecture and make their way to the top of the lighthouse to enjoy the view and the fresh air…

'Be *very* careful before you walk up the steps,' she said. 'I have cleaned them with an experimental cleaning product. They are *very* slippery, and you might – slip.'

'I have a feeling,' Adi said, 'that we had better listen to the history lesson.'

Maria was delighted, helping us understand the printed information displays that chronicled every footstep of each commission representative to Sulina, and how the town grew in political and cultural significance, and how the ethnic constitution changed over time, and its powers waxed and waned. But if

I fidgeted, she looked wounded and despondent. And when my
eyes wandered to the adjacent information display prematurely, she
squealed with displeasure.

Politely I asked whether, once the first room had been absorbed,
Adrian and I might be permitted to ascend?

'Well. If you insist. But do not – slip…' she warned.

We did not '– slip', such good fortune affording my first proper
glimpse of the sea since arriving in Romania. Between us and
the riverbank sat a ship-breaker's yard, and there was something
curiously satisfying about watching the dismantling of old Black
Sea beasts, undone with blow torches, a spark of destruction. The
full extent, also, of the old commission's demesne also emerged, the
houses built for its big and not-so-bigwigs, the customs sheds, and
the dry dock now repurposed for private and commercial use.

'And look,' said Adrian. 'That – recreation ground – is where
I spent some happy times on a school exchange as a teenager.'

Later we strolled far beyond the dunes and marshes to Sulina's
cemetery out on the edge of town, stroked gently by breezes that
have rolled through the length of Europe to cosset headstones such
as that which reads:

SACRED TO THE MEMORY OF KATHARINA, THE
BELOVED WIFE OF
WILLIAM SMITH, BUTCHER OF THIS PLACE
WHO DIED AUG 18TH. 1865 (OF CHOLERA)
ALSO EMILY ROSE KATHARINA, AGED 51 WEEKS
AND ELLEN BARBARA, AGED 5 WEEKS – CHILDREN
OF THE ABOVE
ALSO WILLIAM SMITH, BORN IN AYLSHAM,
COUNTY OF NORFOLK ENGLAND
WHO DIED 3rd DECEMBER 1865 AT SOLINA, AGED
37 YEARS

It's a sad marker of four short, grieved lives. But also interesting for
other reasons. It is not the usual lot of Norfolk butchers to live and
die in places like Sulina, the town at the very end of the Danube. And

Katharina is not a Norfolk name; far more likely that his beloved wife was courted locally. There are other English people, of both sexes, buried in the same graveyard, mostly victims of shipwrecks.

But other occupants of this small but eclectically composed necropolis include a Romanian princess, a German surveyor, Russian poets, French hydrologists, Greek master mariners, Egyptian shipwrights, and any number of Ottoman bureaucrats, their headstones engraved in Ottoman, pre-Atatürk script and embellished with a red-painted, carved fez, presumably to indicate official or administrative importance.

The freight vessels still come and go, but the population is one-tenth the size of what it was at its administrative high watermark, for after the Second World War – during which everyone had bombed Sulina, just as everyone had traded in it in peacetime – the Communist government looked to new ways of accessing the Black Sea: a canal between the Danube bypassed Sulina, slowly imposing upon it a torpor, which Bart, for one, had long predicted, if possibly overexaggerated.

'Yes!' he wrote, 'This city is doomed … cities have their lives and deaths … The gate of Sulina is closing forever. Abandoned, Sulina disappears…' It will become, he wrote, 'just a small village of fishermen on the map, forgotten, on the shore'.

On our second afternoon in the city that had not quite atrophied to the extent Bart had anticipated, we crossed the Danube in the little boat – longer and beamier than a *canotca* but not greatly – that is the regular ferry between the north and south banks of the port.

On the north, it lands at a point at which a little creek meets the river. There's also a shop, a general store selling cigarettes, chocolates, newspapers (what one might have once called in London a 'fags and mags' shop, and is, in Romania, a *magazin mixt*). Outside, sitting on its step, a group of drinkers sat listening to *manele* and playing with puppies. We walked a towpath along the tree-lined bank of the creek, into a small *quartier* of narrow thoroughfares with names like Black Sea Street, Fisherman Street, Sturgeon Street, and houses, none more than a storey high, and none really constituting anything more than an exaggerated hut.

We strolled about, gabbling to each other. In Adrian's company I had no fear of being thought a 'talker', for if I was, he was in spades.

I pointed to how one householder had fashioned a fence of reeds, by gathering their ends together in plastic bottles cut in half. It all made for a nice photograph.

Adrian pointed out a rusty handcart. 'There is a special place in the heart of every Romanian for such a thing,' he sighed. It also made for a nice photograph.

And a voice said, 'Excuse me, are you speaking in English?'

Three boys were playing football at the edge of the houses, where the tiny suburb gave way to waste ground, beneath the shadow of the shell of a huge factory; exoskeleton, as it were, of some stranded leviathan exiled by the past.

We had seen the boys but had walked past without engaging. Youths playing football at the edge of houses bordering waste ground tend to be bored, and can be lippy, I've found...

The smallest looked to be only eight years old. Of the other two, one was freckled, stocky and evidently not in want of nutrition, the other was pale ('peaky'-looking), other than his too-red lips, and skinny. All ribs and elbows.

'If you're speaking English, can I hang out?' he asked, or, indeed, almost pleaded.

He and the other older boy shared the name of Andrei. Both were twelve, and plumper Andrei had lived in Sulina all his life.

Ribs-and-elbows Andrei had been born in the province of Wallachia, but his family had moved to England when he was six.

'Whereabouts?' I asked.

'In London. I think we lived in Neasden, Willesden. Places like that, really.'

'When did you come back?'

'We had to come back last year. My dad had been in prison, and when they released him, he was deported.'

'Did you live in Sulina before?'

'No. But my mum didn't want to go back to Wallachia. We ended up here and she liked it.'

'Are you happy to have moved back?'

'I'm not sure, really.'

He and Andrei, and Andrei's little brother, whose one purpose in life at that moment appeared to be to throw a ball in the air as high as he could and try to catch it, were all great friends. But Andrei missed speaking English, and the company of some of his old London classmates.

'And, you see,' he said, 'life here is just so different.'

This he didn't really need to point out, I thought, as we walked in the shadow of the skeleton of the factory which, he said, 'had been bombed by the Germans during the war'. (Though Adrian wasn't so sure that it had, but I think Andrei was right.)

Beyond the houses was a spattering of ponds, marshy ground, and horses grazing at the cusp of the reeds.

That the ponds were alive with frogs (and snakes, said Andrei) was a testament to the underlying vitality of the delta, I thought, challenged as it was by the considerable volumes of domestic and industrial waste heaped on it casually, almost drunkenly.

'I love the ponds because there are so many animals in them. Sometimes we go fishing for little fish. We make boats out of those...' said Skinny Andrei, pointing to a large rectangle of expanded polystyrene, packaging, once upon a time, for some kind of household appliance, but not intrinsically seaworthy. Or even pondworthy.

'Oh God,' I said.

'Please don't do that!' said Adrian. 'It's so dangerous!'

'I know,' said Andrei.

Andrei, Andrei, Andrei's little brother and their friends lived the life of Huck Finns and Tom Sawyers, or of kids playing in bomb sites in the East End or Liverpool at the end of the war. Feral, free, epic and empowering, playful and perilous.

But Andrei despaired of all the rubbish, shaking his head as an old lady in a headscarf, trailed by a dozen waddling ducks, tipped a wheelbarrow full of household waste into one of his beloved ponds.

'The thing is,' he sighed, pronouncing it *fing* after the west London fashion, 'the older people just don't know. They don't understand about looking after the environment. They just dump stuff.'

'BUT' – he raised his finger, as though just remembering that hope springs eternal – 'we're gonna start a li'l club…'

'Fing! Li'll!' said Adrian. 'I love it!'

'… to look after the ponds, and marshes…'

The woman and her ducks waddled away, but as she did so a man started approaching us.

Andrei and Andrei brushed their foreheads with their forearms in an exaggerated show of amused horror.

'He is so MAD!' said Andrei.

The man rolled toward us, trousers fastened at the fly-button with a safety pin, and his stripy V-neck jumper greasy and holey. He held a harmonica to his mouth, through which he blew energetic gypsy tunes.

We stood and listened, somehow discomfited by his presence but hanging on every wailing note, which was rich and sad, if also, as Andrei had warned us, mad. Every so often he would lower the harmonica and laugh maniacally, before eventually, his medley having come to an end, he also went away.

The five of us walked slowly up Fishguts Avenue or whatever it was called, back up to the left bank of the Danube. Larger Andrei and Adrian were soon locked in conversation in Romanian, Adrian mostly talking and Andrei listening intently, while I listened to London Andrei, and plumper Andrei's little brother straggled behind us, throwing the ball high in the air, and then almost falling over backwards as he watched its descent into the basket of his small hands…

'When we lived in London,' Andrei said, 'we moved about all the time. And sometimes my dad would go to prison.

'My older brother is nineteen now. But he has issues. He gets VERY ANGRY. He's got problems. Sometimes he smashes the place up. My dad smashes the place up sometimes too, when he gets drunk. But he doesn't do that very often.'

By the riverbank were tied all sorts of boats, pontoons and broken, jagged things. The Danube rushed by in its ineffable hurry.

Andrei and Andrei showed us a jetty from which, he said, sometimes, when it was really hot, they jumped to cool off.

'*Oh God*,' I muttered.

'You really mustn't do that!' said Adrian. 'There could be anything in the water. You could cut yourself. Or hit your head on something. You could die. Really, really easily.'

'Yeah,' said Andrei. 'I guess you're right.'

Andrei's little brother threw his ball high into the air again, and nearly wobbled from the quayside (but didn't), and soon Adrian and Andrei had resumed a conversation that held them both rapt.

'What are you talking about?' I asked Adrian.

'Life,' he said.

'What are you telling him about it?' I asked.

'That having the right attitude is everything – and that they mustn't become limited by their surroundings.'

'Quite,' I said.

'And that they really shouldn't jump into the Danube, especially if they can't see what's beneath the surface.'

'Absolutely.'

'And that they shouldn't take any shit from anyone.'

'Yup.'

Soon we walked over another little bridge spanning one of the creeks running from the river into the flatness of the surrounding delta, finding ourselves on what could have been an abandoned sports field turned to pasture.

Cows grazed. The boys played in the concrete shell of a structure which had entirely dispensed of whatever intended function it had ever possessed. A freight ship lumbered quickly up the river, and the boys threw stones at it, Andrei's little brother putting down his ball momentarily to take part. And then we all ambled back to the ferry crossing.

'But things were a bit better in London. Shall I tell you why?' asked Andrei.

'Why?'

'Well,' he said. 'You know, I'm not very well.'

'Oh.'

'I have some kind of a blood syndrome.'

'Ah.'

'That's why I look so thin all the time.'

'Right.'

Indeed, Andrei really didn't look very well. At birth he said, he weighed nearly nine pounds! Now he weighed less than anyone in his class and he couldn't run as fast as any of them.

Whatever it was that afflicted him, he couldn't remember the exact name of it. But in England, he went for regular check-ups, and had injections and treatment. In Romania, you couldn't get that kind of treatment without paying extra – which his family didn't have,

'Still,' he said (and the finger was raised again, this time wise and priestly), 'I know that you can't always get what you want from life. In some ways, I've had a good childhood. One time, I was out in the marsh one evening, and I was surrounded by jackals…'

(In Letea, a man had told us that jackals were crossing the border from Ukraine into the delta with increasing frequency; there was a theory that they were being displaced by the fighting in Donetsk between Ukraine and the Russian-sponsored separatists.)

'But I had a cigarette lighter… and I had to frighten them away.'

He mimed how he had stood holding the lighter as the jackals surrounded him, and how they barked and yelped, but he growled at them and they fled.

I didn't believe him for a moment, but in his reconstruction, I saw Kipling's Mowgli holding the tiger, Shere Khan, at bay, and Morrison's drunken friend killing the pirates who had ruined his life.

'And another time, my mum hired a whole funfair for my birthday. Honestly!' he said, wide-eyed and dishonestly. 'All for me! I woke up, and it was all around me. There were rides and there were dodgems…

'Oh. I don't know,' he added, 'maybe things will be easier when I get older.'

By now, we were joined by another of the Andreis' friends, a girl in the same class at school. She wore a headscarf and had a freckled face of great candour and sensibility. As the Andreis explained who Adrian and I were, she took it all in, nodding with precocious and non-judgemental sagacity. Like, I thought, a doctor hearing a patient explaining their symptoms but not wishing to leap to conclusions.

Andrei said that he felt quite confused about who he was. 'Because sometimes I feel like I'm Romanian, and sometimes I feel like I'm English. And sometimes that makes me feel like I'm neither, so that means I'm from somewhere completely different!'

He translated it back into Romanian and the girl nodded again, as if to say, 'I understand how it must be for you.'

We waited while the ferryman filled his boat with, mostly, adolescents heading across the river for a night out. I hoped that, in a few years' time, both the Andreis and the wise girl with the freckles would be on that boat – and Andrei's little brother close behind.

The three of them (four, counting Andrei's little brother) struck me as possessing extraordinary intelligence and maturity, and it made me feel intensely sad, in particular, of course, for Andrei. And not only on account of his condition, but more, perhaps, for his own awareness of it.

'It was great to meet you,' I said.

'Great to meet you.'

'Really great.'

And we boarded the ferry again.

The 'Germans' did, after all, turn out to be German. As the days passed, our speculation as to their 'mission' had become ever more finely tuned, until we alighted on the putative explanation that they were old friends from school or university and, as the shadow of middle age had crept upon them, had resolved that they should have some sort of adventure. 'One lawyer, one accountant, and a doctor. Or an engineer,' I decided. Adi was OK with that.

Eventually, we found ourselves sharing a near-empty restaurant with them, and it would have been impolite not to ask. We were right, in the main. One, though he had originally trained as an engineer, now handled 'legal matters'. Each summer for the past however many years, they had taken two weeks to paddle as much of the Danube as they could in that time, marked the spot at which that fortnight's journey had ended, returned to Cologne, and the next year started from where they had left off.

When we first saw them, they were being towed into Sulina, having fought a losing battle with an incoming tide.

Now they had come to the very end of the journey, eliciting, said the engineer who handled legal matters, a species of post-Danubial tristesse.

'When we were first planning to do something like this, it seemed so ambitious, it was like: "It can't be done." But now that we've done it, now we have to do something else.'

'What do you think you'll do?' I asked.

'I don't know,' he said. 'Maybe something. Maybe next time the Orinoco. Or climb up something. Or maybe nothing at all...'

And the Danube, which always and never gets to the end of its journey, plodded along behind him, it too having fulfilled its task.

8

Snagged in Snargate

I'll never fathom why I keep coming back to Snargate, given that the place is scarcely any larger than its name, consisting, as it does, of a pub and a church, two forms of long-tried solace separated only by tarmac. But it's a good place to start a walk.

Saturday afternoon in late September is, by which I mean I am, preoccupied by a tumult of thoughts and half-finished sentences. Perhaps the remedy lies in the austerity and counsel of the Marsh, which, were it personified, would have little truck for such things, one imagines.

I set out from the chestnut tree that leans from the confines of the churchyard. A dozen charming black-faced sheep take note of me, and I follow the path leading north, running alongside a sewer, towards Cuckold's Corner.

Fat-winged, long-legged craneflies whir up from the ditchwater. It's too late in the year for frogs in any numbers. In late June they would have been thudding into the ditch with each step. September's frogs are occasional and wary.

The bulrushes are coming apart, giving way to feathery fronds of platinum…

We – that is, the path and I – pass at a decorous distance from Whitehall Farm. Through a break in the hedge, I can see a shed in a state of gratifying near-collapse, a semi-open structure requisitioned for and burgeoning with hay for winter.

At the edge of the road, a small footbridge crosses the next anonymous sewer, and I take a left turn towards Cuckoo Farm, and then north again, in the direction of Ham Farm (wondering, was this ever Hamon's farm?) but then reach it, which means either that I've missed the turn for the footpath, or that it has been taken away.

Perhaps that was to save disappointment, for the path now crosses a potato field recently plundered; a few specimens have been left behind, looking like Lilliputian skulls, in the ravaged soil, which is black and spent.

A week's deficit of rain means, at least, that there's no clagging on my boots and the going is easy, if unpretty.

About Ireland it has been said that 'the frame is pretty but the canvas dull'.

I wonder, sometimes, whether the same might be said about the Marsh, and wearing, as it were, the wrong state of mind, I suspect others would agree. But that would be to overlook the cracks in the paint, the fissures in which the hedges are rich and red with dog-rose hips and haws, purple with sloes and black with berries from the brambles, or at least, the shrivelled corpses of berries – they were at their finest a month before.

I cross another of the little footbridges so helpfully placed by Kent County Council. It has a bar at shin-height to prevent sheep from escaping their allotted fields, though I bark mine upon it, and it has been so reclaimed by vegetation that, by the time I've traversed the sewer, not only does my barked shin throb, but my legs tingle with bramble stings.

At the lip of the sewer on the other side of the bridge is a neatly dug hollow filled with turds – this is badger territory.

The next field is little more than a few acres' rectangle of wheat stubble, affording only the singular, but quickly exhausted, pleasure of crushing the straws underfoot.

The ambient air is neither warm nor cold. The road is now far enough distant that the grumble of passing cars can no longer be heard.

In the sky, way beyond the edge of the Weald, somewhere above the Downs, floats a loosely dispersed bouquet of hot-air balloons.

Another little bridge, and here the grasses in the sewer are soft and frondy, like feather dusters.

In the next field over, the mortal remains of some crop I can't identify sit among dark and brittle furrows.

Redemption comes in the form of goldfinches, bouncing brightly above the blight, in a small and busy cloud of their own making.

A flock of wood pigeons rises with effortful clumsiness and wheezing wings from a beet field.

In a bare-boughed tree, a mob of rooks reposes, sleek as robber barons, blinking heads slung louchely beneath the high shoulders of hunched and folded wings, all dark looks and dagger-beaks.

A pair of dragonflies, copper-coloured, rests on the bark of a tree stump.

I'm grudgingly thankful for what the Marsh gives, for its insights into the futility of trying to put a finger on the point at which Nature and Man go their separate ways.

That the Marsh was created by the latter to extend the reach of the former is borne out by its sharp angles, the unerring cross-hatching of its waterways. There is a wildness in the brambles, in the sloes and in the finches, but this is Nature at its most strained.

I sense the rooks shrugging cruelly, their ink-dark claws shifting scratchily on tree bark.

Having retraced my steps, I'm now within a whiff of the church again. The black-faced sheep take note of me once more, and scatter lazily, woollily.

Whatever I had set out to find, I didn't. But I have souvenirs, few though they are. A half hopheads, tea-stain and old ivory-tinted petals even now disintegrating in the side pocket of my corduroy jacket, a fairy-boat of a feather from a swan, a fat conker (so pleasing to the eye, yet deficient in utility, culinary or otherwise).

And lastly, the greying oval that I find, protruding from the grass, which I pluck at the stem with a hollow snap... All this comes home with me.

'Is it poisonous?' asks my wife.

It's lying on a plate on the kitchen table.

'No.'

'Are we going to eat it?'

'I'll cook it tomorrow.'

But already, though only hours earlier it was full and firm, the shaggy ink cap is darkening. By morning, it has as good as wholly dissolved in its own blackness, and I throw it away.

9

Of Rime and Mire

Lemminkainen, grave and thoughtful,
Long reflected, well considered,
Where the snow-shoes could be fashioned,
Who the artist that could make them;
Hastened to the Kauppi-smithy,
To the smithy of Lylikki,
Thus addressed the snow-shoe artist:
'O thou skilful Woyalander,
Kauppi, ablest smith of Lapland,
Make me quick two worthy snow-shoes,
Smooth them well and make them hardy,
That in Tapio the wild-moose,
Roaming through the Hisi-forests,
I may catch and bring to Louhi,
As a dowry for her daughter.'

'Rune XIII', *The Kalevala*, Elias Lönnrot,
translated by John Martin Crawford, 1888

The etymology is not wholly certain, but possibly, Suomi, the Finns' word for their own country, means 'Land of Swamps'. How could I not visit?

But there was little I could find about Finnish swamps. I ordered a copy of *The Kalevala*, Finland's fantastical verse epic, which duly thudded through the letterbox. But it was not the translated version.

On the internet, summertime 'swamp wrestling', apparently a gay-interest spectator sport, appeared frequently. Of the swamps and their 'meaning', the library and other non-Finnish sources were scant.

And though there are elements of the lives of the Sámi (who do not like to be called 'Lapps', a word they consider to have derogatory connotations), with which the world is familiar, such as the reindeer herding, their colourful costumes and the clumsily imposed association with Santa Claus, anything that might shed light on the intricacies of their social and inner lives was in short supply.

'Dear Tom.'

So began a lovely email (in response to my own, which verged on the beseeching), from Päivi Magga at Siida, the Sámi cultural centre in Inari, the town considered to be the 'capital' of Sámi Finland.

Of course, your question is not an easy one. But I have been thinking how I could help you.

So, you want to know about swamps and marshes in Sámi tradition, social economy and culture.

Swamps and marshes are of course important reindeer-herding pastures. Especially in early spring and in the summertime, swamps and marshes are first places to become green, and reindeer start to feed in the wetlands during the calving time. Even the female reindeer with their newborn calves prefer swamps because they can see if something endangers them. The last summer we had was very hot and dry, so the wetlands have been very crucial for the reindeer.

It is said that the swamps 'work' for us Sámis. That's because mosquitoes help to draw the reindeer together when it is calf-marking time. And mosquitoes need wet places to hatch. And the reindeer escape mosquitoes to open places, like mountains and large open areas...

In the wintertime, the swamps and marshes are important for herding reindeer, because they are open spaces where you can keep an eye on your herd. You can see them, see how they are, and whether they're in good shape and whether any are missing...

Also, a very important berry, the cloudberry (*Rubus chamaemorus*) grows in wetlands. People pick berries for their own use and to sell. The selling price can be 12–20 €/kg, when, for example, the price of blueberries (*Vaccinium myrtillus*) is 1,40 €/kg. They are very delicious.

When I was child it was important income for our family, and so it was in many other families also.

Often, there are springs located in swamps and marshes. Those are important places to get fresh water. Springs again have many cultural meanings related to our belief system. Springs have also been used as a storage or as a cellar before electricity, and still today when you are in the forest in summertime, you can do so.

In early times, people have put some wood material to the wetlands for keeping them fresh and flexible. But about this I have only read from books, I don't know more about this.

And I'm sure you already know that wetlands here in Sápmi [which is the Saami people's word for their land] are important nesting areas for migratory birds…

Spring, summer, would seem to be the most delicious, freshest, greenest and keenest months in which to visit Lapland. But…

It's late October when I arrive with my son in grudging tow. And the birds have mostly fled the woods, the fells, the bogs, mires and marshes.

Not everyone has fluttered off in horror at the approach of winter. The tits in the trees, great and Siberian, are puffed up, fluffy and vivacious. As we drive unsteadily along an undulating tongue of iced tarmac through the forest towards our lodgings, a willow grouse throws itself before the headlights. And at a pee stop by a bridge en route, we dislodge a Siberian jay.

In the stream beneath the bridge is a pair of dippers hopping from river stones into the river itself and back. And a diver, red-throated, serpentine and sleek, prowls the slack water. Dippers and a diver. Dipping and diving.

They say that the whooper swan is the last to leave, refusing to do so until the lakes are wholly locked beneath the ice. And as we stood, the evening of our arrival, by the shores of Lake Kittilä, hunting for the flickering green of the aurora,[1] their calls, not quite a honk, nor yet a quack or a bark or a howl, but something of all of those – a whoop – came easily across its still, still liquid surface from the lake shore some miles away, where they had made a summer home. By the time we woke the next morning, the freezing had begun, and by the following evening, great cracking sounds shook the shallow bowl of the depression in which the lake sat, the ice sheets pushing up against each other, one eventually sliding beneath the other in capitulation. By Thursday – our fourth day – the whooping had ceased, and the swans were already a day's flight south.

We had arrived between seasons. The *ruska,* autumn, when the foliage turns coltishly red and the birds gather for their great migrations south – was some weeks past. And the thick snows had yet to arrive. All week long, the mercury had hovered around zero, plus or minus a few degrees.

I was awed by the prospect of the cold, and of being alone in it with my thirteen-year-old son.

He is not the kind of son to hang on his father's every word; rather, he'll dash it to the ground, despairing at the imbecility of the generation that it's his burden to succeed. So sometimes we snarl and other times we're kind, and mostly we exasperate each other, pushing and pulling apart like the ice sheets.

It showed on the day that Ludo and I set out on a trail through the Lemmenjoki National Park. It was only twelve miles or so, and the sun would shine, and the wind was at rest. But he is no great fan of a big hike, which smacks to him of the kind of thing his father would make him do for his own good. And he would.

Lemmenjoki covers nearly 1,200 square miles of roadless wilderness. In the 1870s it entertained a gold rush, the seams thought exhausted by the turn of the century, until the fever

---

[1]Which, to our great disappointment, roundly eluded us.

returned in the 1940s when, I read in a pamphlet published by the
Finnish National Park service:

> In the summer of 1945, three brothers from the Ranttila farm
> by River Inarijoki – Niilo, Uula and Veikko Ranttila – set
> out towards Lemmenjoki to find gold. Following the advice
> given by the 'reindeer lord' Kaapin Jouni (aka Jouni Aikio),
> the brothers focused their search on the lower reaches of River
> Morgamoja, right by the mouth of River Vaijoki. They did find
> a fair amount of gold, and more prospectors arrived at River
> Lemmenjoki the following summer. Rumours of big strikes
> escalated, and the discoveries were publicised in the papers – the
> production company Suomi Filmi even made a short film about
> gold panning that was distributed to cinemas around Finland.

Looking at photographs of Lemmenjoki in anticipation of our
arrival, I trembled at the prospect of the two of us on its high fells
above the treeline. 'But what if…?'

I worried, before we set out, that Ludo hadn't eaten enough, that
his stamina might fade.

'I'm not eating reindeer,' he'd said the night before.

'But you have to eat the reindeer, because that's what there is to
eat. It's what people eat. Reindeer.'

'How can you eat a reindeer? That's just awful.'

'So what do you think you should eat, given the few alternatives?'

'Pot Noodle.'

'How can you eat Pot Noodle? That's just awful.'

I made sandwiches and put soup in a Thermos and brought crisps
and a chocolate bar. Hungry, tired but eager, halfway through our
walk, I imagined, we would sit upon a hummock or a boulder at
a place with a commanding view and restore our flagging energies
with victuals plucked from a knapsack.

A middle-aged father's fantasy of earning his son's admiration,
of bond-forging, strengthening. And how it dates him. '*Knapsack.*'

Thinking back to a time of swirling vapours of model glue, and
first whiffs of cigarette smoke, I wondered whether that age, thirteen

prime, and with connotations of, at the very least, awkwardness, represents a kind of first run at 'middle age', a swampland between childhood and adolescence proper, where infant joys are mostly exhausted and redundant or despised, and the intoxicating and other delights of later adolescence not yet within reach.

Thirteen as a point of departure. A breakpoint with childish things. In my own case, I laid aside pursuits that I thought would no longer pass muster in the world beyond myself, in the world of other men, and the eyes of girls, but which I would come back to later, having failed in my pursuit of, or failed to care about, 'passing muster'.

The beginning of the path began unremarkably. More of an amble than a ramble through old-growth pines and some birch trees, one of the few deciduous species that can survive so far north, in the taiga forests. Though late morning, the sun had yet to rise above the treeline, and bestowed its light obliquely, casting long, weak shadows, lost among each other on the forest floor.

Ludo, who will always protest the injustice of being made to walk, stopped at each frozen puddle and brook to test its weight with a stick or a stone or a foot. 'Don't put your boot through the ice. Freezing water will spill over the lip, soak into your sock and make the next seven hours an agony,' I said.

He grumbled about it. Surely a day of huge discomfort was a reasonable price to pay for a full second's worth of wholly sensual pleasure.

I worried about him dawdling. It was a long walk. If spellbound by puddles at the outset, would we ever get to the end of it? And yet soon he marched ahead, bored of the puddles, while I found myself snagged on the mysteries of the forest floor. He rolled his eyes as I tried to steer them towards a tiny forest in its own right, of rime-cloaked trumpet lichen on the bark of a fallen tree, each perfect cone brittle and improbable and unlike any lichen I'd ever given consideration to before… not that I ever had many,[2] and

_____

[2]Later, intrigued and entranced, in an article on a Finnish website titled, 'Lichens are most sensitive', I discover that 'lichens are the result of symbiosis between algae and fungi, a

thick beds of moss, and heather-like plants still carrying berries. Not cloudberries, which had all been plucked and devoured months ago, but crowberries. Small, black, honorary members of the Corvidae clan.

I tugged one from its stem and it was hard and unburstable. The frost had come suddenly on the forest. Mushrooms, mute colours sharpened by it, caps snapped from their stems by it, were as little more than effigies of themselves, alchemised, as if by chefs or other gods of great ingenuity and mischief. Everything had been placed on hold until the birds returned. There was only the crunch and the soft snap of our boots on the trail, and the frozen moss and undergrowth to trouble our chilled ears. A curious silence. What might death sound like here? I find myself asking. A hard noise, or soft? A sudden splintering? Or the sigh of something giving way? Or a shriek?

'We haven't seen any animals,' Ludo said.

'No. No animals.'

No animals.

The path wound first through conifer, and then more open birch forest and the wetlands – mires – emerged where the trees thinned, striated in places into mysterious hollows known as *flarks*, caused, possibly, where peat slips beneath the bog (though no one knows exactly), the quality of reflection of the surface water nuanced by the extent of the frost.

There is nothing indistinct about these mires, which are clear and sharp and lush. I would like to be among them in late June when spring hands the baton to summer and those expensive cloudberries are just ripe. But in sort-of-autumn they're no less generous, though the gifts they bear are of a different kind. I leaned against the trunk of an old-growth pine, shuddered as a passing cloud obscured the sun. Let the trickling of a stream, rising through the moss with a crystal song, hold me like a sugar cube in silver tongs... In all of this

minute ecosystem in which the primary producer, an alga, and a first-degree consumer, a lichen-forming fungus, live in close interaction...'

I can find beauty and wonder. But it isn't my prerogative to find these things in it or to give it meaning. That is for the Sámi.

The Sámi, who are the only ethnicity to possess a status as an indigenous people in the European Union, inhabit the area that is known as Lapland, though they know it as Sápmi. It covers a huge expanse of the sub-Arctic, including hundreds of square miles of Russia, Norway, Sweden and Finland.

But even in the parts of Lapland most closely identified with their culture, such as the town of Inari, where the Sámi Parliament building is located, they are in the minority. And even in Finland, Sámi culture is best known by its outward manifestations.

Perhaps the identity of no other people in Europe is as tautly and tightly defined by their relationship with another species as the Sámi's has been since even before they began to 'domesticate' huge wild herds that once roamed the northern steppes and taiga – in an era that, though long distant, distilled distinctly familiar forms of bigotry.

Nearly two millennia ago, Ptolemy said of the Sámi that they:

> [lived] in astonishing barbarism and disgusting misery: no arms, no horses, no household; wild plants for their food, skins for their clothing, the ground for their beds; arrows are all their hopes; for want of iron they tip them with sharp bone. This same hunting is the support of the women as well as of the men, for they accompany the men freely and claim a share of the spoil; nor have their infants any shelter against wild beasts and rain, except the covering afforded by a few intertwined branches … Yet they think it happier so than to groan over field labour, be cumbered with building houses, and be for ever involving their own and their neighbours' fortunes in alternate hopes and fears. Unconcerned towards men, unconcerned towards Heaven, they have achieved a consummation very difficult: they have nothing even to ask for.

In the 700s, Paul the Deacon, a historian in the court of Charlemagne, described them, and the climatological conditions in which they lived, in scarcely more flattering terms. He wrote,

They are not without snow even in the summertime,
and since they do not differ in nature from wild beasts
themselves, they feed only upon the raw flesh of wild animals
from whose shaggy skins also they fit garments for themselves.
They deduce the etymology of their name according to their
barbarous language from jumping. For by making use of leaps
and bounds they pursue wild beasts very skilfully with a piece
of wood bent in the likeness of a bow. Among them there is an
animal not very unlike a stag, from whose hide, while it was
rough with hairs, I saw a coat fitted in the manner of a tunic
down to the knees…

I had been trying to arrange to meet with Petri for some months
before arriving. Whenever we spoke on the phone, there had
been noises off, of barking dogs, growling engines, indeterminate
outdoor rumblings, which precluded any meaningful or coherent
communication, and he would say, 'Can we speak later?'

I think that he would have preferred not to meet with me. 'This
isn't the season for tourists,' he would say, leaving me to protest,
feebly, that I was a writer, and thus an exception. Yet my hopes
rested on Petri, for though he is not the sole member of the Inari
Reindeer Herders Association, the others seemed still less reachable.
And he, he said, was the only one of them that spoke English.
Some were not entirely comfortable with Finnish.

The great autumn round-up was over, and the reindeer were out
in the wilds. In May, the insects would hatch from the bogs and
streams and swamps, and drive the reindeer to distraction, and to
the fells above the treeline to calve.

Then the herders would come, rounding up the calves, separating
them from their mothers, and with a sharp knife cut their 'earmarks',
a sequence of big and small cuts and slits denoting ownership of
each beast. Sometimes the herders bring their children – it is a rite
of passage for young Sámi to cut their first earmarks. The child will
lie on the bleating calf, and, under the tutelage of his parent, make
the little mutilations. The calf and child will rise bloodied, bleating
and bound for life.

When we did meet Petri, he was standing outside his white-painted, timbered house, which lies at the end of a long drive passing through forest and heath. He had said that he might be cutting up reindeer, and I wasn't sure how that would go down with Ludo.

But he was waiting for the school bus from which his young sons would jump, hopping on their bikes, to pedal a few dozen yards to the nearby cabin in which Petri's eighty-eight-year-old father lived. Three reindeer skins, still bloodied, were pegged to the side of an outhouse. A couple of heads were stacked against a fence, not as trophies, but only incidental to the process of skinning the bodies and cutting up the meat, a chore from which Petri, who looked tired, and whose gloves were as sanguine as the heads, had just emerged.

'Hi Petri,' I said.

He looked uncertain as to what I was really doing in his front yard, despite, or because of, our staccato correspondence, such as it was, prior to my arrival. And when I explained again, he looked more quizzical still.

We walked over to a round enclosure where a dozen reindeer trotted, chewed hay and gazed back at us with eyes that were dark and luminous and pure.

'They're beautiful.'

'Yes,' said Petri. 'Beautiful.'

I couldn't help but also glance at a reindeer head cast casually into the yard for the dog to play with.

'And so many different colours.'

'Yes, and different shapes of antler. That's why we have so many words to describe them.'

He said that this was the time of the year that it's right to bring the reindeer down to the fells, the swamps now being firm enough to bear their weight. He and his fellow herders would choose which are to be slaughtered, and which dispersed into the forest.

In the past, the timing was wholly dictated by the vicissitudes of the seasons. The weather could change quickly. Summer might end overnight, and the onset of the frost was sudden, which meant that the reindeer could be slaughtered at their optimal weight and the carcases would freeze naturally. Regulations imposed in the 1980s obliged the owners to have their reindeer transported by truck to state-of-the-art abattoirs; the carcases, once dismembered, would be stored in huge refrigeration units.

Following the logic of the modern supply chain, reindeer meat served in the restaurants[3] of the town of Inari may have been 'reared' in the fells and forests overlooking it but slaughtered and processed several hundred miles away.

Now, in any case, the change of seasons is even less reliable than in the past.

'Real winter, proper snow, should be here by now. Not this little snow,' said Petri. He gestured at the light but picturesque frosting that made everything slightly sparkle. In the forest, he said, the reindeer would feed mostly on the frozen mosses and lichens, breaking through the snow with their hooves to create feeding patches for themselves and their weaning calves. Without snow, everything starts to fall apart.

Inside, Petri's house was clean and spare. Its centrepiece was a large television. On the wall hung photographs of his children in traditional Sámi costume. Reindeer, or parts thereof, were conspicuous by their absence.

I guessed that Petri was in his early or mid-forties. When he was young, he said, he had travelled around the world – the United States, Asia, Europe – on a year-long 'Grand Tour'. I imagined the kind of novelty effect he must have had in a nightclub in Los Angeles or at a Sydney beach party. He had enjoyed it, he said, but since then never had any cause to leave Finland, or even Lapland. Looking after the reindeer was far too demanding.

In the summer and winter, he takes tourists on day trips to get an insight into Sámi life, and see the reindeer and the sled dogs. That

---

[3] There are few. One is a pizza joint. But dried reindeer is a recognised topping.

kind of thing, he said, had become necessary because herding was not terribly profitable any more. But it had to continue because, he said (and Larry Cooke, had he been there, would have only concurred), it was about family, continuity and identity.

He wasn't a forthcoming or gushing man. I expect that neither of those are part of the Sámi way. That confidence must be won.

On the step, we shook hands to say goodbye, and around our feet a little dog called Handi, of a type bred for bear hunting, was frolicking with that reindeer head. (It did look fun…)

I asked Petri a question, which only in retrospect seemed crass: 'How many reindeer do you have?'

'How much money do you have?' he flashed back.

Ah yes.

It was a clumsy and obvious breach of etiquette. He was perfectly good about it. The Sámi are used to accommodating outsiders. But they may be reaching the limits of their indulgence.

When Päivi Magga, who had written me the nice email, and I finally caught up in person at the Sámi Museum, she asked me whether I'd been able 'to meet very many people while you've been in Lapland?'

Implicit was that they should be Sámi people. For Lapland is, if not in law, in name, habit and soul *their* land…

'Um. Not really,' I said.

It felt cathartic, confessing that this trip had not quite been as successful as I had hoped, for whatever reason. Bad planning? I could scarcely have blamed the birds, which were doing as they always do. Had I really wanted to see them I could have checked their schedules.

She said, 'You have to realise that every week we have requests from around the world to be put in touch with Sámi people. From writers and documentary makers and photographers. And we just don't do it.'

Which makes perfect sense. There are in the world, but for the most part in Finland, Sweden, Norway and Russia, fewer than 100,000 people who would call themselves 'Sámi'.

Even in Finnish Lapland, the part of the region most closely identified with Sámi culture, there are only around 10,000. That they should fall prey to their own curiosity value would be to add to the list of considerable threats to their livelihoods and to the sense that they have of themselves.

My sense was that the Sámi didn't want to shy away from the others' interest so much as that they wanted to control it. For which, I can't help thinking, Santa and Rudolf share some of the blame.

It isn't that the Sámi have failed to keep pace with the changing world, which has been flung at them for hundreds of years. And yet, Sámi languages, of which there are several, still retain very, very many words for 'snow', and for 'reindeer', and to describe kinship ties, geological features and states of mind. 'Yoik' singing, an art form that tries to convey the truth about a given thing that lies beyond words, is not only hauntingly beautiful, but quite unique, and something too special to be bandied about freely to curious outsiders, however sympathetic they may appear.

And while proselytisers long ago robbed the Sámi of a polytheistic religion, based, like that of other northern peoples, such as the Inuit, on worship and respect of nature, somehow they've outflanked the strictures, idiocies and indignities imposed by externalities, whether in the form of taxes, missionaries, settlers, pettifoggers or travel writers.

The sophisticated and well-curated museum in which we sat drinking coffee and eating cinnamon buns, and from a picture window of which we looked out at the town of Inari (which, even though it was now quite covered in snow, is not an obviously prepossessing place), was testament to that, and to the (entirely unprovable) rule that there exists an inverse correlation between a small population and its cultural richness.

The museum's permanent exhibition was given over to Sámi history and culture, early animistic beliefs, a way of life that moved with the seasons, and the symbiotic relationship with reindeer, but almost as much of the content was intended to make the point that being a Sámi is no barrier to being a member of twenty-first-century society, especially as – just as Boston once had the reputation of being the world's largest Irish city – Helsinki, not tiny, sleepy Inari, is, at least by dint of numbers, Finland's de facto Sámi capital.

There are Sámi filmmakers and writers and academics and actors, and there are gay Sámi, and Sámi of all political orientations. In other words, they experience the multiplicity of identities that the modern age imposes on all and any of us. Some Sámi immerse themselves in their indigenous language or relearn skills lost by their forebears; for others, their '*Sami*-ness' goes largely unvoiced.

Päivi herself embodies this potential that being Sámi holds for complexity and richness. Magga is one of the great Sámi herding families, and her husband is a full-time herder. She feels her Sámi identity keenly, and writes about it as an academic in papers, such as 'Belonging to Sápmi – Sámi conceptions of home and home region', where she reflects on how Sámi concepts of place and home are quite different from mainstream Finnish, and, by extension, European ideas,

> An old dwelling site, spring, *siedi* (sacred place) or boundary of a grazing area may go unnoticed by most people, but their significance and value are apparent to Sámi by virtue of their traditional knowledge. What to others appears to be the wilderness may be a cultural environment ... regardless of whether one can see concrete signs of human activity.

It is the concrete signs of others' human activity in the terrain that have posed the greatest threat to the Sámi as a people and the meanings they invest in the landscape. And the current danger is greater than it has ever been.

In the Middle Ages until the early 1600s, the Sámi way of life was protected from incursions by 'mainstream' Scandinavian society by edicts preventing farmers from settling in what had historically been regarded as Lapland. After the lifting of the prohibition, the Sámi gradually became a minority population in their traditional homelands, also edging northwards as a natural response to the encroachment. In 1751 a boundary was fixed between Sweden and (what was then) Denmark-Norway by treaty, but their right to free movement was protected by a provision called the Lapp Codicil, which also established that they were to enjoy equal rights as citizens on either side of the border, even in times of war.

A century later friction between the regional powers, Finland, Norway, Russia and Sweden, hardened the borders. The rights enjoyed under the codicil were stripped away and, as Päivi has written, 'The reindeer herder Sámi could not continue with their way of life based on the yearly cycle of the reindeer as they were forced to choose which country they wished to be registered as citizens of. This resulted in forced migration and resettlement within the Sámi home region.'

The first half of the twentieth century brought little respite to the Sámi. In 1917, modern war was visited on these peaceable people for the first time, and it revisited between 1939 and 1945 with a particularly devastating impact on the Skolt Sámi, the group that lived close to, and across, the Russian/Finnish border. In the post-war period, Sámi endured forced assimilation into Finnish and Scandinavian society, and hubristic, ecologically chauvinistic infrastructure projects played havoc with Sámi places and thus their sense of home.

One in particular, the damming of the Álta River, became a watershed in Sámi identity, Päivi told me. It caused the loss of swathes of mires, bogs, forests and grazing.

The Álta sits in the Arctic Circle, in the north of Norway, the government of which had been pushing for a dam and hydroelectric plant from the early 1960s. But it was opposed by Sámi, and indeed, non-Sámi, pro-Sámi activists and environmental groups, who were alarmed by the prospect of the Sámi village of Masi being submerged and the disruption or severing of traditional grazing routes.

In 1979 the government issued the necessary permits to proceed with the dam's construction, and the anti-dam movement scaled up its protests, culminating in threatened hunger strikes outside the Norwegian Parliament in Oslo, and the construction of a huge wall of ice, 2,000 miles to the north in Álta, to which the 'antis' chained themselves, vowing to freeze to death in situ before giving up their fight.

A day after meeting with Päivi, I visited Tiina Sanila-Aikio in her office in the Sámi Parliament building, called Sajos, a rather magnificent, timber-clad jewel of modern architecture, boasting soft curves and a kind of discreet grandeur well suited to its purpose.

Tiina is the president of the Sámi Parliament. She is also young, clearly highly capable, and sings in a heavy metal band, and in a sense embodies modern Sámi identity.

During the war, she told me, her grandparents, then children, were among the many Skolt families fleeing Russia and attempting to resettle in Finnish Lapland. But it was difficult. Their families had lost their herds, their homes and their social networks. They were teased and felt isolated on account of their unique accents and habits, even by some other Sámi. After the war had ended, the Finnish state tried to complete their assimilation into mainstream society. To 'Finnish them off', you might say.

But the Sámi are not naïfs, and if their voice isn't heard, that's less a reflection of their powers of articulation than it is of their numbers and what they're up against. With growing concern, they have realised that if they fail to muster the requisite volume, their entire way of life and cultural existence, despite or because of its many permutations over centuries, is in the balance.

In 2018, the Finnish and Norwegian governments announced that they had settled on the route of a railway, which will be built to run from the town of Rovaniemi, capital of Lapland's gloomily burgeoning Santa industry, to the Norwegian Arctic port of Kirkenes, and which will, in effect, cut Lapland in two.

> The Arctic railway would improve Finland's logistical position and accessibility as well as promote connections with the whole of Europe. It would be an alternative transport route to be used in Finland's imports and exports. The deep-water ports of the Arctic Ocean that are ice-free throughout the year would also open up a new connection to the Atlantic Ocean and Northeast Passage ... the Arctic railway [will mainly carry] ... minerals, fish products, raw wood and wood industry products ...

… proclaims a press release on the website of the country's Ministry of Transport and Communications.

But the Sámi see this as prophesying their downfall.

The railway, slated for construction by 2030, will prevent the movement of the reindeer and destroy whole ecosystems. As Tiina told me, 'The reindeer cannot cross the tracks, and they will not go through tunnels. To lay the track it will be necessary to excavate the tundra and support it with concrete foundations, cutting through the watercourses, and the wetlands, and the forests. Even the prospect of it is making Sámi people ill, both physically and mentally. It is like a death sentence.'

The 'driver' for the railway, as it were, is the fact that warming global temperatures leads to more of the Arctic seas being ice-free for more days each year, and that a shipping route to Asian markets, running along the Russian Arctic coast, is now viable.

This creates a vicious circle: the railway makes possible further resource exploitation, ergo greater carbon emissions, ergo melting of the Arctic ice.

'The funny thing is,' she says, 'that Finland loves to portray itself as this really "green" country, supportive of human rights. But when you look at the way it treats its own environment – and the Sámi – it isn't really!'

And, she says, given the scale of investment going into the project, the government can afford to commission sophisticated 'impact studies', which others might describe as 'greenwashing'.

The Sámi are not entirely alone. For some decades they have enjoyed support and solidarity from other indigenous groups, including First Nations peoples in Canada and Native Americans in the United States, who have fought so many similar battles.

But even pooling their collective resources, any conflict that pitches the Sámi and their supporters against the governments of Norway and Finland will be asymmetrical, especially given the capital incentives that propel the railway apparently ever onward…

Above the treeline, the Lemmenjoki walk became more forbidding.

'We're not going up there, are we?' Ludo asked.

A line of poles, each topped with a Maltese-cross shape, marked the way of the steeply inclined path to a high ridge. Unimpeded by trees, the now-not-dormant wind careered along the fell. We, the heather and the brambles shivered.

Had I been my own father, I would have asked the same question. I could barely bring myself to acknowledge the truth of it.

'But we must have reached the halfway point, surely?'

'Um,' I said. According to my reading of the map I'd brought, we had not.

'Bloody hell,' he said, commendably moderating his language, considering.

We stopped and ate the sandwiches I'd brought, looking down at an eternity of unbroken forest.

The halfway point, when it came, was marked by a pile of stones on a spur. From here, the trail descended steeply into the valley of the Lemmenjoki. I picked my way carefully. Ludo as good as cantered down it. Now I was holding up the party.

We passed a frozen pond and took great delight in skimming stones across its surface. And then, for the last few miles, the path traced the spine of a steep-sided, wooded ridge studded with Iron Age pits, which, literature from the National Park service informed me,

> … were often dug by the edges of forests, along the migration routes that the deer used to move from summer pastures to the winter pastures in pine heaths … The deer were driven towards the pits along a route running parallel to the pit chain then frightened from the sides to run towards the pits. The pit traps could also be dug on a spit or across a neck of land, crosswise to the direction the deer would travel. With this method, the kill remained limited as the deer running at the end of the herd could cross the pits safely as they filled up. In chase hunting, the deer would fall into the pits, not being able to get up quickly enough or at all.

I was moved, deeply, by the quiet *cris de coeur* that came both from Tiina and from Päivi. For decades, Western culture has wrung its hands at the way in which, in supposedly less enlightened times, our forebears played havoc with indigenous peoples, whether in the name of science, Jesus, ignorance, ill-informed good intentions or plain old greed.

We rue, we agonise, we make films and write books and vow that we've learned the lessons of our ways, but here in the north, the old occidental afflictions return, largely out of sight, except from those who'll bear their brunt.

10

Worth Its Salt

In an island of bitter lemons
Where the moon's cool fevers burn
From the dark globes of the fruit

And the dry grass underfoot
Tortures memory and revises
Habits half a lifetime dead

Better leave the rest unsaid,
Beauty, darkness, vehemence
Let the old sea-nurses keep

Their memorials of sleep
And the Greek sea's curly head
Keep its calms like tears unshed

Keep its calms like tears unshed.
                    'Bitter Lemons', Lawrence Durrell, 1957

Through binoculars, from where I stood in the backyard (between the thrum of a generator and crates of empty bottles) of one of those quasi-Greek, quasi-English pubs, a dozen yards from the forbidding checkpoint for entry into the Sovereign Base Area, they resembled nothing less than a few score of albino spermatozoa doing a music-hall turn. Tap-dancing. Or standing on their feet.

They didn't look very pink, but that had been leached out of them by the distance, a good mile, maybe more, that stood between us. The heat haze accounted for their wobbliness. And the vastness of the Limassol Salt Lake, upon which they took their delicate and hesitant steps, pregnant with the very purpose of being a flamingo, accounted for the difficulty I had had in finding them.

Cyprus possesses two salt lakes, amorphous crushed pearls of intense salinity pressed into its southern shoreline, the one separated from the other by fifty miles or so. In summer it hurts the eyes to look upon their hot, lunar surface. In the soft Levantine winter (I am told), they are tranquil and lush.

Of them, the chronicler Anthoine Regnaut said in the mid-1400s, '[They] furnish all the countries – even Italy, Calabria, Apulia and Romania, with salt.'

A travelling silk merchant from Douai, Normandy, Jacques le Saige described, in the early 1500s, the miraculous 'great frozen marsh' from which salt came 'of itself' and without need of a still. To the island's Venetian masters, they were worth fortunes, as they were to the Ottomans, who inherited their monopoly. To the British into whose lap they also fell, they were a nice little earner.

They are invaluable to the flamingos that arrive in great droves each year, mostly flying away again by late spring, leaving behind a small, ambassadorial flamboyance for the delectation, presumably, of ornithologists.

It was a story about salt that had lured me to Cyprus, a country I'd always wanted to visit, intrigued by the Green Line – the de facto boundary between the Republic of Cyprus and the territory occupied by Turkey, by the mishmash of Greekness, stiff-collared Britishness, sultry Turkishness, by the connection with Lawrence Durrell, by the fact of it being thrust so far eastwards and its 'strategic position'.

I'd long thought of it martially, but never marshily.

But I found some justification in what my friend Jimmy Roussounis told me of his grandfather, for whom the acquisition of a sackful of salt had come at some cost.

Roussounis *grand-père*, he said, 'was a big man in the village.' (The village being that of Kato Arodes, in the west of the island, north of Paphos, close to Lara, where big turtles lay their eggs and their progeny pop out of the sand.)

'In what sense?' I asked. 'Physically big? Or figuratively?'

'Both, as far as I can gather. Physically big. Generally respected. Formidable. Respected.'

'Right.'

'Salt was worth a fortune – because of the British monopoly. So one day, he took his donkey down from the village to the shore, beyond the beach where the turtles lay their eggs, and scooped up salt from the rocks and then headed back to the village with the donkey's saddlebags stuffed with it. Back at his house [Jimmy would show me the house later, when I arrived in the village. Solid and square], he carefully packed it into crevices in the walls.

'But he had been reported, informed upon, to the British.'

'Someone being a jealous neighbour?'

'I guess so… and the following morning, a very junior British officer and a Turkish military policeman – divide and rule, you see, the oldest trick in the book – thumped on the door and began to ransack his house, looking for the salt.

'They went through everything, overturning the bed, and the bread oven, and my grandmother's trousseau, the loo, the outhouse, and when they couldn't find or think of anything else to ransack, he asked them, "Have you quite finished?"

'Clearly the quality of the information they had was so good, they thought that if they just kept on going, they'd find it.'

'Did they try the cellar?' I asked Jimmy. He ignored me.

'My grandfather told them that they were welcome to start again, and that if they found the salt, he'd go with them quietly, to Nicosia, to face charges. If, on the other hand, they *didn't* happen to find anything, he'd leave them in a whimpering heap in the street.

'And a whimpering heap it was.'

The next day, all those years ago, Jimmy's grandfather was arrested and taken to Nicosia to be tried for assault. Half the village came along for the ride. He spent a week in the cells, and 'I'll have you know,' said Jimmy, 'the lawyer who defended him, Ioannis Clerides, would not only go on to stand in the first independent Cypriot presidential elections, but his son, Glafkos Clerides, would become President of the Republic!'

This all happened, Jimmy, guessed, in the late 1950s, as, prim, doltish and snobbish but generally benign, at least in its own estimation, British rule teetered beneath calls for *enosis* (union with Greece), and independence, and tension between Greek and Turkish Cypriots became fractious.

There is this – salty – irony that Cyprus's reputation as a limb of Greece is made a little tepid by its association with the British, by its driving on the left-hand side of the road, and the Sovereign Base Area, with its attendant pubs and tattoo parlours.

But to characterise the relationship between the island's original occupants and its colonisers as a case of the latter diluting the former is to misconstrue it. In almost every village below the Green Line, there's a form of tribute or commemoration to the lives of young men and women from EOKA – the National Organisation of Cypriot Fighters – who died in the attempt to oust their overlords.

In Jimmy's village, Kato Arodes, in the Paphos mountains, those men are Georgios Papaverkiou (a cousin of Jimmy's), Iakovos Christodoulides, Charalambos Philippides and Demetris Georgiou. Their bronze busts stand on white marble pedestals by the church, and the young men they represent, once brimming with youth and zeal and vim, are still remembered personally, as it were, by the photogenic nonagenarian priest.

Whether Kato Arodes feels its changes deeply but quietly, or lightly, or fitfully, isn't something that I can know as a fleeting visitor. But the sense in such places is that while they may be momentously altered, upended, emptied or elated, the sour-sweet odour of fig trees will settle in their narrow streets, old ladies will signal degrees of approbation of goings-on with a *po-po-po*, and the baton of village history will pass in the coffee shop as men fatten and age and disappear, first over the lip of life, and slowly (ever so) out of memory.

Jimmy and I had been neighbours in London. We would meet for lattes and croissants in a faintly ludicrous and expensive café, having deposited our children at primary school. But he moved to Cyprus to avail his family of the better education, longer holidays and 'Greekness' – and it was a curious reorientation of my perception of Jimmy to see him in the *kafeneion*, which serves only two kinds of coffee – syrupy 'traditional' or watery Nescafé – both at glacial pace. Just as he is in London, Jimmy, who would be embarrassed to think it, is known and loved. His hand the villagers eagerly clasp, his thoughtful greeting of *yassou* is one they like to hear and return. Jimmy's generational tendrils stretch deep into village history; he makes sure they stay well-watered.

Our little pilgrimage began in the late afternoon, as soon as it was sane to go out. Between village and sea there was scarcely a single building to interrupt a rolling vista of olive trees and thorny, scented plants. It was a charming deficit, delighting the eye, but the cause of the occasional clenching of a coffee cup in the *kafeneion*.

The area has been earmarked as a national park. Some, at least, of the inhabitants of Kato Arodes have cried foul. Why should they be precluded from enjoying the fruits of development that have enriched the lives of so many others?

'You see how it is,' said Jimmy. 'For Cypriots, buying land, developing it, selling it, sends their children to university, or to become lawyers or doctors or work in America.'

Others argue that the national park will bring demand for accommodation and restaurants nearby. There are already 'jeep safaris' which, each day in holiday season, deposit a 4x4 load of 'adventure tourists' to the village, where they stay for a while and try to take a picture of the nonagenarian priest, and trundle off again.

But the entrepreneurial spirit is lacking. Nearby Fasli has five tavernas and a trinket shop, while in Kato Arodes people argue, and shrug, and think about these things, but nothing happens.

Perhaps it is time to bring back a pace or two of donkeys. Kato Arodes has been donkey-free for decades. The last donkey man had sold his beasts when they slipped into obsolescence, for very much less than he might, had it not been for the internal combustion engine. But it broke his heart to be without them, and he soon bought them back, putting himself and his grey companions out to grass, where they petered out of village history moons ago.

Thus it was without one that we followed the track down the mountainside, descending through largely abandoned orchards and scrub and the clamour of crickets towards the cool blue.

Huge, wine-dark clouds tumescent with grand-paternal wrath (I thought) loomed up and over the Paphos mountains, rising over the crescent moon of Lara Bay, where a man called Georgios worked to nurture the broods of turtles that emerge each year from the shore.

Georgios was modestly famous. For forty years he had come to help the turtles, scaring away developers and other beasts, welcoming back the green and loggerhead mamas, noting where each, with weeping eye and ox-strong flipper, had buried the gift of its own species for posterity deep in the cool sand.

Short, but trim and bronzed, he had a Cousteau-esque youthfulness amplified by the presence of his companion, a gravely attractive young Italian woman.

'Foxes!' he told us. It is from their predations that the eggs were protected by the curious contraptions, like the upturned skeletons of buckets, that he and she (as earnest as only a clipboard and M.Sc. in marine biology can render one) were placing above each nest. Like an old turtle, Georgios returns each year, drawn by some ancient yearning...

'Salt?' we asked, and he waved us towards the outer edge of the crescent. 'Out there. Beyond the rocks.'

And we picked our way, first along narrow paths, iron-red among olive-green thickets of shrub and following the edge of the broken-biscuit extremity of the bay, looking down (with envy, not condescension) on the family gaggles that had negotiated the perilously inclined slopes to little coves, where aunts and mothers made sandwiches, children made castles, and everyone made free with the sea.

My first attempt at reaching the *tekke* by the banks of the Larnaca Salt Lake was thwarted by a roadblock manned by a vanload of police.

'Come back later,' they said.

So I did.

I had only visited a *tekke*, a Sufi lodge or place of worship, once before, in Albania, and there I had met a young, garden-proud dervish, with whom I smoked roll-ups and drank raki in a room painted luminous green.

But the Hala Sultan Tekke – the Mosque of Umm Haram – seemed to belong to a different, raki-free category of *tekke*. This was a spare-looking, honey-coloured building replete with dome and minaret, set amid palm trees, simply and elegantly adorned both inside and out.

A mosque guardian, wearing a very sober and grey robe, a skullcap and a lustrously shining beard, was in attendance at the gate, and on the flagstones beside him sprawled a velvet-coated, jade-eyed cat of the finest order of felines.

I asked the man about the *tekke*. Was it positioned so close to the lake because that provided a source of fresh water for the luxuriant gardens built around it?

No, he said, it was where it was because *on this very spot*, moments after arriving in Cyprus, while accompanying her husband, an officer in the service of the warrior Moawia, Umm Haram, foster mother of the Prophet Muhammad, fell and tragically died.[1]

And that seemed a much better reason to build a *tekke* than the one that I had come up with.

In the tourist-office photographs, it is invariably depicted when the water is high enough to reflect the mosque's splendour in the lake's silvered surface. Artful placing of flamingos adds to the fairy-tale vision, though, perhaps, not so many of the (very many) pilgrims that visit are fussed about flamingos. My way had been barred in the morning, the mosque guardian told me, because a

---

[1] And wife of one of the most high-ranking officers of Moawia who 'led two disastrous raids against Cyprus in 649 and 650 AD' (according to the Cyprus Department of Antiquities.

large group was visiting from the de facto Turkish Republic of Northern Cyprus, a trip arranged in such a way that the normal protocols had been waived.

The view towards Larnaca is less pretty, giving way to the aeroplanes ascending from or descending into the airport, and the not very spectacular skyline of the city itself.

Whether they care for it or not, every passenger on a Larnaca-bound aeroplane is acquainted with the salt lake, for the landing strip was built in such a way as to bisect it. Up until 1974 the island's main airport was at Famagusta, which fell to the north after the invasion. The republic needed a new airport and the salt lake was volunteered. Geopolitical necessity, apparently, pushed aside any concern for the annual arrival of the flamingos, but they continued, and continue, to return each year, seemingly nonplussed by the hurtling cylinders in the skies above.

There is, famously, even a black flamingo, blessed with a surfeit of melamine, to keep the twitchers twitching.

It being June when I visited, there was no water in the lake – and hence no shimmering reflections – to distract my ruminations upon the contents of those planes as they roared and soared off to Moscow, full of bankers and *biznismen*, and Manchester, replete with ex-pats, and London, gorged on doctors and lawyers and restaurateurs.

The lake bed was a salt-sand crust that collapsed beneath my weight and clearly stood for no standing upon. But I proceeded apace upon the path around its circumference, amid the distant bleating of goats and other beasts, and the chirruping of crickets.

In the past, I knew, the lake's treasured salt had been zealously guarded. Quite how it could be *effectively* guarded I couldn't tell, given the extent of the perimeter. Perhaps with observation towers?

The use by the British, during their monopoly, of Turkish military police was symptomatic of the playing-off of one group against another (as Jimmy had pointed out) that would feed into Cyprus's tensions later. But the lake lost its political heat when the decision was made in the 1980s to cease production of salt. If you go down to the lake today, you're more likely to be told off for disturbing the flamingos than for pilfering sodium chloride…

I wouldn't have thought to come to Aradippou (the emphasis is on the last syllable: 'Aradip*pou*') had I not spent the morning in the Larnaca archives and museum, housed in an elegant Ottoman building at the end of the seafront promenade with its KFC, TGI Fridays and Pizza Hut, and mostly ignored by those for whom the sun is only ever a blessing.

In an office bulging with boxes full of cutlasses, old maps and deeds, chief archivist Antigone said she would help me fulfil my poorly articulated quest, and we located an article written for the *Cyprus Mail* in 1958 about Larnaca Salt Lake which related how, 'Tenders for the collection and storing up of salt are invited by the Comptroller of Customs every summer, and the contract is usually awarded to the lowest bidder. This year's contract was awarded to Messrs. Antonis Chr. Mouskos and Xenophon Zacharia of Aradippou.'

It described the technique of dividing the lake into sections, each one of which was to be 'worked by eight workers', who cut pathways into the salt and the layer of mud beneath until firm ground was reached, sometimes at a depth of two feet. The pathways were then laid with alternate layers of salt and old sacking to provide a firmer foothold for the workers, who were provided with rubber boots and gloves 'and expected to make around 40 shillings per day'.

Each year, it said, the treasury received around £70,000 through sales of salt – the government selling it on the spot at '27 mils per *oke* in bulk', mostly in its raw state, to tanneries and producers of sheepskins.

Surely, thought the correspondent, it would make sense to process the salt for sale abroad, as had been the custom in the not-too-distant past, for, 'I feel sure it may find its way into the markets of our Middle East neighbours where not so long ago, it was in good demand. Memories of picturesque sailing schooners loading salt alongside the Larnaca Salt Jetty are not altogether lost in the past.'

If they weren't 'altogether lost' then, they certainly are now, for no one to whom I spoke could remember where the salt jetty is.

And salt, unlike halloumi and investment-fund management, isn't one of Cyprus's golden geese.

Though not directly related to the salt lakes, the other stories in the paper provided historical context:

'11 Greek Cypriot girls arrested in a sweep during Operation Matchbox'.

'Three Greek Cypriots – described as EOKA terrorists – were killed last night in fierce gun-battle near Lyssi'.

'A British soldier's machine gun was stolen from a Turkish cinema in Nicosia'.

'Greece has formally turned down Britain's modified plan for Cyprus'.

The *kafeneia* of Cyprus are where men in their varying degrees of oldness have sat, suited, semi-marmoreal, playing backgammon, reading newspapers, slyly gossiping, harbouring secrets and grudges and measuring out what remains of their days in tiny cups of coffee, from, if not the dawn of time, at least since the Ottomans introduced the dark kernels from which they take their name.

Every national event or shift in tempo, the advent or closure of each historical epoch, whether of lasting magnitude or flash in the pan, has been marked in such places. Raising voices – and sometimes the price of coffee.

The revolt against the Turks in 1821, the British occupation of 1879, the first demands for *enosis* in 1931, the burning down of the Government House, the emergence of Archbishop Makarios, the beginning of the EOKA campaign led by Georgios Grivas, the panicked British response, independence in 1961, and the Turkish invasion of 1974, which separated the island into the Republic of Cyprus and the Turkish Republic of Northern Cyprus – the *de jure* existence of which is only recognised by its sponsor. Each has reverberated, rattled through, sweetened or embittered the coffee in every *kafeneion*, each one a keeper of some of the greatest treasures of the Greek-speaking world, if only you care to enquire of their whereabouts.

In truth I was shy to, walking into the main square in Aradippou, with no Greek and no introduction, which seemed to boast a *kafeneion* at each corner, the habitués of each being either somnambulant, engrossed in cards or squinting at a newspaper.

A point of purchase revealed itself only when I approached a man sitting with his peers beneath an awning, who shrugged and smiled, gestures kindly combined, apropos of nothing.

I said hello. A man opposite, of similar age, perhaps between seventy and eighty, said in a thick voice, vowels bent a little by years in, I guessed, Australia, 'He won't understand you. He only speaks Greek.'

Oh, I said. And explained that I was interested in the salt lakes. I had read an article from six decades ago about it, and I wanted to meet someone who had worked them before the extraction ended for ever.

'He did. Vassily. He worked the salt lake at Larnaca.'

It was, I thought, peculiarly serendipitous that I should walk into a village square, approach one elderly man with bright eyes, and discover that he was the very person to whom I wanted to speak. But it was so.

The man who spoke no English shrugged again, quizzically, and the man who did leaned forward to speak with him. There was another shrug, and more leaning into the age-muddled ear, and then vigorous nodding. He turned to me. And I asked him how it was. He couldn't have been very old…

'No more than a child!' he said, through the interlocution of his Australian-accented friend.

Oh, he said. It was horrible work. Each summer for three years, when the heat had desiccated the lake and the tenders were opened, he would sign up to do it. But it was a kind of torture – for him and his donkey, Stella.

'… beneath the sun in August,' he said, looking and pointing upwards, so that I should be left in no doubt as to the position of that heavenly body.

He spread his hands expansively and looked into my eyes.

'Everything. Everything was white. And how the salt burned our skin.'

Vassily mimed being afflicted by the stinging, burning, desiccating agony, wincing, voice rising, eight-decade face puckering and furrowing like a closing drawstring bag... but fell back into the kindly smile befitting a man among his friends, with coffee to hand, and half a mind on the World Cup, and half on the North Macedonia question, which had the Greek-speaking world in its thrall...

'And my little donkey, Stella, used to work so hard... so many *pite* [cakes] of salt that I had to lift onto her back, to meet our quota.'

'Was it all worth it?' I asked Vassily.

'In three years I saved a hundred and twenty pounds. And by the time I was twenty I had bought my first five acres of land. And when I was twenty-one, I bought a tractor...'

'And look at him now!' said his friend, who had translated everything for me, and who had been shucking oysters in Adelaide ('and loads of other stuff') since 1961.

'A big man!'

Vassily nodded and shrugged and smiled, as if to say, 'Yes, perhaps it was worth it.'

He was only seventeen – a child – when he had answered the call to gather huge cakes of salt that could be lifted from the Larnaca lake, as Cyprus simmered with the injustice of the house-masterly despotism of colonial rule, and Greeks and Turks were finding new differences with each other, and the British were still milking the fruits of a salt monopoly they had taken from the Ottomans, and the Ottomans from the Venetians.

Cyprus, of course, has not yet disentangled and perhaps never will disentangle itself from Britain, and if sometimes the telltales of that strange relationship are picayune, they're no less telling for that.

The Akrotiri Peninsula lies just south of the city of Limassol. Virtually all of it is under British administration, part of the deal struck when Harold Macmillan's government granted Cyprus independence in 1960. For the most part, it's possible to cross between Cypriot and British lines without interruption, but there are enclaves which, because they're especially, and British-ly, secret, require visitors to pass through checkpoints, bearing the appropriate permissions. Elsewhere, mysterious antennae, like those of gargantuan moths, appear to have taken root and sprouted, sieving the Mediterranean air, catching 'chatter' from the Middle East.

From Akrotiri, the Royal Air Force has flown sorties against Saddam Hussein and the so-called Islamic State. It is, I read in a defence trade journal, 'vital to the military capabilities of the UK and for the security of its subjects across the world'.[2]

It also provides employment and economic liveliness to local people, and if there is disgruntlement about the presence of the British on Akrotiri, it's mostly about the terms of the deal, under which Britain 'leases' the peninsula[3] for not very much money at all.

Geologically speaking, the peninsula is, as peninsulas tend to be, curious. Limassol's freight docks sit at the north-east corner. Running south from them is a long stretch of sand called 'the Ladies' Mile', frequented, once upon an equestrian-minded, colonial time, by British officers' wives astride their mounts.

The 'Mile' is now punctuated by beach bars, which, environmentalists say, shouldn't be there, for they scare away the turtles, which would, were it not for the deckchairs and the glitzy lights, avail themselves of the soft sand to lay their eggs.

Running parallel to it is a dirt track, and long hollows of salt and sand, like dry lagoons, all eventually converging but then broadening into a confusingly directionless plain.

The western shore is also beachy and flat in the south but rears up into cliffs from which soar vultures. At nearby Kourion is an ancient site with a temple to Apollo and a rather wonderfully preserved amphitheatre, which, when I visited, had been put to colourful use

[2]The sovereign bases, I read in the UK Defence Journal, 'accumulate strategic relevance and are of constant use by the Armed Forces which has more than 3,500 personnel serving in Akrotiri and Dhekelia, branches of the Army and Royal Air Force are permanently located there, and the Royal Navy's vessels pay regular visits to the enclaves ... Their role is vital to the military capabilities of the UK and for the security of its subjects across the world.'

[3]https://www.sbaadministration.org/index.php/background

by a well-choreographed contingent of diaphanously garbed models for a fashion shoot. The non-sea-facing part of the peninsula is made up, no less delightfully, by orchards. And a marsh.

Where the salt lake was austere and expansive, the marsh is smaller and intimate, its rustling reeds whispering their affinity with an English fen.

Vakis, who is a farmer in the village of Akrotiri and who also works at the environmental centre close by, told me that if I drove to where I could see his cows, I could help him feed them. I had driven past them earlier. Delightful, clever-looking little bovines with rusty-red coats and big, kindly eyes.

Possessing not a single facial hair, neither eyebrow nor lash, Vakis looked somehow ageless, but his love for his cows and the marsh was evidently well established.

'They are part of the same hydrological complex,' said Vakis. 'The marsh and the salt lake. They feed each other. They're linked to the same aquifer.'

I had parked my car close to his four-wheel drive at the edge of the meadows that made up part of the marsh 'complex'. Seeing Vakis, the cows trotted jauntily towards us, swaying their hips and heads, and mooing hungrily.

At his instigation, I helped him shift hay bales, each straw of which glinted in the warm evening sun. I would have liked to have stroked the friendly cows, but they weren't pets.

'For decades, the marshes were ignored. It meant that the invasive plants took over, sucking up the water, killing off the insects, and making it less interesting for the birds…'

The British administration's instinct to improve everything that they found in Cyprus meant that in addition to other environmental ameliorations, they took to planting eucalyptus in marshy areas to suck up the 'excess' moisture. This was, in part, a well-meant effort to reduce the incidence of malaria, but the gung-ho intervention in the natural process was resented by the local population. As in much of Europe, malaria presented a risk to anyone living in proximity to still water, but it was regarded as part and parcel of life, not something that needed to be addressed urgently, Vakis said.

'We know that there were people paid by the British to plant eucalyptus, who at night ripped out the saplings and were arrested and punished for it. In some ways, these people were early environmentalists,' he said. 'They understood that these new species would destroy their wetlands and their ways of farming and fishing.'

Vakis tested whether the electric fence was working by touching it with his hand. It was. He laughed and recoiled. The cows all had their calves with them, almost weaned.

'As well as looking beautiful, these cows have only one real purpose in their lives – to eat the invasive species and bring back the natural plants. So we don't have to separate the calves from their mothers very often, because we're not relying on them for milk… But sometimes we do.'

He nodded to a calf tied on its own, on the other side of the road. Tomorrow it would be 'taken away'.

We busied about, or rather, he did, while I tried to keep up, like a son following his dad about. He said that while these were his cows, he was also encouraging other people to graze cows on the marsh. The herd was an ancient Cypriot strain that one used to see in the mountains, but agribusiness was taking over. These cows weren't suited to those kinds of intensive farming conditions, but in the marsh they thrived.

'My task, really, is to keep the local people engaged. A lot of people in Akrotiri gave up farming years ago. But if the marsh is going to survive, we need projects like this – the cows, and we need people to take an active interest, because in the short term, there isn't especially any money in it.'

The British effort to subdue malaria had only ever been partially successful. The eucalyptus forest, it turned out, also created conditions in which some species of mosquito could thrive – alongside other species such as rats. They also introduced acacia – weird, yellow and Australian – as a weapon in the war against the wetlands.

Ironically, British bird lovers are among those leading the charge against these ebulliently rampant aliens. In the case of acacia, the fight is not only with the plant itself, which is tenaciously fecund, but with Cypriot hunters, who value the plants for their ability to disguise the fine-filament nets they use to illegally catch songbirds, and construct irrigation networks of water pipes to encourage their growth.

We filled a trough with water and watched the cows cluster around it, and with a hose we cooled off a bull called Jimmy who had been watching his beloved cows amorously from a pen. He was a small bull, and not aggressive but 'ripped', as they say, noble-eyed and Minoan in aspect, his dewlaps soft, rippled and supple.

'There are lots of other challenges,' said Vakis. 'The aquifer was lowered in the 1980s when they built the Kouris Dam, which created the lake that provides water for the city of Limassol. And there is the possible problem of the casino. Cyprus is finite because it's an island, and there are limited opportunities to grow economically and for development. But as an island, we're addicted to trying to do it.'

The casino, fed on Russian finance, will, when it eventually sprouts, resemble the unplanned offspring of an Aztec pyramid and a water park, and is no mean cause of disagreement between Cypriots. In anticipation of its existence, the company had already built a smaller, temporary casino to meet demand, pending the completion of the much-vaunted wonder.

A group called BirdLife says,

> The Akrotiri Peninsula is a unique wetland and is home to many wonderful birds, plants and habitats protected under national and European laws. While media coverage has very much focused on the economic and job creation benefits of this touristic development, little has been said about the environmental impacts of this huge project on the peninsula and its wildlife. These have, sadly, been brushed away, in the name of profit.

They have particular concerns for the fate of the red-footed and Eleonora's falcons, the impact upon which would be very much greater than anyone had allowed for.

But the potential for job creation is real. As Jimmy (Roussounis, not Vakis's bull,) points out, there are lots of young, educated people in Cyprus who would struggle to find a job without leaving the island, were it not for the casino. 'The salt lake and the marsh can look after themselves. They're not going anywhere.'

Vakis will fight hard for his marsh. The cows are just part of it. He's also encouraging local women to weave baskets from the marsh reeds and has initiated a scheme by which passing tourists can knock on their doors, meet with the basket weavers, and hopefully buy a basket.

And of course, there's the environmental centre where Vakis works, with its conscientiously curated digital exhibits and factsheets, and which earnestly undertakes all sorts of important research, measuring alkalinity levels and spawning rates and microbial action.

Vakis spends a great deal of time filling in grant forms, showing important people with purse-string power around the marsh, explaining how their money would be spent on improving not only its biodiversity, but making it accessible to visitors: people who live in Limassol or Larnaca, but might not otherwise visit, or tourists, passing between, say, the beach club on the Ladies' Mile, and Simon's Cat Sanctuary on the other side of the peninsula.

'Watch this,' said Vakis, and he walked back to his truck, where he hoiked out a bale of hay almost indistinguishable from the other bales, and headed back to the cows, who bucked and mooed with giddying excitement. 'This is the organic hay. They just *love* it. It's locally grown on the marsh and absolutely delicious.'

The cows fought to get at the hay, chewing with palpable delectation. They dispelled in a chomp any notion that cows might be indifferent to subtleties of taste.

And, brushing the sole of his foot against the pasture, he showed how, where the cows graze away the introduced species, slowly the native species return, needing no other encouragement.

Larnaca Salt Lake also possesses a 'satellite marsh', at a nondescript place called Oroklini, just north of the city where it thins into a loose agglomeration of half-built or not-obviously-intentioned buildings, and carelessly and unglamorously placed cheap hotels. And a fire station.

There's a layby (just the kind of place that you might pull in to, perhaps take a drink of water, a pee in the bushes, or check, using your phone or, in the distant past, a map, that you're on the right track for the airport) from which you can access an observation tower, its dozen or so steps leading to a bird hide that sits on the platform at the top, the rectangular aperture of which looks out at a small marsh, bounded at its southern edge by the grounds of a hotel possessing the perfect proportions of a cereal box, to the east by what looks indeterminately like farmland, and to the north by a path, behind which a small village, shiny white and new, follows the contours of rising ground.

Despite all the surrounding caveats and the whine and hum of the road, this little marsh, a small lake buffered by reeds and rushes, is good for ten or so minutes' gazing. Even if you're not ornithologically inclined, the black-winged stilts, the startlingly red legs on which they stand, and the fluttering, zoetropic antics of the spur-winged lapwing are enjoyably improbable.

There are some ducks on the surface, constrained in their paddling by an encrustation of green-and-yellow scum, and a pair of swallows is making feints at the ripples, the water-boatmen and the whirligigs. The mess of grey rags flung into the bushes at the opposite end of the lake turns out to be a colony of night herons on closer inspection. The plastic bags with which they share those bushes are plastic bags.

That Oroklini Marsh inhabits reduced circumstances is hinted at heavily by the green metal fence, intended, it seems, to prevent its diminution, but also the reclamation of its surrounding hinterlands.

That, you might say, is what happens to such places that fail to attract the love and custodianship of a Vakis.

After a few hundred yards or so, the scrub at the outskirts of Lara Bay gave way to a shelf, a plateau, of ragged rock. Neither Jimmy nor I were wearing particularly sensible shoes, having failed to anticipate the sharpness we'd find underfoot, and we picked our way with geriatric deliberation over this uncompromisingly igneous platform.

The sea, clapping and smashing itself against it, was blue steel except where it splintered into spray. And in small wells in the rock, the salt had become viscous, in varying degrees, or encrusted, where the process of evaporation was almost complete. I felt a surge of pity for Jimmy's grandfather's donkey if it, also, had ever been here.

And I thought how funny it would be if either Jimmy or I were to fall. But both of us have decades' experience of taking too much care…

Closer to the edge, the pools widened and deepened, and the salt deposits were more significant.

'Here,' said Jimmy, squatting close by one such, like a burst and oozing abscess, and into which we peered.

Jimmy put a hand in.

'It's hot,' he said.

I put my hand in.

'It is. Really hot.'

'Geothermal hot.'

'Scorching.'

He put his hand in again…

'Ouch.'

And opened his palm, letting the grey-white sludge fall on a slab of rock, before taking some between his finger and thumb, and tentatively placing it between his lips, and wincing appreciatively.

'What's it like?' I asked.

'All good,' he said.

II

Under the Glacier

As we picked our way back through the marsh we kept hearing a single desolate creaking sound – like a creaking gate as Maisie said – which it turns out is a plover. This land would really make a very good setting for Hell, it reminds me of Gustave Doré's illustrations to the Inferno. The sphagnum moss everywhere gives the effect of ruins and you can imagine the souls of wicked philosophers sitting here and there on the sharp stones, their beards covered with lichen, repenting their false promises.

Letters from Iceland, W. H. Auden and Louis MacNeice, 1937

Vakis and his beloved cows put me in mind of the sweet hay in the floodplain for which Ragnhildur's great-grandmother came to Ausa, the Icelandic farm where Ragnhildur now resides with her mother and a flock of sixty sheep.

'After her first husband died,' said Ragnhildur, 'she found herself, an attractive widow with a young son in tow, looking for a new future. She chose my great-grandfather not for his personal qualities, although those were perfectly fine, but for the meadows that belong to the farm, and the hay. You could call it a "marriage of convenience".'

It was nine o'clock, but in early June, the sun, which in summer always leaves enough of itself to dispel all but the darkest of midnight thoughts, is still high, and we were sitting in the kitchen of Ausa feasting deliciously on mutton and potatoes raised and grown respectively on the farm. It was cosy and homely inside Ausa. I could only imagine how necessary that might be in October, or December, or March...

My son was watching the Icelandic football team, which was trying to narrow the gap with Norway in the European Football Championships.

Ragnhildur's mother, who was over eighty, hadn't said a word to us, indeed, seemed to regard us with some scepticism, and ate quickly before disappearing to the lambing shed to attend to new mothers (ewe mothers?) and mothers-to-be.

'You see, when survival was so precarious...' said Ragnhildur (she had finished eating, but I was serving myself with MORE delicious home-grown Icelandic potatoes and mutton), '... every decision must be carefully taken. Even marriage!'

Ausa, and other nearby farms, such as that belonging to Ragnhildur's neighbour Dagny and her husband, sit on a thumb of land defined by the course of a big river, the Hvítá, and that of a smaller watercourse, the Andakílsá, in the estuary of the fjord Borgarfjörður, where the rivers converge with the lake Vatnshamravatn among floodplains, marshes and hayfields. Collectively they are fed by a glacier that sits high in the mountains which, when the weather is kind enough to permit it, reveal themselves as icy-cloaked and monochromatically austere.

Ragnhildur grew up on Ausa. Dagny married into her farm, but she also came from a rural background. Both women now worked at the nearby Agricultural College of Iceland, Ragnhildur lecturing in environmental studies and Dagny looking after its comings and goings. It's about a two-hour drive north of Reykjavík, on the island's west coast; a spare landscape, which, in concert with the sky, quickly turns moody.

We had visited Dagny before dropping in on Ragnhildur. Her farm, at the very edge of the floodplain, beneath the protective, almost fraternal shadow of a steep black mountainside, is a little bigger. She has some sheep, but also indulged in the national addiction of horse-breeding, which she acknowledged, 'is really like a form of gambling.'

Through a picture window at the back of Dagny's farmhouse we gazed up at a black wall of rock against which fulmars dance and skirl. Sometimes, said Dagny, a white-tailed sea eagle plunges out of the clouds and carries one of the gulls away.

Ludo was eleven then, with wild, dirty-blond Viking hair, and we were staying at the Agricultural College, term being over and there being a surfeit of spare rooms. Even at midnight, the sun made light work of the flimsy curtains, which was disconcerting, and the night birds calling in the meadows became day birds.

When Ludo, who had no truck with the midnight sun, was asleep, I walked out into the meadows where the bar-tailed godwits were nesting, and the snipe drummed, or as they say in Iceland, '*Hrossagaukur hneggja.*' *Hross* means horse. And *hneggja* means neigh. Like a hross. Or a horse.

Neither neigh nor drum quite convey the bizarre, infuriating sound of the snipe, pushing themselves up into the sky, and then whirring as they fall. And up. And whir as they fall. And so on, like mechanical toys thrown by a child obsessed with the empirical confirmation of gravity.

There are dozens of *hrossagaukur* nesting in the hay meadows, their busy-ness unimpeded by darkness, and their vocal call – the sound of the summer, they say in Iceland – that of a person trying, with little success, to inflate a rubber dinghy with a cheap foot pump...

Snipe and godwit are the big hitters now, so many other birds having already passed through on their way to the 'real' north, somewhere above the Arctic Circle, to Greenland maybe, or Arctic Canada. In any given year, there might be sixty species feeding and sheltering in the estuary, and the hay fields, and water meadows, among them *spói*, and *tildra*, *fálki*, *smyrill* – and even the elusive *straumönd*...[1] Some white-fronted geese were still milling around. But these were the stragglers, and they'd be off too, before long.

[1]Whimbrel, ruddy turnstone, gyrfalcon, merlin and harlequin duck.

We had crammed some obligatory Icelandic things into our itinerary before reaching Andakill. A boat trip from Reykjavík to look for whales had been quite gruelling. Our first and last sighting of a young humpback breaching was exciting because it meant, we hoped, that the captain could turn back, his queasy complement of passengers relieved that they could report that their churning experience of the North Atlantic had not been entirely in vain. And pony-trekking in the Icelandic fells was almost as dreadful, beneath a fusillade of hailstones and rain.

At Hvanneyri the weather cut us a little slack and we took a long walk at the fringes of the estuary, rocky, ragged and grassy.

Perhaps it was the expansiveness of this unfolded landscape, so alien, if accustomed to the confines of the Lilliputian English countryside or townscape, that encouraged us to speak openly about our gripes. Ludo's most immediate grumble was that we were here at all, in this barren place. That we were without Mum (who hadn't wanted to come). And that there were so few other people, and Nothing To Do.

And he had others, all deserved. How we had moved from flat to flat too many times in his eleven years, and it was unfair of us to make him change school, and that you could scarcely call this a 'holiday', so many of the commonly accepted attributes of such a thing being absent. Though I had the sense that none of these complaints fully sounded the depths of a discontentment akin to the smouldering anger of the landscape around us.

It was good walking, not strenuous, but demanding a little foot-thinking ahead of time, between the black rocks and boulders, though it was softer towards the estuary, where the hay fields began. And the scent of the hay and grasses, rich and pungent, and the breeze from the cool and god-like mountains. Here we could speak and be heard, and reflect and be silent. I thought: How admiring of him I am, for his wisdom and courage, and willingness to call me out… and how peculiar it is to be here at all.

In part we were 'here', such as it was, for the soft-scented hay. For not all hay is equal. Only recently, Ragnhildur told me, had she discovered how special is the hay that grows at the edge of the estuary, some of which sits on her farm.

For many years, local farmers have bought the feed they need from agricultural feed merchants, including hay imported from wherever it happens to be most cheaply grown.

But the Andakill hay is a feast of minerals, scoured from the rock by the glacier that feeds the estuary, and released in the meltwater. The hay absorbs it, and you can even smell the difference.

We could, for now we were in the barn with the ewes and the lambs, and she held in one hand some, as you might say, common or garden hay, which smelt hay-*ish*, but only ordinarily so, and in the other, hay harvested from the meadow not a few hundred yards away.

The latter, a stalk of which she broke, was pungent and spicy, the difference between a processed cheese and a cave-aged Roquefort.

So highly prized, she said, was the hay in the days preceding not only industrial agriculture but good roads and lorries, that a system had evolved over the hundreds of years, by which farmers whose land extended to the meadows where it grew ('They didn't *own* the land – but they inherited the *right* to it') and who had more of it than they could possibly use to feed their own stock, bartered it with farmers further away, who would take it away in exchange for their labour or produce.

In a society like Iceland, which is both fiercely individualistic and also traditionally attracted to collective problem-solving and 'standing together', she said, there's an abhorrence of excess. What cannot be used should be shared.

Which is not to negate the recognition of self-interest, as her grandmother's example showed, so much as to place it within a framework that encourages mutual recognition and equality. If always keeping an eye on the main chance.

Which is how Ragnhildur came to live at Ausa, where her sheep enjoy sweet hay, from a meadow fed by a glacier.

VUE PRISE DANS LE DISMAL SWAMP.
Gravure de Boeber, d'après une photographie de M. Shaler.

12

More Sad Stories Than All the Sunshine Can Make Bright

About thirty paces from me I saw a gigantic man with a tattered blanket wrapped about his shoulders, and a gun in his hand. His head was bare, and he had little other clothing than a pair of ragged breeches and boots. His hair and beard were tipped with gray, and his purely African features were cast in a mold betokening, in the highest degree, strength and energy. The expression of the face was of mingled fear and ferocity and every movement betrayed a life of habitual caution and watchfulness.

David Hunter Strother, journalist, writing for *Harper's Magazine* in 1856

Only minutes after the sting of insect repellent had faded, continuing along my towpath walk in the Dismal, I did indeed have an encounter with a bear (though not a whole family, thank God), strolling out of the swamp onto the towpath a dozen yards ahead of me. It wasn't so big. And, though I knew and know little about the length and longevity of ursine apron strings, I had the sense that I wasn't in danger from any outburst of maternal protectiveness.

It swatted at a butterfly, fossicked at the verge, and ambled and shambled. It was, hang it, cute, and had me spellbound for the few minutes it spent in the open before hunkering back into the undergrowth.

There lies an irony in Colonel William Byrd's long association with the Dismal Swamp, his boundary-marking exercise and his grand designs for the swamp's exploitation, in so much as he, chiding though he was of the credulous ignorance of those who lived at its edges, had little greater personal acquaintance with it than did they.

By the time that it came for Byrd and his fellow commissioners, representatives of both states – North Carolina and Virginia – and their team of surveyors and labourers, to embark upon their mission, failure to agree a boundary had been the long-standing cause of any number of jurisdictional, legal and commercial frictions.

While at the face of it the politics was local, the larger world beyond also had a bearing, because while Virginia belonged to the British Crown, North Carolina was in the private ownership of descendants of courtiers to the House of Stuart, to whom it had been granted by Charles II, thus magnifying what might otherwise be regarded as an administrative chore between neighbours.

Even after the terms of the boundary had been agreed, the plan for demarcating it, a task that would take the surveying team straight through the heart of the hitherto uncharted Dismal, was bedevilled with sniping and fractiousness.

In a letter to its North Carolinian counterpart, the Virginian side of the commission assured its colleagues in the endeavour that, 'because there are so many Gentiles on your side of the border who have never had an opportunity of being baptised, we shall have a Chaplain to make them Christians ... Whoever of your Province shall be desirous of novelty may report on Sundays to our Tent and hear a Sermon.' The Carolinians replied that they would so give notice 'to all lovers of novelty', such waspishness setting the tone for the entire enterprise.

Byrd's 'secret' version of his *History of the Line* only flimsily masked the identity of his colleagues with names that betrayed their respective characters ('Judge Jumble', 'Shoebrush', 'Puzzlecause' and 'Dr Humdrum'), but bestowing upon himself the handle of 'Steddy'.

Even on the allotted day that the survey began, the states' representatives squabbled as to whether the starting point should be a spit of sand on the north shore of the Currituck Inlet. Or not.

The Virginians only conceded to the North Carolinian request that the cedar post marking the beginning of the boundary should be 200 yards from that point when they saw it was in their own state's interest to do so. And thus, equipped with theodolites, astrolabes and a huge length of chain, they set out over mountains and marshes and rivers and farms.

Each evening, 'Steddy' reported, they generously refreshed themselves with the rum and whiskey with which both states had furnished them, to 'toast the success of each following day', and gradually lost, in the border lands, much of the decorum they had possessed in surer jurisdiction.

They passed 'pretty girls, as wild as colts', but carried on their journey with 'diligence' nonetheless, though a week into the endeavour, wrote Steddy/Byrd, he and 'Shoebrush' surprised a 'dark Angel' walking in the woods, whose copper complexion and fine shape made her appear as though she was 'a statue in bronze by a masterly hand'. Had Steddy not been there, he suspects, Shoebrush's interest would have taken a dangerous turn.

Not all the region's inhabitants bore the hallmarks of semi-Divine creation. North Carolinians, he wrote, ate so much pork, that they not only smelled 'piggy', but were 'hoggish in temper', and grunt instead of speaking. This, he opined, suggested that the Jews were wise to forbid the eating of swine's flesh in a hot country, given the pernicious effects of doing so.

Passing through a small settlement, he found that while the women were busy knitting, spinning and weaving, the men were seized with the 'distemper of laziness … sloathful in everything but the getting of children, and in that only Instance useful members of the infant colony'.

On 14 March 1728 they reached the margin of the swamp, where Byrd was amused by the ignorance of the inhabitants, scarcely acquainted as they were with 'this mighty Swamp', notwithstanding they had 'liv'd their whole lives within Smell of it.'

They 'pretended', he said, 'to be very exact in their Account of its dimensions and were positive it could not be above 7 or 8 miles wide but knew no more of the Matter than Star-gazers know of the Distance of the Fixt Stars.' And yet, their fearful minds abhorring a vacuum, they imagined it to be brimming with 'Lyons, Panthers and Alligators'.

Still, Byrd was pleasantly surprised to find his surveyors keen to be chosen to form a team that might be sent into the Dismal, mindful as they were of the 'Immortal Fame' sure to await them, regardless of whether they emerged from it.

But he himself was not without misgivings, though not on his own behalf, because he would not be joining them. Each man was to carry between sixty and seventy pounds of provisions; any more would be 'unconscionable', given that they were to 'lugg them thro' a filthy Bogg'. By way of medical supplies, they were furnished with 'Peruvian-Bark', which one presumes to be Talbor's cinchona, rhubarb, rattlesnake root, and a Native American emetic called Hipocoacanah, to be taken for 'fevers or Fluxes'.

Byrd (Steddy), Meanwell and Puzzlecause of the Commissioners had the grace to walk with their surveyors half a mile into the swamp, leaving Firebrand and Shoebrush to 'toast their noses' over a good fire, to 'spare their good persons'. The deeper they travelled, the taller grew the reeds, and more thickly interlaced with bamboo-briar. The 'spungy' ground became 'moist, and trembling under our feet like a Quagmire', so much that a ten-foot pole could be run into it without effort. After three hours of making little headway, the party stopped for refreshment. Steddy, Meanwell and Puzzlecause said some stirring words to their men, who answered with three 'huzzahs'; Steddy reminded them that he would be right alongside them, were it not for his concern that he should be a burden. And the party divided.

He had, at least, every sympathy for them. Half a mile, he said, might not seem far, but these 'Poor Men' had every reason to believe that it was. They had no firm footing. Every step made a deep impression that filled immediately with water. And while they laboured with their hands to cut down the reeds, their legs were hampered by briars. The worst of it all, given the heat, was the teasing breeze, the friendly touch of which they were prevented from feeling by the reeds, though it whistled among the branches of the white cedars...

Later, in the relative safety of their camp, Colonel Byrd's sleep was troubled by his conscience. It rained hard, and the wind was strong, and his fellow feeling for the poor 'Dismalites', as he called them, and whom he now imagined to be half-drowned, 'rendered the Down we laid upon uneasy'.

The uneasy Colonel Byrd was now in his early fifties. His personal estate included all the accoutrements of a Virginian gentleman: a comfortable house in the village of Westover; orchards full of cherries, apples and apricots; fields heavy with the scent of the tobacco flower and its leaves; livestock; a wife he adored, flourished and bickered with; children he doted upon; property and trading interests on both sides of the Atlantic; and substantial and ever-worrying debts. And slaves.

There were 30,000 black slaves in Virginia by 1730. Whether it remains politic to make the distinction that was made at that time between those who were 'enslaved' and those on contracts for indentured labour is a nice point: on the one hand, indentured labour was so demeaning and depriving of liberty that it was, to all intents and purposes, slavery. On the other, it was a condition of labour that knew no bar on colour. Many poor European emigrants were in Virginia on that basis.

Since 1619, when the first Africans were brought to Jamestown, numbers of both white and black immigrants had steadily risen. But ethnic diversity, and conflict, in the Dismal Swamp preceded the arrival of both. By this time, Chief Powhatan and the Algonquin people whom he led had extended their territory to the edge of the swamp, pushed out other tribes, such as the Chesapeakes, Nansemonds and Recehecrians, and yet, by the time settlers arrived in any considerable numbers, native people were so few that they could be safely romanticised, as they were by the Irish bard Thomas Moore in his poem 'A Ballad: The Lake of the Dismal Swamp'.

The *mise-en-scène* is Lake Drummond. The theme is a sad legend about a princess who died before her wedding. The inspiration is the rumour of strange lights upon Lake Drummond…

> They made her a grave, too cold and damp
> For a soul so warm and true;
> And she's gone to the Lake of the Dismal Swamp,
> Where, all night long, by a fire-fly lamp,
> She paddles her white canoe.
>
> And her fire-fly lamp I soon shall see,
> And her paddle I soon shall hear;
> Long and loving our life shall be,
> And I'll hide the maid in a cypress tree,
> When the footstep of death is near.

Thus speaks her grief-stricken intended, who believes her fled from her grave to the lake, where they can be eternally united. And sets out to find her…

> He saw the Lake, and a meteor bright
> Quick over its surface play'd—
> 'Welcome,' he said, 'my dear one's light!'
> And the dim shore echoed for many a night
> The name of the death-cold maid.
>
> Till he hollow'd a boat of the birchen bark,
> Which carried him off from shore;
> Far, far he follow'd the meteor spark,
> The wind was high and the clouds were dark,
> And the boat return'd no more.

It concludes with the comforting thought that 'oft' from the shore, the pair can be seen 'at the hour of midnight damp', crossing the lake by a fire-fly lamp, paddling their white canoe…

One day, in woods at the edge of the swamp, Byrd and his fellow commissioners came upon a family of mixed-race people he described as 'mulattoes'. He suspected them of being runaway slaves, whom their 'righteous neighbours' would not report, rather allowing them to settle on their land in return for their labour, 'well knowing their Condition makes it necessary for them to Submit to Any Terms'.

It wasn't only maroons, he thought, that were likely to be hiding out in these wild, marginal territories. Debtors and criminals, had, he wrote, not only been indulged, but encouraged, as part of a masterplan by the government of North Carolina to swell its population. It was a strategy he admired: the Romans did no less, he pointed out, 'and from that wretched Beginning grew … to be Mistress of that part of the World'.

The colonel[1] was born in Virginia, his father being an English-born 'Indian trader' and planter. Young Byrd was sent to a grammar school in Essex for the first part of his education. This was topped off with a spell at Middle Temple for a legal education, and with business experience in the Netherlands. He returned to the land of his birth in 1704 after the death of his father, whose considerable wealth he inherited and consolidated, and in doing so became what the Old Virginians called A Person of Note.

In 1726, after a five-year spell back in London, he returned with a wife, Maria, to retake his place in the emerging autarky of Virginian life, the tone of which had been set, or at least represented by, the likes of Robert 'King' Carter, an ambitious egomaniac, and member of the Council of Virginia from his early thirties.

Carter had a singular talent for using his connections to reward himself, his sons and his sons-in-law with valuable tracts of land, some 300,000 acres of it, including fifty farms and 750 slaves he came to own by the end of a life which he had largely enriched, financially speaking, by importing and profiting from the trade in slaves.

Byrd, and his wife's brother, John Custis, with whom he spent a lot of time, were friendly with 'King' Carter, and politically

[1]'Colonel' being little more than an honorific. He was in charge of a local militia, but it was seldom called upon to do anything.

allied with him. They would visit his house by the river, with its shipyard and wharves, drink from his excellent wine cellar and dance minuets. Three of Carter's children married three of Byrd's.

By no means was Byrd an abolitionist. His plan for draining the swamp was premised on the labour of slaves, and it might be assumed that the 'servants' to which he refers in his cypher-written diary, were, if not slaves, scarcely in possession of their own liberty. But he was unnerved by the numbers of slaves being imported by boats like the *Liverpool Merchant*, which would dock on the York River with upwards of 700 people from the slave coasts of West Africa. Buyers, he reported, of both sexes, would board the instant the boat was tied to the quay to inspect the 'produce': men at the front of the hold, women aft, children in between. All were naked or wearing scraps or beads.

The enslaved people of Virginia, thought Byrd, would 'rise in revolt' if they found the man to lead them. The only way it might stop would be if the king (George, not Carter) outlawed it, for the slave ships were British. The traders themselves, he said, were the epitome of venality, and would sell their fathers, mothers, brothers '& even the wives of their bosoms, if they could black their faces & get anything by them'.

Of a similar mind, Custis wrote that he wished the trade might be ended but, 'it is so sweet to those concern'd and so much concerns the trade & Navigation of great Brittain, that it will bee next to impossible to break the neck of it'. French demand for tobacco, British credit, cheap and easily obtained labour assured the continuance, and the expansion, of the trade. '[It] is a very melancholly thing seriously to consider it,' he sighed.

I, too, crossed the border that had been demarcated by Byrd, Puzzlecause, Shoebrush and Dr Humdrum. I saw and heard nothing hoggish about the inhabitants of the Carolinian side, who surprised me, as I passed through the first township that I encountered, seconds after leaving the State of Virginia, by waving at my car. It was charming, I thought. Perhaps both parties were desirous or lovers of novelty...

And I stopped at an 'eatery' somewhere on the road and ate, gratuitously, a kind of lime pie, and asked a man to confirm the direction I was supposed to be heading in. With a gnarly, farmer's hand, he pointed me in the direction of the 'Desert Road', which I only mention because of his pronunciation of it, 'des*art*', just as how it once was spelt.

The route had taken me south down the White Marsh Road, and then onto the 'Desart' Road, and around the southern edge of the swamp, and north again, flanking the eastern side of it, towards a state-park entrance. It was quite late in the day, and the ranger warned me about the dangers of being 'in the wilderness'. But I was frustrated by the path that ran parallel to the course of the Great Dismal Swamp Canal, from which it was separated by a screen of trees. On the other side of the canal runs Highway 17, a fast, noisy road that broke up the songs of the swamp and dispersed them with the clamour of its traffic.

The Great Dismal Swamp Company was incorporated in 1763[2] by George Washington, his brother and a band of 'subscribers', all prominent Virginian gentlemen, inheritors all of a vision, not unlike Byrd's, to enrich themselves at the expense of the swamp and the labours of others.

Like Byrd, Custis, 'King' Carter and their ilk, their lives were as interwoven by family relationships as they were by commercial entanglements. And all were on the lookout for new opportunities to make fortunes, or hedge investments in, or offset debts incurred by other schemes and crops such as indigo, tobacco and turpentine.

To show their enthusiasm for the venture, each member of the company committed to providing between two and five slaves, whom George Washington personally valued according to his perception of their capacity to produce profit. Shrewdly, he

[2] *The Fabulous History of the Great Dismal Swamp Company* is excellently told by the American historian Charles Royston (New York: Vintage, 2010).

accorded greater productive capacity to his own slaves than he did
to those owned by his colleagues.

Next the company rented a plantation just beyond the swamp,
where the slaves were to build structures for their own dwelling,
raise livestock and grow corn, before proceeding with the next stage
of the endeavour, digging a canal (the self-same canal along which
I had had the encounter with the bear and flirted with butterflies),
ten feet broad by three feet deep, and five miles long.

Washington mustered the fifty-six slaves that his fellow shareholders
had contributed in July 1764. Most were men, but one investor gave
up a young couple – Jack, who was tall and slim, and Venus, short and
stout. The noted ability of both was their patter and loquacity, which
could be 'troublesome', and not conducive to productivity, indeed,
the complement of enslaved workers was 'the worst collection that
ever was made ... the refuse of every one of the Estates from whence
they were sent', said a local resident. None of the shareholders was
prepared to risk his most valued assets on such a scheme.

The fortunes of the Dismal Swamp Company shareholders would
fluctuate over the years, in or out of step with global markets and
trends, whether for hemp, sugar or timber. And always tobacco,
the dangers of which were being noted in Virginia, where its use
was prevalent and odour omnipresent. One investor had recently
bought a book that advocated a global prohibition on its use.

The first purpose of the first canal was to drain excess water
into Lake Drummond. But the Washington Ditch, as it came to
be called, enabled the conveyance of produce such as 'shingles',
wooden tiles sawn from lumber, shipped out by narrow barges,
punted or dragged, and known as 'lighters', to towns such as
Norfolk, Suffolk and Port Elizabeth. Connectivity to the seaboard
meant that goods could be sold elsewhere on the coast and beyond,
in England, the umbilical cord to which remained strong.

More canals were built: first, the Riddick Ditch, and in 1802, the
twenty-two-mile-long Dismal Swamp Canal, linking the swamp with
the ports of Albemarle Sound and Chesapeake Bay. Even among local
whites, the treatment of the black slaves by the Company became
infamous. In the early years of the twentieth century a woman tourist

was given as an explanation for the swamp's name that it was because there are 'more sad stories [in the Dismal] than all the sunshine can make bright'.

No sane or free person would volunteer to carve a canal from an insect-addled, snake-worn and in every way impossible swamp. For decades, the slaves of the Dismal Swamp had remained, historically speaking, voiceless, their lives only documented in contracts for sale or rent, or rewards for capture. But eighteen years before General Beauregard fired the cannon shot from Fort Sumter, thus opening the hostilities that became the American Civil War, a group of abolitionists launched a salvo against slavery in the form of a book that they published: the autobiography of a former slave born in the Dismal Swamp.

> I remember well how our mother often hid us all in the woods, to prevent master selling us. When we wanted water, she sought for it in any hole or puddle formed by falling trees or otherwise: it was often full of tadpoles and insects: she strained it and gave it round to each of us in the hollow of her hand. For food, she gathered berries in the woods, got potatoes, raw corn…

So begins the *Narrative of the Life of Moses Grandy, Late a Slave in the United States of America.*

Moses was born in the swamp, and his recollections of its hardships, and sometimes atrocities committed in the effort to fell trees and dredge canals, stretched back to childhood. 'The ground is often very boggy,' he wrote.[3]

> The negroes are up to the middle or much deeper in mud and water, cutting away roots and baling out mud: if they can keep their heads above water, they work on. They lodge in huts, or as they are called camps, made of shingles or boards. They lie down in the mud which has adhered to them, making a

[3]Moses himself was illiterate, and the publishers of his book acted as his amanuenses, giving rise to some accusations of introducing dramatic licence for their own purposes.

great fire to dry themselves, and keep off the cold. No bedding whatever is allowed them; it is only by work done over his task, that any of them can get a blanket.

And he catalogued the cruelties imposed by those that had made it their habit to do so, such as the overseer, M'Pherson, who, he recalled, would single out the weakest slaves, unable to perform allotted tasks.

I have often seen him tie up persons and flog them in the morning, only because they were unable to get the previous day's task done: after they were flogged, pork or beef brine was put on their bleeding backs, to increase the pain; he sitting by resting himself, and seeing it done. After being thus flogged and pickled, the sufferers often remained tied up all day, the feet just touching the ground, the legs tied, and pieces of wood put between the legs. All the motion allowed was a slight turn of the neck. Thus, exposed and helpless, the yellow flies and musquitoes in great numbers would settle on the bleeding wounds.

Little of Moses' own life was spent working in such conditions, for in his teens he acquired a reputation for his ability to manage the boats, ferries and lighters plying the waterways of the Chesapeake, the canals and the tributaries of the nearby Pasquotank River, becoming known as 'Captain' Grandy, a title that befitted him better, arguably, than Byrd's rank of 'Colonel'.

But, in Grandy's early years, he saw one brother sold to slavery and his mother tied to a peach tree and whipped for grieving. Another brother, sent to find a 'yoke of steers', died of exposure in the swamp, where he was found 'through a flock of turkey buzzards hovering over him; these birds had pulled his eyes out'. In his own childhood and youth, he said, he was repeatedly whipped and starved.

Though kindnesses were not unknown. Not all owners (or temporary owners, for slaves were frequently leased out) were bestowed with equal degrees of depravity. Moses said that a

Mr George Furley furnished him so generously with clothes and food that, 'he would not have left the place to go to heaven'.

The hardest blow came when Moses' wife, whom, he wrote, he 'loved more than life itself', was sold by their hard-up owner. He watched her being taken away in a chain gang, her new owner levelling his pistol at him to prevent a last embrace.

The pro-slavery lobby tried to defend itself against allegations of brutality, saying that they were exaggerated by the abolitionists, and that such actions would not have made economic sense, given the economic value of the "assets", who were worth very much more alive, than dead or incapacitated.

Also, the slave economy of the Dismal was complex. It suited the owners to hire out their slaves to the labour gangs on a seasonal basis, this being an easy way to profit from their labour without the necessity of managing it. It equally suited the gangs to exploit the labour without making the capital investment needed to purchase the slaves.

The system could even be profitable for the slaves themselves; once they had met their quota for shingles, they were permitted to sell any surplus and keep the cash. In the worst of the summer heat, they returned for two months of each year to be with their own families.

And they had the opportunity to subcontract work to the runaways who lived at the fringes of what, for want of a better word, passed as 'civilisation', for, away from the canals and the labour camps, the swamp remained as impenetrable and inhospitable as it ever had been, and on account of it, a last hope of freedom for runaway slaves or maroons. There were poor white families who also subsisted on making shingles in the swamp and they too would employ maroons.

Black and white swamp-dwellers were equally capable of exerting leverage on their subcontractors through fear. In 1856 the *Harper's Magazine* journalist and illustrator David Strother visited the swamp, and though he didn't venture far beyond the canal towpaths, he did fall into conversation with a slave called Joseph, who described how the maroons possessed hidden huts in the swamp, and that, 'When the shingle negroes employed them, they made them get up logs for them, and would give them enough to eat, and some clothes and perhaps two dollars a month in money. But some, when they owed them money, would betray them, instead of paying them.'

Strother asked Joseph whether the runaways were ever shot.

Yes, he said, when the hunters saw a runaway, if he tried to get away from them, they would call out to him that if he did not stop, they would shoot, and sometimes kill him. 'But some on 'em,' he said, 'would rather be shot than be took, sir.'

Not all maroons lived on the fringes of, or depended upon, the shingle trade. A man called Charlie told a journalist at around the same time as Strother's excursion that there were families living settled lives, having built homes and communities on higher ground, who lived by making furniture and musical instruments, built bark canoes as the indigenous people once had, trapping wild hogs and cows, and attending prayer meetings led by a preacher known as 'Ole Man Fisher'.

'Dar is families,' said Charlie, 'growed up in dat ar Dismal Swamp dat never seed a white man, an' would be skeered most to def to see one.' Of the slaves who exploited their fear, he said, they 'got jist as much devil in dem as white folks'.

Daniel Sayers, the leading academic expert on the Great Dismal Swamp, suspects that black runaways weren't wholly alone in the swamp, and that it had become the redoubt of many others – Native Americans, English or Irish indentured labourers, debtors and felons – for whom freedom, of a sort, caveated by agues, alligators and other hardships, was preferable to servitude, beatings, rotten salt pork, prison, chain gangs, coffle, rape and forced labour. But at heart, the evil that the swamp perpetuated was about racial distinction and the old system that perpetuated it.

Some years, the white South would be gripped by fears of slave insurrection, and at such times the swamp was feared to be the heart of the slaves' 'intrepidity'. In the Great Dismal, local newspapers reported, gathered 'lurking assassins' and 'outlaws' and 'desperadoes', always on the cusp of revolt, mayhem and savagery, a dark threat to the genteel and mannered civilisation of the antebellum South. But for others, the 'dark' versus 'civilised' opposition was reversed. 'Dark' was the perpetuation of slavery; 'civilisation' could only flourish if it had been wiped out across the South. Meanwhile, in the northern states, Grandy's book sold in huge numbers, as did prints depicting the hunting of runaway slaves with dogs, and similar outrageous reminders of the perfidy of the Confederacy.

In like vein, Harriet Beecher Stowe made the swamp the setting of a follow-on from *Uncle Tom's Cabin*, a book called, *Dred, A Tale of the Great Dismal Swamp in Two Volumes*.

But this time the eponymous Dred is no 'Uncle Tom', but a firebrand modelled on two real-life insurrectionists, Denmark Vesey and Nat Turney, the zeal and fury of whom Stowe attempted to capture in her creation's

> large eyes [which possessed] that peculiar and solemn effect of unfathomable blackness and darkness which is often a striking characteristic of the African eye. But there burned in them, like tongues of flame in a black pool of naphtha, a subtle and restless fire, that betokened habitual excitement to the verge of insanity…

Like Byrd, Beecher Stowe (also known as the 'Crusader in Crinoline') had no need to venture into the swamp herself to draw a line. For her audience, and those whom she intended would be won to the cause, its ills were self-evident, or would become so, once perceived.

Dred is a multilayered book. The title character, surprisingly, doesn't steal the story, which revolves mostly around the complexity of relationships between rival (white) Southern families, who, like Grandy's masters, are sometimes cruel, sometimes kind, but mostly use both qualities in the pursuit of their own ends.

But while *Uncle Tom's Cabin* pointed the finger at individuals for their cruelty, *Dred* says that it is the enshrining of iniquity, and inequity, in the Southern statute book that wrests moral responsibility from the hands of individuals and cuts them the slack to behave as they did. Change the law, and behaviour and mindsets will change.

I tried to stay colour-blind in the environs of the swamp. But no outsider visiting the Southern states arrives with their vision not tinted by what they know about the slavery, the Klan, the Jim Crow laws and subsequent history, including the battle to end segregation, which some would argue has yet to be fully won.

Virginia is not what they call 'Deep South', but the tropes are visible. Highway ammo stores and liquor stores; towns divided along lines of race and class; Confederate flags sagging unembarrassedly in the still air…

The hotel at which I stayed, the lowest rung on the ladder of the hierarchy of a well-known hotel chain, sat, with no pretence at being anything other than conveniently situated for access by automobile, by the highway on the outskirts of a town that itself resembled the outskirts of nowhere, or anywhere.

In the hotel lobby, a boy, dressed in a smart black suit with a black tie and shirt and crew-cut blond hair, handed me an invitation to join a Bible study with the Suffolk Baptist Church. The leaflet posed one of those difficult questions: 'How do you know you are not bound for Hell?'

It seemed that the church was being rebuilt on a plot of land adjacent to the hotel and that, pending its completion, the congregation were using the hotel's facilities. And so in the foyer they sat, congregating, and mute. Even the children seemed to have been sucked into a slow-moving whorl of well-behaved torpor.

In the evenings the swirling river of tail lights and headlights and sirens was so intimidating that I could scarcely venture further than an American-Chinese buffet restaurant within a few hundred yards' walking distance from the hotel. Here I could listen to burbling soft rock and eat as much gloop as I liked for $13 (including soft drink. No refill).

I felt, dare it be said, quite marooned.

There were, it was said, maroons living in the swamp long after General Edmund Kirby Smith signed the terms of the Confederacy's surrender. Some were second or third generation and had never been enslaved. Many had escaped noticing the Civil War, its roots, and the abolitionist movement. All stepped out of the swamp to face the realities of reconstruction, the Jim Crow laws, the Ku Klux Klan, race riots, and the continuation of segregation by any means other than slavery. And William Byrd, George Washington – and Donald Trump – have yet to Drain the Swamp.

13

But Doth Suffer a Sea Change

No spot than this, more desolate remains,
Yet with the place my fondest wishes
Dwell,
For deeds of manly daring fling strong
Chains
Of memory around it: I could tell
Of honest Truth and Love, with fewest pains
All linked to Dungeness – Heaven bless
It well

From *Dungeness Ballads*, Joseph Castle, coastguard chaplain at
Dungeness, 1800s

Is it surprising that the Marsh, with all its damp overtones, should
be bordered by the only desert ('des*art*'?) in England, as Dungeness
has been described? Or merely a question of balance?

The latter perhaps. A nice contrast.

As deserts go, Dungeness is neither sandy nor wholly deserted.
And it would be glib and inaccurate to say that there's nowhere
in the world like it, for apparently there are two places, one in
New Zealand and one in Japan, which almost resemble the great
heel of the peninsula, twelve square miles of shingle ridges, the
culmination of 5,000 years' hard graft on the part of the forces of
longshore drift.

Until modernity made a clean sweep of such things sometime in the nineteenth century, local people wore special shoes made of wood with a perpendicular backstop as a means of making any kind of meaningful progress over that shingle. And a cart with wide-rimmed wooden wheels, exaggerated to the point of ridiculousness, was needed to replenish its pubs with supplies from the Kent breweries.

In winter, when the sea kale judders in the clasp of a southerly, and the telegraph wires are keening and wailing, the place is unbearable. But unbearably lovely.

Why is it all so compelling? I wonder this each time I'm moved to be there, lying on the surprisingly comfortable crest of a shingle wave. There is nothing like the contemplation of a billion pebbles to baffle an otherwise overburdened train of thought.

Dungeness has become a gathering place for the knowing to wander and poke among its fishing boats and huts, discarded detritus, strewn, burnt things, to wonder at the way its composition plays with perceptions of scale and qualities of light.

The rub lies in it not being public land in the usual sense. For over a century, its estate was owned by a family called Tufton; it has changed hands several times over the decades and has even been in the possession of a railway company.

In 2017 it was acquired by the French energy giant EDF. But the 'privateness' doesn't intrude. Rather, it bestows a distinctly anti-municipal largesse, which is fitting, given its accidentality and overwhelming skies.

Towards the sea: sprawling over the tawny ridges, shipping containers, repurposed for keeping fishing equipment. Rusting winches for hauling in the buxom, beach-launched boats. And a pantheon of wildflowers. Viper's bugloss and Nottingham catchfly and especially the aforementioned sea kale, which, apparently, tastes rather good if you place it beneath a small cairn of stones to blanch it, then boil it up like cabbage.

But alas no longer the bogbean, stinking hawk's-beard or far-too-modest least lettuce.

There is, on either side of the single-track road that leads up to the lighthouses, a casual arrangement of cottages that have about them an edge of Ur-ness, the geometry of a settlement that never quite became purposeful.

Some are placed in such a way as to conform loosely to laws of community. Others have sunk into the shingle where they ran out of steam, only in part metaphorically, for all these, once, were train carriages, decommissioned by the Southern Railway and sold to its employees for £5 or £10 for their potential as holiday chalets in the teen years of the twentieth century.

It takes a keen eye to see those origins. The carriages have been widened and heightened and shortened to fit their owners' needs. They've accrued right angles as they've grown up and out into more orthodox dwellings.

Scarcely any are inhabited by 'native' fishing families or pioneers from the 'early' days. Only a handful are lived in for more than half of the time. Mostly they can be rented from websites, or from friends of friends who live in cities and 'need' the respite from their own lives that Dungeness can offer. And the aloneness.

On one cottage, the following is written on a piece of paper posted on a window: 'Next door: Stop trying to look into my bedroom!'

By the beach there's a pub called the Pilot Inn, the origins of which I've heard lie in the carcase of a ship lured to shore by wreckers sometime in the seventeenth century and repurposed as a watering hole. A new form of transport you could say. But the best known of Dungeness's dwellings is Prospect Cottage, owned until his death in 1996 by the filmmaker and writer Derek Jarman.

It is one of the first buildings you see on entering the estate, its clapperboard charcoal-black and window frames yolk-yellow. The garden in which it sits has about it something of a Shinto shrine, only subtly accentuating, not usurping, its natural surroundings. The photographer Howard Sooley, who worked to create a book about it, said that 'the garden is the landscape. It ends at the horizon.'

Often the cars slow as they pass Prospect Cottage, unsure as to whether their attentions are welcome, or even worth giving, given how quietly spoken are its charms.

Some years ago it was mostly the likes of those who came to pay their respects not only to Jarman, but everything he loved about Dungeness – its naked, world's end-iness – that found themselves here with their sketchbooks and cameras and projects, and *knowing*.

Such savants are often among those in the queue at the hatch of the Snack Shack, where three young women under the firm control of the daughter of a local fisherman serve lobster and crab rolls, and fresh grilled fish of an excellence generally alien to a nation where the serving of tired food has become elevated to an art form.

There is no cheap seaside cheer here. Which is not to say you can't buy an ice cream, but bright, bare Dungeness has a kind of gravity, as befits a place that domiciles the nuclear power stations (Dungeness A and B) that, from the cliffs close to my home in Hastings, appear to pop out of the sea, on account of their thirty-or-so-mile distance, and the low-lying spit of land at the tip of which they sit, exuding a strangely docile potency, as if biding their time.

They retain that power even up close: bright, boxy, surrounded by shingle and high fences. Depending upon your viewpoint, they're a toxic abomination or a glamorous addition to the Marsh. Indeed, so innocuous a presence are they on that bare extrusion of land as to be verging on the benign.

From a lay perspective, there's little between them. Surrounded by the same perimeter fence, they resemble the generic, incomprehensibly complex behemoths of humming grey-white mystery that they are. But if you look at their insides, they're quite different.

Dungeness A is an old-fashioned, gas-cooled, Magnox-clad (magnesium-aluminium alloy) power station. It became operational in 1965, and after forty years of service was put into retirement, or rather 'decommissioned'. From 2006 until the present, its reactors have been 'defuelled', their spent rods freighted away to Sellafield for reprocessing. The only Magnox power station still functioning in the world is in Yongbyon, in North Korea.

Dungeness B has two reactors, one coming into operation in 1985 and the other in 1987, despite the completion date having been set for 1970. It is an *advanced* gas-cooled reactor or AGR.

'We've hit the jackpot this time!' said Minister of Power Fred Lee when he told the House of Commons about the wonders of the AGR in 1965.

Nuclear power in Britain was dragged into existence on the coat-tails of nuclear weapons research in the fraught post-war order, with the geopolitical climate rapidly chilling and the Iron Curtain beginning to close. Nuclear energy for civilian purposes was initially a mere by-product of the programme to create weapons-grade plutonium.

Always, the machinations of the nuclear scientists and policymakers, and the military-industrial interests invested in it, were secretive and only partially accountable. The first annual budget of the Atomic Energy Agency (AEA) in 1954 was £53 million, potentially a significant strain on the purse strings, given that rationing only ended in the same year.

Parliament had only the lightest insight into and control of its operations. But the following year, the AEA published an exciting 'Programme of Nuclear Power', which proposed commencing from the very outset with a multiple of power stations. Four would do, to start, each to be built by a different 'consortium', the pompous but thrilling word kicking around to describe a business group. Megawatts were the thing.

After the 1956 Suez Crisis, Britain, France and Israel's disastrous attempt to intervene in Egypt's nationalisation of the Suez Canal, the rush to energy dependency seized the government's reins, just as food security had a decade or so previously. (More wheat. Fewer sheep.) The race was on for more power: where the target of the first programme had been 1,200–2,000 MW by 1965, now it tripled, to 6,000 by the same date.

As bureaucrats and consortium members proceeded with their Promethean task, over-expectation, budget overruns, delays and infighting were the inevitable spoils. As was the discovery that early, intoxicating, forays into the world of designing nuclear power stations didn't always marry neatly with reality.

The outputs of the Magnox reactors were not as impressive as foreseen. Each new project demanded not only larger reactors, but two of them. Larger reactors needed larger plate-steel pressure vessels, which became exponentially harder and more expensive to run. The notion that nuclear power was a shortcut to cheap home-grown electricity soon went up the chimney.

The second cast of the die, the *advanced* gas-cooled reactor model and Lee's 'jackpot', spelled the end of the hubris and overspend. Or so Fred Lee believed/told the Commons, or both.

Seventeen years passed between the date Dungeness B was ordered and its first reactor being functional, and a further two years before the second reactor hummed into life. The build cost was five times over the estimate, and its output a fifth less than had been projected.

'In the lexicon of the British nuclear establishment,' wrote former nuclear physicist and chronicler of the atomic age Walt Patterson,

> Dungeness B has always been discounted as a desperately
> unfortunate anomaly. History, however, suggests the contrary.
> Dungeness B was not an anomaly … [but] merely the most
> conspicuous and long-running cock-up in a virtually endless
> catalogue of cock-ups … There were of course a few bright
> spots; but there was, and still is, a quite extraordinary variety
> of egregious embarrassments, cruelly at variance with the lofty
> long-range aspirations of those who first introduced nuclear
> power to Britain.

By email correspondence, Walt told me that there was little opposition to the construction of the Dungeness plants, fears about low-level radiation having then yet to seep into mainstream consciousness.

The promise of jobs has always sustained local support for nuclear power in Dungeness. But Hansard records that residents were concerned by what the movement of shingle and coastal erosion might do to the power stations. And in 1958 Conservative MP Sir Alfred Bossom asked the Minister of Agriculture, Fisheries and Food whether,

Since it has been officially announced by the Chief Planning Engineer of the Central Electricity Generating Board that no assurance can be given that there will not be danger from radioactive dust emitted from the proposed new nuclear power station at Dungeness, how far provision has been made to safeguard the health of the population and livestock in that district from contamination of the crops or water supply; and what compensation will be provided, and in what form, for such damage as may occur from this cause.

In a debate in the House of Lords on 'The English Landscape and Electrical Development', Henry Strauss, 1st Baron Conesford, insisted that, though he was as strong an advocate of electricity as anyone else he could think of, taking a very different view of progress to 'that excellent Tory, Dr Johnson, who ... it may be remembered, objected to canals', such things as pylons, though they can 'stride rather nobly across the scene', need to be placed in such a way as to confer their great benefits 'on our people without destroying unnecessarily things of the greatest value'.

The English landscape, he pointed out, was beautiful, but subtle, and uniquely vulnerable, and as easy to destroy as it would be for 'a lunatic to ruin a picture in a great gallery by taking a hammer or chisel and destroying it'. May I remind the House, he asked it, of what happened at Dungeness?

Dungeness A is out to grass, and Dungeness B has moved recently from a period of 'extended outage' to a new, defuelling phase. EDF, which has custody over the entire Dungeness estate, appears to manage it, to its credit, with apparent sensitivity. Where the nuclear industry was once all secretive boffins and 'Men from the Ministry' in mackintoshes, the French company strives to be transparent, producing brightly coloured newsletters and community reports, welcoming schoolchildren and organising bug hunts, and addressing minor concerns around things like the accidental discharge of space-age-sounding elements like the isotope tritium, which presents a radiation hazard if ingested.

One recent memo reassured residents that,

> Samples analysed during routine quarterly sampling of
> groundwater at Dungeness B indicated levels … above the
> agreed Environmental Agency investigation level of 100Bq/l.
> This has been identified and isolated to one small area on
> site. Work is well underway to resolve this issue and the
> Environment Agency and Office for Nuclear Regulation
> site inspectors are being kept informed of the progress
> being made…

There are other potential causes of concern.

Already EDF is obliged to continually re-place (deliberate hyphen) the shingle, packing up into freight containers what the sea has moved along the coast, and carrying it back to where it began, to maintain the integrity of the sea defences. In 2014 residents established an action group to prevent an EDF plan that would have seen up to a hundred quarry lorries each day, according to press reports of the time, 'coming along the 3.1-metre-wide unmade road for five days a week, trundling right past their front doors'.

'Diggers', (said the report), 'will be out too, along a 300-metre stretch of seafront, pulling out up to 30,000 tonnes of shingle a year to dump it back into the sea a few miles away down the coast.'

All the while the power stations sit, white elephants cooling their toes in the shingle, zoological specimens that have lost their curiosity value but continue to be serviced and fed, their excreta carefully packaged and taken away, on the specially purposed train that comes down from Appledore, to be 'reprocessed', while all around it pylons are caught in the act of 'striding rather nobly'.

But perhaps there isn't enough nuclear stuff going on at Dungeness.

In 2001, after the attack on the twin towers in New York, the Dungeness Visitor Centres were closed as a precautionary measure. They were reopened in 2013 as part of a public relations exercise accompanying a push for a new power station – Dungeness C.

In 2011 an article in the *Financial Times* described 'paradoxical' local support for the project as a kind of 'reverse Nimbyism', quoting the widow of a fisherman as saying that her husband always said he felt, when he was out at sea, that the lights of the power station 'were welcoming him home'.

Since then, Dungeness has been removed from the list of candidate locations for another power station, because the government has concluded that the site is special, and its unique features would be irrevocably altered by the addition of another letter of the alphabet.

The shingle, it points out, isn't just a heap of old stones, but, 'exceptional for the succession of unique shingle habitats that they [the ridges] support as they demonstrate the evolution of the habitats over time', and has thus been designated, and protected, 'for its annual vegetation of drift lines, habitats and perennial vegetation of stony banks habitats … considered to be one of the best areas in the UK and the most diverse and extensive examples of stable vegetated shingle in Europe.'

More quarrying, and freighting, and re-placing would damage them, geomorphologically speaking, irrevocably, for 'once pristine vegetated shingle is disturbed it will never fully recover to the same quality of vegetation community'.

Plan C is not the only possible outcome for Dungeness that's been put paid to – for now.

In 2012 Shepway District Council produced a pamphlet entitled 'Romney Marsh's Nuclear Heritage', part of its canvassing of local opinion on a question of significance not only to Shepway, but to the nation at large, which was whether Romney Marsh 'should host a Nuclear Research and Disposal Facility?'

In other words, would their community like to be the custodians of the nation's nuclear waste for the next 100,000 years?

The council itself, it said, had no 'formal' view as to the desirability of doing so. But it thought that local people ought to have the 'option to consider the opportunity'. No decision would be made lightly or quickly; the communities involved could pull out of the project right up until the time that construction began.

But construction of what?

It was too early, said the document, to describe such a 'facility'. Unquestionably, it would entail a great deal of digging, even on a scale that would dwarf the digging demanded by the construction of the Channel Tunnel.

The waste would be stored at between 200 and 1,000 metres beneath the ground in 'vaults and tunnels'. At ground level, it said, 'there would be research, handling, office, transport and other facilities covering an area of about 1 square kilometre'.

Everything would be 'state of the art'.

The proposal pitched job creation against a whole suite of unknowns, raising complex imponderables, difficult enough for fully fledged ethicists, geologists and other 'ists' to get to grips with, let alone the combined populations of a smattering of rural villages and hamlets, and for the most part deprived towns, who had never asked to be so asked.

On the positive side, the document enthused, the nuclear industry had been 'a familiar part of Romney Marsh' ever since Dungeness A started generating electricity in 1965, and a huge source of revenue for the area. Over 1,000 people, it said, were employed by it, and about £46 million was put into the local economy each year. All of which would taper off as and when the reactors were decommissioned.

Were the 'disposal facility' to be built, it would provide 'skilled employment for hundreds of people over many decades ... long-term jobs that would help offset the loss of employment from the closure of the power stations.'

And further, in recognition of the essential service provided by the 'host community', the government might provide 'community benefits' such as better housing, recreational facilities, and investment in healthcare and education, to take the edge off the stigma of acting as the nation's nuclear garbage can.

But it made no mention of half-lives, or the possibility of leakage, or the yawning expanse of time during which the 'facility' would need to be kept safe and intact. (Even the most 'state of the art' facilities may look a little stale after the lapse of a few centuries.) All that aside, it was generally to be regarded favourably, though for the sake of balance, it mentioned that while many august institutions 'support' geological disposal, 'organisations such as Greenpeace have their doubts about its effectiveness'.

Kent Against a Radioactive Environment said that, 'If the Romans had nuclear power we would still be guarding their waste.' They and others also argued that the Marsh is too geologically unstable to support such a project. For some, the Great Earthquake of 2007, which measured 4.3 on the Richter scale, remained fresh in the memory. In Dymchurch it cracked windows and sent chimney stacks tumbling. An acting fire watch manager in Folkestone had reported, 'We had been sat at the breakfast table and it felt as if someone had driven a lorry into the fire station. It was a major impact. It shook violently.'

Clearly, if Romney Marsh was a 'quake zone', it was no place to dump nuclear waste. And in any event, it's a hard thing to foist on a community that doesn't want it. In China in 2016, the Lianyungang Municipal People's Government baulked at a similar project. Even Beijing was forced to back down.

I rang Councillor David Godfrey (of the famed Godfreys of Lydd, whose early ancestor had had the falling-out, hundreds of years ago, with Hamon about failing in his obligation to keep the dykes in workable condition) to talk about the project because his name cropped up in the literature. He, evidently, was a fan, and he said he was surprised at the negative responses to the consultation. Anyone born after 1965 had lived alongside the nuclear industry and should be used to the rumbling past their windows of waste from Dungeness A and Dungeness B on its way to Sellafield.

But, he said, the government had been too vague about the promised 'benefits' the scheme would bring. And there was another concern, which was that while there was a general assumption that the facility would be somewhere around Dungeness, and far from the (relatively speaking) denser population centres, that wasn't guaranteed. In their inestimable wisdom, the planners, were the project to go ahead, might break ground further afield, at Appledore or Brenzett. Or Ivychurch, Brodnyx or St Mary in the Marsh. Only then would the Marsh know upon whose doorstep the diggers were set to dig…

Given all that, he could understand why some people were less than keen. But, he said, he genuinely worried about what might be next, economically speaking, for the Marsh. In December 2017, plans were announced for a new 'garden town' at its edge, called Otterpool, with the potential of homes for 12,000. That could create jobs locally, but only for as long as the project lasted, and it wouldn't generate any long-term employment prospects. And then, of course, there was uncertainty over Brexit, one of the quite possible consequences of which was that, without an arrangement for free trade or a customs union, it might be necessary to create holding space for road freight awaiting inspection before boarding the ferry at Dover. This could stretch back many miles into the Marsh. Whether an 'opportunity' lay therein or not, Godfrey wasn't sure. But it wasn't a pleasant prospect. A nuclear waste facility would be neater and cheaper.

The more difficult question, though not one that Godfrey attempted to answer, lies in the nature of the duty of care owed by one generation to its successors.

The obligation to our children, their children and even their children is palpable; we may yet live to become loving great- or even great-great-grandparents. But beyond that, to the inhabitants of the shiny future in their weird clothes and jet-bubble transporters, listening to their unlistenable music and doing whatever they do, notwithstanding that we have bequeathed them their DNA, is it reasonable that we should now be attempting to second-guess their abilities and their concerns? Nuclear disaster may, in time, be averted or avertable by an as-yet-to-be-discovered technological breakthrough. Or even pale into insignificance in the face of some existential threat that we have only begun, or even have not yet begun, to imagine.

Barring accidents, the risk of a radioactive leak over the lifetime of the next few generations is low. But it rises over the coming millennia. We are dwarfed by the possibilities of the atom – all that energy is scarcely conceivable without the disciplined and ever-unfolding imagination of the very brightest physicist. But even without one, it seems unlikely that a government consultation, with its bullet points, stakeholder-friendly jargon and dissembling fudge, is up to the job of ensuring that, in the course of the next few thousand years, everything will be OK.

Many are the stones that such a thinking exercise turns over – around the essence of time, the duality of Man and Nature, and even where 'God' sits in this conversation, if at all.

All of which may be abstract and existential, but just as Derek Jarman's garden flows seamlessly into the horizon, so do the big questions flow from and to the little ones. The future of the power station is impossible to consider without reflecting on the nature of our legacy, and the nature of our *nature*, and who on Earth we think we are, and a host of other, big, baggy, ontological ghosts, which always seem to absorb our punches with neither complaint nor reward.

By late afternoon of a day in August at Dungeness, a vein of ships' fumes and general fug marbles the breeze from the Channel. The pebbles cool quickly, the Snack Shack is done with its customers, and the Ness's remaining visitors are perched on the shingle, watching anglers cast their lines into the sparkling unknown.

14

A Dip in the Dowels

Far away, in the south-east corner of Kent is the Romney Marsh. A flat, sheep-nibbled kingdom with oak posts and rails, and windswept salty churches.

John Betjeman, *Discovering Britain With John Betjeman*,
Shell Series, 1956

The Dowels is one of those last remaining plots of unploughed Marsh, a microcosm of how it all may have looked before *before*, in time out of mind.

To its west, it borders a section of the Royal Military Canal, and is, as an Environmental Assessment of 2016 says perfectly adequately, 'a tranquil and peaceful landscape, with little modern development. The landscape feels open, and areas of wetland and wet pasture give it a variety of textures and colours.'

Perhaps of anywhere on the Marsh it is the hardest to 'place' chronologically. Its most noticeable architectural feature is the pocket-sized church at Fairfield called Thomas à Becket, which sits on what was once as good as an island before the construction of a tiny wooden causeway just before the First World War. It has a square-based pyramid for a small belltower, a steeply sloping roof and heavy eaves, while the interior, with its oak ribs and beams, evokes the belly of Jonah's whale, albeit equipped with box pews and a triple-decker pulpit.

The red-brick, lichen-roughed church exerts a pull upon the sheep in the surrounding field. They lean against its walls, in their lee.

It is an old church, and it isn't. The original timber-and-lath frame was built shortly after the death, and dedicated to the memory of, its namesake and turbulent priest in around 1200. Six hundred years later brick replaced timber. In 1912 much of it was rebuilt again. So convincingly ancient is it that it has appeared several times on television. But it's all over the place, epochally speaking…

The sense of entering a time-tableau extends beyond the hallowed grounds to the rest of the Dowels. The sheep are not any old sheep. They are Romney sheep. Sheep upon which, according to the wholly unbiased Romney Sheep Breeders Society 'the sun never sets'. The breed is mentioned in the Domesday Book and has, as Rob Montje of the Internal Drainage Board wrote in an early chapter of his dissertation on Romney Marsh, evolved over the same span of the Marsh. Like hunter and prey, he writes, 'the two are inextricably linked and well suited'.

They are famous around the world for being sound of feet, resistant to disease and parasites, of strong constitution, good foragers, independent, exceptionally hardy, long lived, of early maturation. And good mothers.

Only the church can rightly be described as a showstopper. But there are other interesting things to be seen, like a wartime semi-cylinder of rusting corrugated iron, almost entirely embraced by vegetation. A crumbling looker's hut. And a shearing pen, after a New Zealand design, only a few decades in age but already acquiring the patina of the Marsh, and within which, with the blessing and encouragement of Les Ramsden, is long established a dynastic clan of pigeons, not fancy but precious to him, and not on any account to be disturbed…

Like Jim Pilcher, but a good decade younger, and still busy and active, Les is a powerful-looking man, one of the most respected sheep farmers on the Marsh, and a legendary shearer in his time.

'There's something that I want to show you,' Les told my daughter and me.

We were driving across the Dowels, slowly cleaving through a
flock of Romneys. And we stopped at a dip, a bowl-like depression
a few yards wide, in the field.

We could see, half a mile to the south, the road running from
Appledore to its station (the two are separated by a mile or so);
and the Engine Sewer, which runs alongside the road. Road and
waterway are only visible, other than when cars pass, on account of
the line of trees that follows them.

'When I was four,' said Les, who was eighty-three, 'my mum
and I were walking along that road. We were living with my
grandparents at the time, in a cottage in a field on the other side of
it. And a huge man ran out of a hut, that was just there – you can
see where the trees are…'

We could.

'He shouted, "Get down!" and my Mum picked me up and
threw us both into the ditch on the other side of the road. A few
seconds later there was an explosion, and we could see flames and
smoke coming out of the field. If she hadn't done what she'd done,
well, I wouldn't be showing you this.'

'This', of course, was the crater where the doodlebug, for such it
was, had landed, and has intrigued Les ever since.

'The sheep won't go near it,' he said. 'Something about it. Very
clever kind of a bomb, the V2. And a very clever people, the
Germans. Such a shame they got hoodwinked by that man.'

Things, said Les, were always falling out of the sky during the
war. Especially during the 'Doodlebug Summer' of 1944, when
Germany began to kick back after the D-Day landings. More
ordinary bombs had fallen from the very start, sometimes because
defences on the Marsh were being deliberately targeted, but also,
as planes returning from bombing raids over London lightened
their loads returning to occupied Europe. He has yet, he said, to
learn not to duck when he hears aeroplane engines. Given that
the Marsh has its own airport at Lydd, replete with a suitably
utilitarian Battle of Britain canteen and a runway from which light
aircraft fly to Le Touquet for lunch, or just pull above the clouds to
gaze upon the riddling landscapes of the estuary and the robed and

disrobed mysteries of the tidal coast, there have been many ducks and flinches over the decades.

Bombs fell. Planes fell. People fell.

On the road between New Church and New Romney there is, by a hedge, at the verge, a memorial to Arthur Clarke, a twenty-one-year-old pilot whose Hurricane fighter was shot down over the Marsh on 11 September 1940. It consists of a headstone – not a gravestone, for his remains were found thirty years after his death – and a little gravelled plot, with a pillar at each corner, which squares it off.

The internet reveals more about Clarke: a sepia-tinted photograph captured a decade before his death, on the beach, he and two siblings flanking his matronly mother Lavinia, all squinting, smiling at a father whose presence is betrayed in the bottom right-hand corner of the image by the faintest shadow of a trilby hat.

Sometimes they fell, but were never, in a sense, caught, like the Polish officers, Pilot Officer Bogusław Mierzwa of 303, 'Kościuszko' Polish Squadron RAF Northolt, and Pilot Officer Mieczyslaw Waskiewicz, who disappeared somewhere off the coast of Dungeness returning from a mission escorting Blenheims that was on its way to bomb France. There are memorials to both, far from the madding crowds in the shingle. But none to the pilots of the Messerschmidts and Heinkels that also fell out of the sky, although they, too, were many – more perhaps.

Thinking about it, there's scarcely an inch of the Marsh into which the war did not insinuate itself.

A man called Martin Morris, who works for Les and whom, I expect, will succeed Les as the Old Man of the Marsh when Les is too old to look after his sheep, told me that after 1945, farmers would detonate the ordnance that the Special Operations Executive (SOE) had hidden in the ditches, to clear them. The SOE had, he said, trained and equipped local farmers to act, in the event of invasion, as a Resistance force, like the French *maquis*, who would use their knowledge of the Marsh, its ditches and sewers and hollows and hedges (for there isn't very much more to it) to frustrate German supply lines and intentions, just as the 'free traders' of the eighteenth-century smuggling era baffled the excise men with their superior and instinctive understanding of the landscape.

A subtle 'tell' from the secret, wartime Marsh: a square-sectioned concrete 'corridor' eight inches or so wide and deep, only visible where it extrudes from the banks of the ditches, otherwise silent and seven decades dormant beneath the turf...

One might write it off as 'just a thing', a relic of some dull and unnecessary work specification. But this unpretty protuberance is a hero of D-Day, a little section of the Pipe-Line Under the Ocean, or the PLUTO line.

The PLUTO line was the means by which Britain pumped oil across the Channel after the invasion of the Continent, hundreds of miles of lead piping unrolled from gargantuan spools called Conundrums, each 'five times the height of a man', laid beneath seventy miles of marshland and across the Channel. At its peak capacity, PLUTO could deliver 1 million gallons to France every day to support Allied efforts.

At Dungeness and around, pumping stations were disguised as bungalows, or bungalows repurposed as pumping stations, the machinations of war masquerading convincingly as the dreary and suburban. Ice-cream parlours also 'did their bit'.

'I remember', Les told me, 'the Irish workmen arriving in the middle of the night, when they wouldn't be seen, building the trenches in which to lay the pipes. And the sound of the spades in the soft earth.'

Surveying, with Les, this old patch of the Marsh, I feel the paucity of my own understanding of this all-too-subtle corner of the sheep-nibbled planet. I see sheep, and clouds, and grass, and wonder at and about the names of the plants in the ditch, and wood pigeons and pollarded willows (are they pollarded? Are they willows?).

But for Les: here he walked with his mum, across fields. To this place his dad returned wounded from the war and could no longer farm. Here Les learned the craft of farming. To here Les came back from New Zealand and turned the art of shearing on its head. And here he built a shearing pen after the New Zealand model, the first on the Marsh, now home to his beloved pigeons. And here, not many years ago, during a freezing winter, he slipped into a ditch and would have drowned had he not just been able to drag himself out of it.

A strong hand and heart crowned him Best Shearer in the World – 390 sheep in a single day. And here he courted his wife Rhona, who had travelled south from the Highlands to work as an au pair, and one day taken her wards to watch the lusty shearers at their work…

And here, right where we were now, was an overgrown wilderness before Les raised the money to take it on and return it to the pasture it had been before the war. In other words, here was a topography of emotions and memories that made it unique to him, upon which also rests the future.

Les's son has his own construction business and no interest in farming, for which his father would never chide him. But in Martin Morris, whom I had met on a ramble on the Dowels and who had made the introduction to Les, I could see that he had more than an heir.

Martin had just retired from the fire service but had worked with Les on the side for twenty years, helping him with his sheep. He possessed an extraordinary aura of intelligence and friendliness. And if you couldn't tell how old he was with any certitude, you'd have to say he was young despite any accumulation of years.

Watching the two of them at Les's shearing sheds, the strength of their mutual regard was very evident.

'Some years ago,' Les told me, after our trip to the Dowels, 'I had to have an operation to remove a tumour. And it happened at the worst possible time because the lambing had begun. I was out of action for weeks. Very low. And Martin said, "Don't worry, I'll look after things." He was still working for the fire service at the time. And he did everything. Absolutely everything, perfectly. Checked on the ewes, helped with the births…

'When I was up to it, I went round to see Martin, and I said, "Martin, what do I owe you for all this? Let me write you a cheque."

'And do you know what he said?

'He said, "Nothing, Les. You don't owe me anything at all. It was my pleasure that I could help you."'

I could tell, when Les told me this, that the memory of it was moving almost to the point of tears.

A tough man, but not a hard man. He abhors shooting. One year he had a troublesome fox in the fields and had it shot on the advice of his neighbours. But when he found the vixen's kits starving in their den, he vowed that he'd never have another fox shot on his land. Nor does he go in for the corporate pheasant shooting that gees up the bank accounts of other farms. But badgers...

'They are', he says, 'cruel beasts. They drag the lambs into their setts and eat them alive – I've heard them down there, bleating before now. It's horrible. And they attack the lambs at the moment they're being born.' Pull them from the womb.

He doesn't like, he says, the point at which the lambs are separated from their mothers, and knows that when they have the chance to, they'll seek each other out, calling to each other, nuzzling with relief when, or if, united.

'I owe everything I have to these sheep,' he says, and he said it in a way that was more than an evaluation of an economic resource that he had mastered, but an appreciation of it or them as – if not individuals – a collective of sentient and lovable things. 'Everything I have.' Which perhaps in the context means 'everything I've lived'. Possession, in the looser, greater sense of the word.

15

Washing Away

Thus ere another noon they emerged from the shades; and
  before them
Lay, in the golden sun, the lakes of the Atchafalaya
Water-lilies in myriads rocked on the slight undulations
Made by the passing oars, and resplendent in beauty, the lotus
Lifted her golden crown above the heads of the boatmen
Faint was the air with the odorous breath of magnolia blossoms
And with the heat of noon, and numberless sylvan islands.

> *Evangeline: A Tale of Acadie*, Henry
> Wadsworth Longfellow, 1847

The man in the silver suit and the pork-pie hat hunched over a piano,
set right by the door at the Three Muses bar on Frenchmen Street,
New Orleans' *avenue du jazz*, singing, as he played, a song with a
refrain that warns that Louisiana is under threat of being washed away.

My wife and son and I sat at a little table among others populated
by people who shared with us two characteristics. They, too, would
have liked, perhaps, to have at least looked as though they belonged
to the enviable tribe of those that actually *lived* in New Orleans,
and were more than the froth of tourists that washes in on the tide.
And they also had spent a day wondering when the rain, alternating
with dirty smears of wind grubbing up the entire south bank of the
Mississippi, and the blotches of fog that had put a dewy dampener

on everything, might call it a day and give way to the comfort of darkness and bar lights.

The daylight hours we had squandered on a drive to the site of the Battle of New Orleans, a large open space which, though it may once have rung with flashing muzzles, war-whoops, death cries and glinting, bloody steel, was damp, desultory and depressing. We'd strolled along the levee, watching the ships coming up and down the river, and pondered the predicament of bankside trees now up to their lower limbs in a rising tide.

Later we'd returned through the troubled Ninth Ward district, broken by Hurricane Katrina and as yet not repaired, past smashed shacks and houses and stores flung on their sides, upside down and down and out, and under the overpass of Claiborne Avenue, a monstrous tongue of concrete, which for all its sins, at least puts a roof above the head of those for whom the likelihood of ever possessing a home was long wrecked by poor mental or physical health (or the insanely astronomical costs of treating them), or any one of a number of wars that awarded veteran status but little else. Or by flood.

Until I caught the refrain describing President Coolidge coming down to Louisiana in a railroad train, I'd guessed the song's subject was Katrina, which over the course of a week in 2005 swept across the city, flooding four-fifths of it, breaking the levees built to protect it from exactly such disasters and killing 1,833 people.

In fact, the song, written and first performed by Randy Newman in 1991, described the Great Flood of 1927, the consequences of which were no less devastating. But it would, could and should resonate with any Louisianan who had lived through a succession of watery catastrophes, such as Hurricane Betsy in 1965, or the Great Flood of 1973, and inevitably, those yet to come – and in each case, the causes are as intermingled as the ingredients of a gumbo,[1] though inestimably less palatable.

The Atchafalaya Basin is a swamp system based around the 140-mile river of the same name and which (the river) begins its

[1]Which typically include okra, filé powder (the ground roots of the sassafras plant) and shrimp, sausage, chicken or anything else to hand.

southward journey just above the town of Simmesport, debouching in the Gulf of Mexico, brushing through the disconsolate oil town of Morgan City, sitting gloomily behind a levee that, though it may protect the town from freak rises in sea level, is no barrier to economic or social malaise.

Bayous, rivers, swamps and levees. The lives and fortunes of southern Louisiana and its inhabitants are wholly sculpted by such features, the levee system being the most overt intervention in a landscape that would otherwise be almost wholly given to river swamp and coastal marsh.

The levees are high-sided dykes that more or less enclose the delta, and were and are built to ensure continuity of water supply and prevent flooding. It is a system that works most but not all of the time.

The cost of the levees is that they prevent the river from following its own course. Without them, the Atchafalaya might have long ago eclipsed the better-known waterway of which it is a distributary. It came close to doing so in 1983, when an abnormally high flood almost burst through the control structure regulating the flow between the two rivers. Had the state government not responded quickly enough, the Mississippi would have changed course.

'The economic, environmental, and cultural disaster that an avulsion [an avulsion being the natural, but rapid, abandonment of one channel and the creation of a new one] would cause is incalculable,' reads a report prepared for the state of Louisiana.

Dean Wilson had asked that we meet in the parking lot of Dale's Trading Post on the bank of the Little Tensa Bayou on the basin's eastern flank.

Dean's sobriquet, self-assumed, but others also use it to refer to him, is 'the Basin Keeper', and his devotion to protecting the Atchafalaya is well known, begrudged even, by those who would otherwise profit from it.

The night before, I'd driven eighty-five miles from the airport, getting roundly lost in the Baton Rouge traffic system before bedding down with my family in the Best Western Hotel in the tiny town of Plaquemine. Squeezed between the highway and the Mississippi, sleep sat uncomfortably between two batteries of horns: those of the trucks that passed so close as to almost brush the walls of the motel, and those of the bleary-eyed ships, bleating through fog on their way towards the Gulf of Mexico.

Driving the last stretch, we felt upon our faces the glow and heat of the flickering furnaces of the Dow chemical works at Morrisonville, which sits on a spur in the meandering river, and breathed in its odorous breath. It all felt tragically removed from the swamp that Dean had promised to reveal, let alone Longfellow's sylvan islands. But the next morning at Dale's, an all-in-one food and gas stop selling everything from boudin, cracklin' and alligator sausages to fishing bait, root beer, Mountain Dew, chewing tobacco and the rest of it, I could tell that I and it were inching closer.

A pickup truck, towing a flat-hulled swamp boat, was parked up by the gas pump. Out of the passenger window emerged a cigarette attached to an arm attached to a woman who asked, 'You the writer?'

'I suppose so,' I said, and she gave a throaty laugh...

She introduced herself as Monica.

'Dean's just in the john,' she said. And soon he emerged from some outside corollary of Dale's, beaming warmth and urgency, and doing up his flies.

When we'd spoken on the phone some weeks before, I'd mistaken Dean Wilson's distinctly non-standard American accent for Cajun. But Dean, though born in Louisiana to a Spanish mother and a father from Ohio, was brought up in Spain, where he worked on fishing boats until he was twenty-one, at which time he returned to his native state, as it were, to ply the same trade.

Having trapped and fished and hunted and generally immersed himself in the swamp, he made a vow of sorts, to protect it from many-headed hydra of collective threats to its health, the *primus inter pares* of these being the oil industry, which has, since the 1930s, dug trenches for pipelines, creating 'access corridors' and building refineries and all the other necessities for its existence.

We drove in convoy along a road that followed the winding course of the bayou, past shacks and sheds and bigger houses, a church and a boatyard, before crossing a small steel suspension bridge, unloading the boat at a launch ramp under the censorious gaze of a moody clique of pelicans. These, Dean said, had flown south from Canada for some winter sun, not that there was much to be had.

It was cold and cramped in the boat. Monica pulled out rain macs that were flappy and inelegant, but in anticipation of worse to come, certainly better than nothing. Dean pulled the starter cord on the outboard, and moved out into the bayou, kicking up spray as the flat hull planed along the broad reaches, an Ariel among the Caliban-like freight vessels that might have come from almost anywhere on the Mississippi River system. Pittsburgh perhaps, or Memphis, Kansas City or St Louis.

The banks of the bayou were dark with trees, and its surface pocked and pitted with a rain shower which was really getting unpleasantly into its stride. A bald eagle cruised above, with menace in its leisure, or the other way around, putting to flight a small party of large egrets. A better man than I, less likely to have been rendered mute by his discomfort, might have said, 'Look, a bald eagle!' But I, not being better than I am, could not.

'Look,' said Dean, 'a bald eagle.' I nodded stiffly, as befits a man shivering beneath a thin cagoul, who is not what he might have been.

I could tell that Dean and Monica were on the prowl.

We came alongside a digger at the edge of a defoliated bank, literally on the verge of toppling into the muddy waters into which its great maw jerkily sank.

Monica cut the engine and took out her camera, drawing hard stares from hard-hatted men.

'You can see how they're digging out the mud and just dumping it into banks. They're supposed to be transporting it out. That's why we're documenting all this.' Monica waved and the men in the hard hats waved back hesitantly, as if uncertain that in so doing, they weren't complicit in something dangerous.

I hate confrontation and was relieved when the boat turned into the intimacy of the swamp, where the wind was broken by a flooded forest of flared-bottomed cypress, willow and tupelo, brushed by low branches from which hung with melancholic grace, like the curls of a dolorous heroine, tumbling fronds of Spanish moss.

Beyond the larger channels, the swamp looked labyrinthine, its unfolding patterns of trees and their reflections Escher-esque and repeating; one might think that perhaps the trees weren't so endless in number as they appeared, that there were only a few dozen, that we were merely enclosed by a mirrored box lending the impression of an arboreal, aquatic infinity…

It was coolly quiet, like being, strangely, in the presence of people at prayer.

Apropos of no more than all the above, Monica said, 'I like being with you, Dean, it makes me feel peaceful.'

'How do you mean?'

'Like, less crazy.'

'But I'm the crazy one!' laughed Dean.

'Well, I'm more crazier than you. It just makes me feel good to be in the boat with you.'

Dean had that effect. He let the boat drift up to a point where it could rest still against the trunks of two cypress trees, and stood, one foot on the starboard gunwale, a hand on the bark of the cypress and the other on his hip. It was, I thought, a pose that was Conquistadorean, but also benign and deservedly proud.

'This is all second-growth forest. The first growth was felled in the nineteenth and twentieth centuries, and while what's here looks established, you'll see that none of the trees have a large girth. The big trees are all gone.'

The trees stood attentive and quiet as though they, too, could learn from a retelling of their ancestral history, and from their trunks his voice echoed lightly and crisply…

'There is so much you can tell from these trees. Such as this dark line…' He pointed up to a tree, 'which shows the change in the growth in lichen. It's the high-water mark of the 1927 flood.'

He talked about the birds of the swamp (though, corroborating my hunch that I have an unerring ability to be in the right place at the wrong time when it comes to migratory species, I saw few), the Mississippi kite, and the screech owls, and the wood storks and woodpeckers, and the painted buntings and the tanagers, and how, in a hot summer, the swamp waters run dry and the big animals move in. Bears and coyotes, deer and antelope, bobcats and armadillos. And about how not all the species are native: how the nutria, large rats, like coypu and AWOL from fur farms, have run rampant through the swamp. And how the Chinese carp have found it so much to their liking that they grow ever fatter, and sometimes leap from the water with the sheer joy of doing so, knocking anglers from their boats.

And there's salvinia, a baize-like weed that sat so smoothly and neatly on the water and through which our little boat had traced interesting patterns, which has come up through the waterways from Brazil.

'It's an invasive species, and it chokes off the native plants and de-oxygenates the water,' said Dean. And, pushing on our way, he stopped by the stump of what had once been an impressively large tree, felled perhaps a century ago, and pointed to the notches and scars that showed how the lumbermen or 'swampers' had tackled these huge trunks, 'girdling' the tree by cutting through its cambium layer and effectively 'killing' it some weeks before felling it, so that it could be floated out of the basin towards the lumber markets.

Funny, flickering film footage from the 1920s shows the 'swampers' defying all the conventions of gravity by swinging their axes as they stand in tiny, untethered pirogues. In it, *pace* Jack and the Beanstalk, David and Goliath, the Argonauts versus the Cyclops, is writ the inevitable victory of the small and nimble over gargantuan clumsiness... for the current and subsequent generations of trees may never throw the long shadows their ancestors bestowed upon the swamp.

Strong, fragrant and insect repelling, cypress, which Florida's Seminole tribe called '*hatch-in-e-haw*' or 'everlasting', is a highly desirable wood for building. The cypress forests of what is now New Orleans were destroyed to feed the growing city's demand for materials. Prices rose and fell with all the stability of a tulip market, with fluctuations determined by flooding and land-clearance schemes, but the general trend being upward, and by the middle of the nineteenth century all the giants, some more than 1,000 years old, 150 feet tall, twenty feet in diameter, had been chopped into little pieces for roofing tiles and clapperboard.

'Off we puffed ... through the little village of white houses ... and away into a dense, gray cypress forest. For three or four rods, on each side of the track, the trees had all been felled and removed, leaving a dreary strip of swamp, covered with stumps,' wrote the man who designed New York's Central Park, Frederick Law Olmsted, in his journal in 1853.

A map of New Orleans from around the same time marks huge swathes of land with the words 'timber mostly felled' and 'timber felled'.

Dean thinks that the risk of the resumption of lumbering is very real, especially if the basin were ever to be left undefended. But it may not be inevitable. An early success of Dean's came when he challenged a company that had been felling cypress and converting the timber into wood pellets, shipped from Baton Rouge to Liverpool, carried by train across the Pennines and ultimately burned in furnaces in the Drax power station in Selby, North Yorkshire.

'We invited the board of Drax to come out here to see the swamp, and to see the trees that were being felled to make their wood pellets. They were horrified. They're among our biggest supporters now.

'This forest that you see was able to regrow. But it couldn't survive a second time. In fact, in lots of places it never came back – where there was swamp, now it's a lake.'

It takes a seasoned eye to smell a rat.

There are connections, said Dean, and contrivances, between the oil interests and private-property owners who have designs on the swamp, and see value not in its uniqueness as an ecosystem, for its natural beauty, or even for the value of its role as a spillway for absorbing floodwaters, as a buffer zone protecting New Orleans and other Louisianan cities from disaster, but as opportunities for timber and land sales and property development. 'All across America, people only see profit in the land. They look at how they can get rid of the messy stuff and build houses,' he says.

It was true that, while the impertinences of the dredging and the pipelines were noticeable and ugly, it all seemed pretty wet to me. But, he said, 'Look through the trees and you can see the raised ground behind them, like hills. It gets higher every year. In places, the swamp is disappearing and being replaced by land.'

This, Dean said, was the result of decades of meddling with the hydrology of the swamp that has accelerated the accretion of sediment, a process which, before the levees, happened when the Mississippi and its sister rivers flooded, bringing silt from across the continental United States, and washing it away, and replenishing it again. Epically, episodically, and without a timetable.

But the inroads, access canals and other conduits that the oil companies have created to pipe the black stuff back and forth across the swamp, from wells to refineries and terminals, in concert with the levees that prevent the floodwaters spilling beyond their bounds, have speeded everything up, and spoil banks alter natural waterflows and habitats and spawning grounds.

But oil means jobs, of course.

In 2018 a consortium of NGOs lost a battle against a joint-venture project that planned to build a pipeline straight across the swamp. It's this pipeline that the hard-hatted, slow-waving workmen were building.

'As much as anything,' said Dean, 'it's the fact that even when violations of the environmental protections occur, which is often, nobody does anything about it. There are laws, but no enforcement.'

So, he says, where it is easier to run a pipeline through a spoil bank than it is to build a trench for the pipe, that is what'll happen, 'So the bank will stay in perpetuity, disrupting the flow of the water, drying out the swamp so that it becomes permanently dry.'

Nor is this disruption any good for fish stocks, or the crawfish fishery – crawfish, once seen as a common Cajun food, now luring tens of thousands of gourmands in holiday season. And if there happened to be an oil spill, that could be most catastrophic of all.

'I'm afraid,' said Dean, 'that the alligators are hibernating.'

'That's fine, I don't blame them,' I said.

'Sometimes they come out to warm up when the sun comes out, but I don't think the sun's going to come out today.'

'No. Doesn't look like it.'

In fact, now it started to rain really, really hard. It was as much as I could do to peer through a small aperture in the hood of my cagoul. But Dean seemed immune to it, pushing the boat fast through a long stretch of the bayou, past another freighter, low in the water and heading back from Morgan City or maybe further out, in the Gulf, and past the egrets, and the pelicans and the invisible, sleeping alligators.

Monica was struggling to keep a cigarette alight. I knew that Dean wanted to get back to the landing, to winch the swamp boat back onto the trailer and get going because that afternoon he was picking up his son from school – in Arkansas – so they could spend the Christmas holidays together. Like Monica, I liked being with Dean. I felt that the basin liked him too.

There is, in the town of St Martinville, on the other side of the basin, upon the bank of the lazily lovely, lovely and lazy Bayou Teche, a large oak tree, sprawling and cloaked in Spanish moss. It represents as much as a monument to Cajunism as almost anything else in Louisiana. More, even, than bumper stickers that read '*Laissez les bons temps rouler*', alligator sausages or swamp boats. The tree is the Chêne d'Evangeline, the Evangeline Oak, and as the sign that accompanies it says: 'This oak marks the legendary meeting place of Emmeline Labiche and Louis Arceneaux, the counterparts of Evangeline and Gabriel.'

To those unacquainted with Henry Wandsworth Longfellow's epic *Evangeline*, the tree, with its garland of a wrought-iron chain suspended from white pillars, can't resemble more than the kind of mournful civic feature whose historical importance is exaggerated by small towns such as St Martinville to attract the interest of anyone passing through. A bid to persuade them to stop for lunch. Or pass the night.

But, if you *have* read *Evangeline*, and been borne along by its solemn dactylic, unrhyming hexameter, the oak represents the

pinnacle of the poem's pathos, and is fully deserving of some
contemplative moments, as is the statue, a few dozen footsteps
distant, of Evangeline herself, modelled by Dolores Del Rio, the
star of the second film of the poem, released in 1929 (and a mere
decade after the first, directed by Raoul Walsh).

There is another statue of Evangeline in the town of Grand-Pré,
in a memorial park, thousands of miles and many degrees of latitude
away from the steamy swamps of Louisiana, in Nova Scotia.

And it is there, in the Maritime Provinces of Canada's eastern
coast, where, since the 1500s onwards, European adventurers
sought their fortunes in its fur-rich fastnesses and fish-brimming
shores, that all the 'Evangelines', real, imagined and in-between,
began their journeys.

The Italian explorer Giovanni di Verrazzano first put the term
'Arcadie' on a map of the north-east coast of North America. He
did so in 1523, years before anyone knew a great deal about it.
For a century or so the word was shuffled around by Renaissance
geographers and mapmakers, before coming to rest sometime in
the 1700s. It actually was a kind of Arcadia, indeed, perhaps, a
multiplicity of Arcadias, before a great cloud of toxic Englishness
spoiled it or them.

The first was that enjoyed by the Mi'kmaq people, who, well
before the raising of the pyramids of Egypt, made the jump across
the Bering Straits, continued eastwards, and, settling in Nova
Scotia, as it was not then called, found it to be a suitable place in
which to build a tolerant and inclusive but well-ordered society,
and develop skills to exploit the generous local resources.

Sometime in the 1600s, settlers began to land on the Mi'kmaqs'
shore, mostly arriving, *petit à petit*, from the western seaboard of
France.

There are Breton seafaring words in modern Cajun, and telltale
songs, habits, recipes and names that point to Normandy and
Poitou, but the Cajun movement, in its grand and magnanimous
sweep, also caught up Scots and Irish and Spanish.

But come they did, in little waves and ever larger ones, across the
centuries and the sea, driven as much by a thirst for adventure as by

politics or poverty, building as they came a patchwork of villages around their largest settlement Grand-Pré, or 'Big Meadow'.

These mostly French immigrants quickly detached themselves from the Old World, within scant few generations identifying as natives of the western, not the eastern, shores of the Atlantic. They settled easily among the Mi'kmaq, and intermarriage was usual, to the extent that the French military began to despair of communities of settlers becoming wholly assimilated into the indigenous community. Mutual attraction was felt between all classes of both societies. After the French soldier and grandee Baron de Saint-Castin arrived in 1670, quickly falling in love with and marrying a local chief's daughter, he effectively joined her tribe, and on the death of her father assumed the title of chief, leading raids to defend Native homelands against the British.[2] The Acadians, it seems, nurtured few nostalgic fantasies about their European roots.

Mi'kmaq and Acadians shared other affinities: for democratic decision-making, lack of deference, and disinterest in financial profit, preferring a system of barter and eschewing capital and exploitation. But this was a worldview tantamount to economic blasphemy to the mercantile-minded English, who bristled and fumed at the intransigence of Native inhabitants and French settlers alike.

In 1731 a doctor and trader called Robert Hale was disturbed to find when he arrived in Acadia that because the indigenous people had no interest in money, nor had the Acadians.

> The Acadians have no taxes to pay, and they trade but little
> among themselves, everyone raising himself what he wants
> except what they have in exchange from the traders. And as
> a proof that they are governed by this maxim, I need only

[2] If British perfidy be doubted, let the example of General Jeffrey Amherst's 'solution' to the 'Indian problem' speak for itself: in 1763 Amherst generously donated blankets – infected with smallpox from dead and dying soldiers – to Mi'kmaq villages, with exactly the consequences he had expected and hoped for.

say that when I came to pay my reckoning at the tavern, the landlord had but five pence in money, though he is one of the wealthiest in the place.

But, and though they wouldn't inhabit their idyll for long enough to greatly profit from it, there was nothing short-termist about the Acadians' hopes for their own future.

Guided by the Mi'kmaq tradition of making weirs to catch fish, augmented with Dutch techniques, the French emigrés embarked on ambitious reclamation projects, exploiting the characteristics of the coast, its rivers and salt marshes, and their own ingenuity and capacity for hard work, to dig dykes, out of which they forged, quite literally, pastures new.

As William Faulkner Rushton[3] wrote two centuries and four decades later, 'By the time of the Expulsion [the Acadian colony] was so self-sufficient that the agricultural production of Grand-Pré's fields alone would have fed [its] entire colony of 18,000 people for one year.'

But the Acadians, not wanting to work harder than necessary, and feeling little need for imported possessions any more elaborate than iron pots, bottles of liquor and bolts of red English cloth, never went on to develop a proto-capitalist economy with its surpluses, money, government, banks and soldiers.

'By 1755,' he points out, 'the Acadians had carved out ... an area exactly the size of Manhattan – and on that land they lived with their livestock, in quietly rude and independent and proliferating defiance of every European attempt to make them go away – or to exploit them while they remained.'

Most ghastly of all, these native-loving, non-capital-seeking, family-minded, un-martial and Catholic dyke-builders were dismissive of British, and indeed anyone else's, attempts to impose governorship. They had to be got rid of.

[3]'New Orleans' most acerbic critic' according to the back cover of his book, *The Cajuns, from Acadia to Louisiana* (New York: Farrar Straus & Giroux, 1979).

And thus, Longfellow transports us to Grand-Pré – conjuring a Tolkienian vision of bucolic contentment and good cheer so complete, that ruin, destruction and sorrow were as good as inevitable.

> Strongly built were the houses, with frames of oak and of
>   hemlock
> Such as the peasants of Normandy built in the reign of the
>   Henries
> Thatched were the roofs, with dormer-windows; and gables
>   projecting
> Over the basement below protected and shaded the doorway…

It was a place where

> Matrons and maidens sat in snow-white caps and in kirtles
> Scarlet and blue and green, with distaffs spinning the golden
> Flax for the gossiping looms…

Here, according to Longfellow, the Acadians '… dwelt in the love of God and of man … free from Fear that reigns with the tyrant, and envy, the vice of republics.' And here, in the bosom of this Arcadia, dwelt the delightful Evangeline.

Black were her eyes, as the berry that grows on the thorn by the wayside (I wonder whether he was thinking of sloes?), and softly did they gleam.

Every boy in Grand-Pré had a thing for Evangeline. Luckily, or unluckily for Gabriel, son of Basil the Blacksmith, she saved her berry-eyes for him.

The two grow up together, sledding in winter, bird-nesting, and passing 'a few swift years' until the time that Evangeline became 'a woman, with the heart and hopes of a woman'.

But as young love brewed, a few miles from the coast British warships lurked, heavy with ill-intent, their cannon pointing (pointedly) at the village, the ships' commander-in-chief having issued an order that the inhabitants of Grand-Pré are to be summoned to the church the very next day. Old Benedict the farmer, ever the optimist, suggested that the British presence might be on account of some 'friendlier purpose' than appearances suggested.

Perhaps the harvests in England
By untimely rains or untimelier heat have been blighted
And from our bursting barns they would feed their cattle and
    children?

But that was not the case.

The potted early Cajun story is that, despite all their best endeavours to remain neutral and aloof from the raging political and military battle between two ancient rivals, the Acadians had long been viewed with suspicion by the English. While there was some recognition of the difficult situation in which they found themselves, i.e., not quite French, but not quite anything else, other than themselves, they were generally regarded as problematic.

In the late 1740s the British won one of their interminable squabbles with the French, a prelude to the Seven Years War of 1756–63, and they found themselves in possession of Acadian, *ergo* French-speaking, territory, about which they were uncomfortable.

In a sanguine attempt to overcome those anxieties, they beefed up their military presence with some fort-building, beginning with the city of Halifax, and attempted to bully their new subjects into taking an Oath of Allegiance under the terms of which, were war to resume, the Acadians would be obliged to take up arms against their fellow Francophones.

The Acadians refused, there being nothing in it that appealed to their nature. They had avoided being governed for over two centuries and were more inclined to take up arms against deer or squirrels than they were people, regardless of either tongue or history.

The point wasn't pressed until a new lieutenant governor, Charles Lawrence, took the helm of the Halifax government, and it was Lawrence whom the British would later blame for what the Cajuns have ever since called *Le Grand Dérangement*. For it was he who, anticipating what would become the Seven Years War, choreographed the expulsion of those he described as 'The French Inhabitants', exploiting every opportunity to exaggerate or manufacture instances of their 'disloyalty'.

There was nothing vague about Lawrence's instructions, which were to devise some ruse for getting the men 'both old and young' into his officers' power, detaining them 'so that they may be shipped off as soon as the boats arrive, to various American colonies … Then ship the women and children afterwards to different destinations far from each other.'

Just to make sure, their homes, and all means of subsistence during the winter months, were to be destroyed. Grand-Pré was not the only community evacuated, but because the officer charged with the exercise kept a diary throughout, it provides the richest documentary material – for historians and poets alike.

In late August 1755, Colonel John Winslow arrived with 300 men and camped at the Church of St Charles. The inhabitants were mostly distracted with their harvest. By the beginning of September, three ships, the very same vessels that Old Benedict surmises might be looking to buy some of the Acadians' bounteous produce, drew into their harbour.

Winslow issued a summons, demanding that the men attend a meeting. He had no French, but a Huguenot (i.e., Protestant) collaborator took some delight in translating what he had to say, which was that he, Winslow, had received 'the King's Instructions' from Governor Lawrence, and that, though it was disagreeable to him to have to do it (and he knew it would be grievous to those that heard it), it was his duty to inform them that their lands, tenements, cattle and other livestock were to be forfeited to the Crown, and they themselves 'removed from this Province'.

Either to avoid panic, or as temporary balm to conscience, he said that not only would he do everything in his power to ensure that neither they nor their belongings would be molested, but also 'that whole families shall go in the same vessel: so that this removal, which I am sensible must give you a great deal of trouble, may be made as easy as His Majesty's service will admit'.

He hoped, he said, 'that in whatever part of the world your lot may fall, you may be faithful subjects, and a peaceable and happy people'. 'As, when the air is serene in sultry solstice of summer,' wrote Longfellow,

> Suddenly gathers a storm, and the deadly sling of the hailstones
> Beats down the farmer's corn in the field and shatters his
>   windows,
> Hiding the sun, and strewing the ground with thatch from the
>   house roofs,
> Bellowing fly the herds, and seek to break their enclosures;
> So on the hearts of the people descended the words of the
>   speaker.
> Silent a moment they stood in speechless wonder, and
>   then rose
> Louder and ever louder a wail of sorrow and anger . . .

But the men found that, while they'd been listening to Winslow's pronouncement, the doors of the church had been locked, and, as the boats began to arrive to take them away, they were only permitted to leave in small numbers to inform their families that they were to be deported. If they failed to return, they were told, the other prisoners would be killed.

Thus over the next few weeks the British soldiers herded the entire population of Acadians towards waiting boats, deliberately breaking up families to prevent their regrouping and returning. The intention was that the Acadian Arcadia should be comprehensively destroyed and the land it sat upon added to the British portfolio.

> Wives were torn from their husbands, and mothers too late, saw
>   their children
> Left on the land, extending their arms, with wildest entreaties...

It would be unconscionable to reveal whether Evangeline meets her Gabriel years later (and it scarcely matters, historically, given that they didn't exist *per se*). But save to say, she travelled long and hard in her quest, as did all the Evangelines and Gabriels and other victims of the *Grand Dérangement*. The families were scattered across the Eastern seaboard of the United States, some finding themselves back in France, which was discomfited by the poor alien beings washed back on home shores by an unfortunate tide, whose long absence had wrought strange things upon the native tongue.

Some found themselves even less at home in England, and others still in the Caribbean.

The territory of Louisiana was so named (*La Louisiane*) in 1682 by an explorer, Robert Cavelier de la Salle, after Louis Quatorze, the Sun King, the French magnanimously claiming for themselves territory on both sides of the Mississippi as far north as Canada. After losing Canada to the British in 1762, France, exhausted by its American military adventures, gifted 'the country known as Louisiana', which then included the entirety of the Mississippi Valley, to Spain. Over the next few decades, as the European nations acted out their power plays with muskets and treaties and trading rights in both hemispheres, Louisana's boundaries would be adjusted accordingly, and in 1803 the territory, a prime fillet of central North America, extending as it did as far north as modern-day Montana and North Dakota and even across the 58th parallel, was sold to the young United States for $15 million.

At least as much as anywhere in the United States, within the state lines of modern Louisiana, African and European cultures danced and spawned novel and exciting steps and passes in the hot and heady subtropics, not so much a melting pot as a punchbowl of new distinctions, classes and elites, and fractions, refractions and factions.

The Creole families were the long-established French that had arrived in the 1600s and retained their courtly manners and *métiers*; the black Creoles, descended from freed slaves (and their masters and no doubt mistresses), figured high in the social order. It wasn't unusual for wealthy black families to own black slaves.

New Orleans, founded in 1718, and chosen by Commandant, and later Louisiana governor, Jean-Baptiste Le Moyne de Bienville for its strategic location on the Mississippi and its relative protection from floods, was from the very start a commercial and ethnic hub out of which were born unique social mores and expectations.

Scrupulous attention was paid to gradations of race and the distinction between 'mulatto' (half-European, half-African), 'quadroon' (one-quarter of African descent) or 'octoroon', and the respective social entitlements due to each. (After a quarter, even eighteenth-century Louisianans would think you were quibbling.) Because of its interracial swirl, New Orleans was famous for its women, who were regarded as among the most beautiful in the world.[4] Of course there was music, voodoo, rich and spicy recipes, and endless intrigue.

It was not into this high-stepping, preening, pimping and primping *quartier* that the plain-talking (but funny sounding), hard-working and exhausted exiles from Nova Scotia would take root. The Cajuns were, instead, drawn to the prairies in the north of Louisiana, where they became cowboys, and the bayous and swamps of the south and south-west.

Perhaps the 'swamp' tag has stuck better than the 'cowboy' label for no other reason than that it's stickier and more unique to the Cajuns. And here was the place to put to use the Acadian canon of country wisdom, and to dance familiar steps to familiar dances and sing familiar songs – highly rhythmic, high-octane, high-octave nasal hollering, strangely hypnotic against the accordion drone and the fiddle part.

There is about Cajun music a kind of Gallic sadness, which is not as sad as, say, Portuguese fado, but sad all the same:

[4] A convention of New Orleans life in the early nineteenth century was that the father of a rich young Frenchman would negotiate an arrangement with the mother of a beautiful 'mulatto' or 'octoroon': that, in return for her favours, the young Frenchman would support the young woman, for, typically, the 'price' of a stylish house and a carriage. On his inevitable marriage to a 'suitable' French bride, his previously favoured lady would keep the assets, and he would be obliged to recognise any children from the relationship.

Oh Madeleine, t'as couché dehors
Oh Madeleine, dehors dans l'grand brouillard
Oh Madeleine, quo' faire toi tu viens pas
Oh ma Madeleine, moi j'connais tu va me faire mourir…

So sing the Balfa Brothers, accompanying themselves in a show of virtuosity that has survived and evolved through four centuries of migration, voluntary and forced, and the inspiration of any number of Evangelines and Madeleines.

And if modern Cajun music has had some of the sharpest, most interesting corners knocked off by easy living and well-meaning appropriation, dig out the hip-wigglingly excellent recording of 'La Valse du Bayou Plaquemine' by the Frères Breaux, 'Catahoula Stomp' by Cleoma Breaux Falcon, or accordion supremo Nathan Abshire's recording of 'La Valse de Riceville'.[5]

But it is another musical style, zydeco, which, as the Cajuns lose their hold on Louisiana's identity, is more reflective of the state's people-scape, in so much as it appears to combine elements of Cajun tradition with black and other musical styles, forging what amounts to less unique but more accessible kind of old-fashioned dance music.

In Cajun country, zydeco is *très grand* at any time of the day. Zydeco breakfasts, between 8.30 a.m. and noon, with two-stepping, waltzing, shouting and eating on Saturday mornings are a particular favourite.

When he met me for coffee, Sherbin Collette was betting his town on zydeco. Zydeco, and the swamp.

---

[5] *Eh, toi, 'tite fille, quoi t'as fais avec moi,*
Te m'a quitté, chere, au soir,
Pour t'en aller chez ta famille.

hé, c'est ma joue rose, qui va voir comment j'suis la aujourd'hui,
Tu m'as quitté dans la misère et le chagrin,
Comment j'vas faire chez moi tout seul.

The accompanying dance scene is simmeringly erotic, notwithstanding its age.

Mayor Collette had a strong grip, and spoke in a thick Cajun accent which, though it scarcely survives the effort to transcribe it, rhymed 'beauty' with 'foody' and lent a hardness to the pronunciation of the definite article.

'You know,' said Mayor Sherbin Collette, 'it took an outsider to show me how beautiful is the basin, the swamp. It was a woman from Missouri. Doin' her Ph.D. And we was out in the basin, in my boat, fishin', and she said, "Mayor Collette, what is it you see?"'

Sherbin Collette is the mayor of the small town of Henderson, which sits right at the edge of the levee; on the other side are the 'numberless sylvan islands' that Longfellow must have imagined: magical so long as you avert your gaze from the majesty of the Atchafalaya Basin Bridge, a twenty-mile-long overpass carrying Highway 10 across the swamp to Baton Rouge.

Henderson is only nine decades old, but it has aged quickly and well. The local economy, such as it is, stands on fish and crawfish. The main eatery, Pat's Fisherman's Wharf, on the corner of Main Street and the Levee Road, is one of those American eateries enjoying such local renown (and a monopoly on dining opportunities) that it genuinely believes its own claims to be 'World Famous'. Strung out along the levee road are two or three places offering the ubiquitous airboat tour of the swamp. In winter the experience is of intense cold, despite the quilts and special padded suits that the proprietors of these establishments provide, and verdant beauty.

The mayor's office, sharing its building and a secretary with the police department, is situated in a raised, single-storey, weatherboarded building on Amy Street, just around the corner from Collette Street. It has a large, covered, wraparound porch, from the roof of which, when I came to visit Mayor Collette, the morning's rain still dripped in sulky drops. A sinuous ginger tom cat greeted me at the screen door; in a cardboard box, his consort nursed a brood of kittens.

Almost every street in these little towns seems to celebrate a local family. In Breaux Bridge, founded in 1799 by the Nova Scotian-born Firmin Breaux, today's local sheriff is one Becket Breaux...

Mayor Collette said, 'And I said, "Well, whaddoo I see?" I said, "Well, over there I see an alligator. And there, I see cypress trees. And I see birds, egrets, and fish swimmin' underneat' the boat…"

'And she said, "But putting it all together, what you see?"

'And I said, "Whaddoo you mean, 'whaddoo you see?'" And she said, "Mayor Collette, don't you see the beauty? This all, the egrets and the alligator and the fish swimmin' underneat' the boat, it's beautiful!"'

'I see,' I said.

'And from that moment, I came to see the beauty of the basin. To want to look after the basin and preserve it.'

Sherbin, said Sherbin, was a fisherman, not a politician at heart. He had only stepped up to the mayoral plate because no one else would, he said. Now he wanted to put Henderson 'on the map'. And he, his deputy, Jody Meche, moustached and rufous-faced, with a fisherman's heft and breadth, told me about the swamp, and divulged their admiration for Dean the Basin Keeper, who, they said, was phenomenally brave for standing up, near-singlehandedly, against vested interests and powerful lobbies.

Mostly they spoke about crawfishing, the factors that impact upon the health of their populations, the sorry state of the market for alligator skins and meat, and the importance of the species – sold as it is in myriad forms: sausages, *boudin*, canned and fresh – to Cajun identity and cuisine.

There are, said Meche, an estimated two million alligators in the swamp, which really went to show what a particularly special place in the world it is, for where else could make such a boast? But what saddened Sherbin Collette was that there are people, children especially, who, though they might live only a mile away from the basin, had never peered over the levee, and seen the aqueous-footed trees, the pelicans and the cormorants… let alone laid a trap for crawfish or hunted in the swamp, or fished for catfish.

'They don't jus' not see the beauty, like I didn't see the beauty. They don't see any of it. They just see a concrete wall!'

But Sherbin Collette and Jody Meche had a plan. Recently, said the mayor, he'd been approached by a consortium of investors from out of state who were interested in building a zydeco museum and cultural centre, 'right here in Henderson'. This, he said, would generate much more interest in local attractions generally, and was very exciting.

Henderson is a tiny straggle of a place, and I couldn't quite that the town was ready for such upheaval. On the other hand, it was scarcely my place to opine.

If Mr Hayes of Hayes Fishery had strong thoughts on the subject, I couldn't say either, as I only understood about half of every dozen, or fewer, words that he uttered. Hayes was wonderfully weathered, clear-eyed and kindly-faced, and I enjoyed being there in the windowless Portakabin, where he had in one part something like a shop with a counter, and another that was all steel tables and hoses and possessing all the cold paraphernalia of a place in which one might sell dead things like fish, frogs or alligators.

Now, perhaps because it was towards the end of the day, the counter groaned only softly beneath the weight of two large catfish, mostly catfish-brown in colour, but rather elegantly yellow-tinged at the fringes and the fins.

A man, tall, black, and extraordinarily sharply dressed, came into the shop. He said he'd come from New Orleans, having heard that Hayes had some big catfish for sale, and he glanced approvingly at the whiskery brace on the counter.

Hayes seemed offended that his customer should think that these puny specimens, each of which, I'd say, if it had legs, would have given a well-fed Staffordshire terrier a run for its money, were 'big'.

'Big' was the catfish that he'd hauled in the other day, which was three times as big, and even that catfish wasn't big compared to the *really* big catfish out there in the basin, that had never yet been, and never would be caught, and even these mythic monsters were undersized, measured against the fish of the past...

But Hayes's customer looked only satisfied with the fish, which, having been haggled over, filleted and packed up, returned with him to a welcoming kitchen, somewhere in the heart of the city.

'Cajun culture' seems to be possessed by a combination of self-congratulation and anxious self-scrutiny that culminates in a kind of destructive self-awareness and promotion, like some of the tropes that the Irish perpetuate about themselves for the sake of tourist money. A television programme called *Swamp People* capitalises on all the caricatures of the Cajun as gun-toting, liquor-loving, 'gator hunting primitives, living in huts on stilts in a literal backwater, and as it does so, painfully belittles its willing subjects, who dumb down for the camera even as they play up to it. My grown-up daughter and her boyfriend took a ride into the swamp and reported how the airboat 'captain' and his deputy fell out after the latter spoke approvingly of it.

'They're nothing but a group of stupid Cajuns doing anything for money, giving their own lifestyle a bad name. I hate that show. They're trash – that show is trash,' the captain said to his chastened mate.

The Cajuns arrived in the swamp with nothing, seemed to be his point, and over a mere two centuries have created for themselves an identity, which, like the swamp, needs to be guarded zealously, not squandered for the amusement of outsiders. And I could see the need to be vigilant against 'swamping' by 'mainstream' Anglophone America.

Whether survival and preservation are the same is a difficult call. And it's one with which the indigenous peoples of Louisiana, who are considerably fewer in number than the Cajuns, are also wrestling.

Several times on the drive to the Chitimacha Nation, I had to stop to call Kimberly Walden, tribal historic preservation officer, who was waiting patiently for us at the national museum, to tell her that I was hopelessly floundering, the road lost in a sea of sugarcane plantations and rain-soaked arable pastures through which it otherwise cut a swathe. Steeped in history as Louisiana may be, outside of the swamp and the marsh the landscape tends towards the featureless. Many tourists in this part of the state are almost certainly heading to the tabasco-sauce factory and adjacent gardens – the patrimony of the interestingly maverick and philanthropically minded McIlhenny family, a member of which played an interesting role in the Chitimacha story.

'What can you see?' Kim had to ask me.

'Nothing,' I'd say. Nothing but sugarcane...

And yet, as one does, we found our way, the route becoming gentler, tracing the soft curves of the Bayou Teche, fringed kindly with oaks, the houses having, as one might have once said, 'a pleasant aspect', arriving at the small town of Charenton, at the boundary of which a wooden painted sign reads, 'Welcome to the Chitimacha Nation'.

It takes only moments to drive the length of the Nation, past well-kept, white-painted houses, in the crook of an elbow of the Teche. But not so many centuries ago, the Chitimacha were the Lords of the Bayou: their presence, their culture and their political influence thoroughly extended into and across the labyrinthine creeks and rivers of the Mississippi river system, and a great deal of what is now the state of Louisiana.

Before the invasion of the Americas, the Chitimacha (the name is thought to derive from words meaning 'men altogether red') made up a large group composed of smaller ones: the Washa, Chawasha, Chitimacha and Yagenichito, and constituted an estimated 20,000 individuals at the end of the fifteenth century, well spread out across the delta.

The boundary of the Chitimacha homeland was originally defined by four sacred trees: the first was at Maringouin, Louisiana; the second southeast of New Orleans; another at the mouth of the Mississippi; and the last a great cypress located in present-day Cypremort Point State Park. Of the four tribes associated with this group, the Washa in 1699 had a single village on Bayou Lafourche in Assumption Parish, with the Chawasha just to the south. However, hunters from either of these tribes could be encountered as far south as the mouth of the Mississippi River.

So writes a historian of indigenous American peoples, who goes under the 'nom du net' Dick Shovel.

But the centre of their political base, and residence of the 'Grand Chief', appears to have been at Charenton, where it remains, and where the archaeological record, particularly by way of middens of shellfish remains and burial mounds, suggests it may have been for at least the past 1,400 years, and quite possibly very much longer.

Long and close acquaintance with the surrounding swamp provided a physical defence against outside threats, and furnished the Chitimacha with a generous diet of corn, pumpkin, squash, alligator, deer, buffalo, shellfish and fish. The living dwelt in timber houses thatched with palmetto fronds; the dead were interred in mounds.

Each village possessed its own central granary, to iron out the vicissitudes of the changing seasons. The largest Chitimacha boats, canoes dug from cypress logs, could carry forty people or more. The art of forging them was revealed, according to Chitimacha legend, by the Great Spirit himself, who, one day,

> took several of the men out to the woods. The Great Spirit told them to take some mud, place it around the tree about shoulder high, set the trunk afire and let it burn until it fell. The mud was packed thigh high so that the fire could not go above it. When the tree had fallen, He showed them how to pick the right part of the tree and length that they needed for a canoe. The Chitimacha were then shown how to burn off the bottom and ends, also using the mudpack to control the fire. When the burning was complete, they were told to take clam shells and scrape all the charred parts off.
>
> With the outside complete, the canoe was set upright; a fire was made on the top of the log for the full length. This was left to burn the desired depth, and if they wanted to stop it from burning too much on the sides, they would pack it with mud so that the burning could go to the right depth. The canoe was then scraped in the same manner for the bottom.

The only apparent deficit in their immediate surroundings appears to have been the absence of the right kind of stone needed for tools and arrowheads. Shovel says that to acquire it, they exchanged agricultural surplus with other tribes, but where a deficit remained, they improvised, sharpening their cane shafts to compensate for the absence of a stone head, or using 'fishbones and garfish scales' as projectile points.

Social life was rigidly structured along a line of matrilineal descent, and distinguished between 'nobles' and 'commoners', in a way that no doubt resonated with the European intruders. And outward appearance was paramount: the foreheads of the males were flattened after birth by binding their soft skulls to a cradleboard; long hair was braided. Bodies, legs, arms and faces were extensively tattooed.

Even before the Chitimacha had come face to face with settlers from across the Atlantic, they had felt the impact of European diseases and provocations that were already changing the world that they lived in, undermining traditional orders and ties, and altering the land and water-scape, for, by the time they'd reached the Bayou Teche, French and Spanish adventurers had become adept in the use not only of violence and physical force but other, invidious methods of coercion: playing off rival groups against each other; exploiting old enmities and destroying fragile truces or arrangements; spreading misinformation – each seeking competitive advantage over Old World rivals.

To do justice at least to their diplomatic instincts, the French saw that, if they were to defend their territory from English designs, the indigenous inhabitants of the Mississippi basin would need to be won over as allies, not antagonised.

The early history of Louisiana interweaves French, Spanish and British ambitions with those of the Native Americans, against a backdrop of a black population increasing, boat by boat, and it's as good as impossible to un-entwine the geopolitical from the personal.

A watershed moment or fateful juncture in the Chitimacha's relationship with the world beyond the Americas, and a downward turning point in their own history, lies in what might be described as the 'St-Cosme' affair, a convoluted saga, the origins of which lay in the tense web of Native enmities, recriminations and counter-recriminations, in part stoked by the French, who played tribes against each other in their push for regional dominance.

According to the testimony of a Frenchman called Penicaut (who is not regarded as terribly reliable), in 1705 a tribe called the Taensa, who had initially joined forces with the Bayougoula in response to slave raids by the Chickasaw, turned on their hosts, killing most of them, apparently attempting to curry favour with the French. Carried by a surfeit of enthusiasm, the Taensa played a trick on a group of Chitimacha families, inviting them to a feast, and then delivering them to the French as slaves.

In the summer of 1707 a Chitimacha war party set out to exact revenge on the Taensa, but on the way they encountered, on the banks of the Mississippi, a little group of missionaries to the Natchez tribe heading in the direction of Mobile, Alabama: Father Jean François Buisson de St-Cosme, two assistants and a Native slave whose name went unrecorded, but whose subsequent actions would prove consequential.

The Chitimacha, apparently incensed by the presence of the slave, killed St-Cosme and his assistants, but let the slave go free. The slave, who, as a convert to his owner's religion would have been unlikely to have been accepted by his own tribe, in any event soon ran into the Grand Vicar of Quebec, who, as St-Cosme had been, and for the same reason, was heading in the direction of Mobile.

The slave told the Grand Vicar everything. In his estimation, while the death of a lesser man could be forgiven, that of a missionary was the last straw, and he gave the word to Bienville, the governor, that war must be declared war against the Chitimacha.

Bienville mobilised a coalition of tribes, the Acolapissa, Bayougoula, Biloxi, Choctaw, Houma, Natchitoches, Pascagoula and Taensa, against the Chitimacha, pushing them ever further south, providing firearms and other supplies to fuel a war of attrition that the Chitimacha had no hope of winning. Not only did the Chitimacha possess no firearms, but the supply of stone that they required for their arrowheads was in the gift of a group allied to the Taensa – now their enemies.

The Chitimacha survived, though in much reduced circumstances, for a further twelve years, until the chief, Le Grand Soleil, as he was known, came to realise that without peace, his people, now very much fewer in number and possessions than they'd been only a dozen years ago, would be annihilated. Many of his people had been captured and sold into slavery. For the French also, it made no great sense to continue with the war.

Bienville used emissaries to sound out the prospect of a peace, and in 1718 – the year of New Orleans' establishment, a *calumet* or peace-pipe ceremony was scheduled, and a treaty-signing.

As Shovel points out, 'The Chitimacha may have been battered but still had style. The grand chief and his wife came to their meeting with Bienville in a huge canoe propelled by 40 warriors.'

But in exchange for peace, the chief and his people were obliged to accept a very much reduced territory and standing. Their time as the Lords of the Bayou had passed.

Subsequent events, post-treaty, were little kinder to the Chitimacha. By 1800 the ethnic mix of Louisiana was – even more than it ever had been – a swirl of peoples from around the world: Spanish, Creoles, African Americans, both slaves and freedmen, Acadians and others fleeing British rule, and American indigenous peoples displaced by wars between the French and the Spanish, and the English, and each other.

In 1776 the Chitimacha had been given a land grant, but much of it was sold over the next decades, largely to pay federal taxes, and they continued to fade from view, intermarrying with the Acadians, the Cajun language displacing their own. After Louisiana's sale to the United States in 1803, the US administration, though it would create a reservation for the Chitimacha, refused to sign a treaty with the tribe, who numbered only in the hundreds, many having married into Cajun culture, the Chitimacha language being lost on the way.

A 1900 census, says Shovel, 'listed only six families with 55 people, only three of whom were full-bloods'.

Adding further insult to all the copious injuries, in the early 1900s the tribe's few children were removed to the infamous

Carlisle Indian School in Pennsylvania, where, in keeping with its founder's philosophy, the faculty endeavoured to 'kill the Indian to free the man'.

As Kim showed us the exhibits in the museum, I sensed both her sorrow for her people, but also huge pride and optimism, tempered with the kind of self-control born of the realisation that as the Chitimacha continue to prosper culturally and economically, they will by necessity be required to be pragmatic and forward-thinking.

Among the exhibits: arrowheads, canoes and pottery, early depictions of Chitimacha, sporting memorabilia and documents. At the entrance stands a fur-swathed, life-size figure of the chief, Le Grand Soleil, who signed the treaty, his hair long and pushed back by a red band, and carrying a feather-adorned *calumet*, a peace-pipe presumably not dissimilar to that possessed by his distant, real-life inspiration.

But the most outstanding and exquisite artefacts are the baskets, woven out of coloured reeds, exacting in their precision and geometry, and somehow ancient, timeless and contemporary all at once. Arguably, it was such basketry that shielded – and shields – the flame of the tribe's identity and continues to do so.

Even as the Chitimacha themselves were disappearing from Louisiana, the baskets, made from what a 1919 writer described as the 'interminable' rivercane in the locality, were, because of their beauty, uniqueness and the extraordinary vitality they exude, exciting interest among anthropologists, connoisseurs and collectors, such as Sarah Avery McIlhenny of the tabasco clan.

In 1915, when the Chitimacha stood on the threshold of destitution and their remaining lands were on the cusp of being sold, a group of the tribe's women approached McIlhenny, who bought the land on the Chitimacha's behalf, ceding it to the federal government, which kept it on trust until the formal creation of a reservation in 1917.

A further and no less important 'gift', or more properly, not a gift, but a restored inheritance, had its origins nine decades ago, but only began to bear fruit more recently.

In 1930 a young but talented Mexican linguist, Morris Swadesh, met, in Charenton, a man called Chief Benjamin Paul, born in 1867, who, with his niece Delphine Ducloux, were, apparently, the last fluent speakers of the Chitimacha language, aside from some elders who could still remember terms related to basket-weaving.

Chief Paul mourned what had been lost and what he had forgotten, especially, he said, '… stories about the west. There were very many stories about the west…'

Swadesh wrote down everything they could tell him: words, stories, history and grammar. Within three years Paul and Ducloux had died, but they had left by way of a legacy the seeds from which the Chitimacha could rebuild their own language.

Even in the eighteenth century spoken Chitimacha was falling out of use, and what remained of it in the twentieth were remnants and place names, snatches of songs.

In the late 1980s, said Kim, she was approached by the American Philological Society, who told her that they had the entirety of Swadesh's copious records, including his notes for a grammar and a dictionary. The tribe soon embarked on the journey of scrutinising the texts and creating lists of words, and in 2008 they partnered with Rosetta Stone, a company best known for promising rapid assimilation of more widely spoken languages, under a programme to resuscitate those that would otherwise be lost.[6] Thousands of hours of effort were put into creating the tools for relearning Chitimacha, in some cases resuscitating, in older tribal members especially, long-dormant memories and forging new ones in the tribe's school.

The Chitimacha have navigated the years since 1915 with care and deliberation, capitalising on opportunities when they've arisen.

As 'big oil' came to Louisiana, in part on the coat-tails of the First World War, it created new opportunities for employment and skills for the tribe: a diaspora of Chitimacha oil engineers and managers works and has worked on projects from Aberdeen to Abu Dhabi. Military service during the Second World War also brought

---

[6]It appears that this programme is now discontinued.

standing: Kim's grandfather, of whom she spoke with palpable reverence, was an officer decorated for bravery, and was not alone among his people in having served with distinction.

In common with other Native American reservations, the Chitimacha own a casino, taking advantage of a characteristic of their sovereignty that exempts them from state prohibitions on gambling. But they've also established a company that provides consultancy services to the US Department of Defense on missile systems and satellite support, and to other firms that operate at similarly high level – which is to say that this century demands new survival strategies: the ability to engage and negotiate with state and federal government agencies, commercial competitors, non-Chitimacha local people, and an outside world with its head full of ideas about what and who America's indigenous people are, or who they think they ought to be.

Often these challenges present themselves as an ongoing series of negotiations.

In 1915, when Sarah Avery McIlhenny helped the Chitimacha arrest the final dissolution of their territory, it stood at around 500 acres. Since then, where and when they can, they've bought more land, tripling the size of their territory. But even where they have the resources to do so, Kim said, so convinced are their neighbours that the tribe is wealthy beyond the dreams of avarice on account of the Green Tree casino that they'll only sell land to them at ridiculously inflated prices. Which means that they now buy 'by stealth', through the offices of a nearby landowner who buys on their behalf. (And those exquisite baskets are not for sale; in fact, just as the tribe is looking to buy back its own land, it's buying back the baskets, woven into which are so many of its treasures.)

And if they're to bring to bear their understanding of the landscape, acquired through 5,000 years of living in the Land of the Five Rivers, that requires that they must negotiate with the Army Corps of Engineers about water management and environmental matters.

Despite the title of historic preservation officer, it was clear that Kim's real role, given her apparent expertise on everything from health and education policy through real estate and environment and planning law, is to help the Chitimacha chart their own future.

After the 2017 pipeline battles in Dakota, which saw Native American groups fending off construction of a pipe which, they said, would have contaminated their water supplies, some radical environmentalists who had been involved came to Louisiana in an attempt to fight a similar war against the Bayou Pipeline, and to co-opt Native American sympathies in the process.

But the Chitimacha have a different relationship with oil from the one that some environmentalists may romantically wish they had. This was not their war. The Chitimacha, said Kim, will serve themselves better by imparting their understanding of the environment to the oil company, but also benefiting from the interaction.

Which is not to say that the Chitimacha have disavowed their past so much as that they don't consider it to be a bolthole in which to hide from the future, and outsiders should not be permitted to define for them either their past or their future.

We had arrived late in the day, and it being the holiday season, Kim had kids to look after and cookies to bake. A short visit to a small but ancient nation. And so many unanswerable questions – about the relationship between a people and their language, and whether, maybe, there exists a genetic aptitude for cultural patrimony. One could see how the thesis could be used in all sorts of dangerous and exclusionary ways. But certainly, the Chitimacha appear to be comfortable with theirs to an extent that lies easily with that supposition, and one can't help but suspect that as modern America continues to reveal new contradictions and conundrums, the people of Charenton's sense of identity will continue to strengthen and grow.

By way of a postscript, I found a testament to the Chitimachas' patience and courteous diplomacy very much closer to home, in the online annals of the British parliamentary record, Hansard.

It was in the form of a petition, sent from Charenton, and signed by Alton D. LeBlanc, Jr, who was the tribe's leader at the time of

its being written, in March 2020, and was addressed to members
of a parliamentary committee debating the issue of the return of
cultural property, illicitly removed and now residing either behind
glass or mouldering in long-unopened drawers, in British museums
and other institutions.

'Today,' said the letter:

. . . you meet on the issue of Cultural Property: Return and
Illicit Trade. [It] is not one easily addressed.

As I am unable to be here to address the House of
Commons personally, I must pray that through my words, an
understanding of our Chitimacha culture, beliefs and history
will be created and touch each and every member.

For reasons unknown or not understood, thousands of our
ancestors were disrespectfully removed from their final resting
place and taken away from their homelands ... We discovered
that there are two of our Chitimacha female ancestors in
the possession of the Natural History Museum in London.
The ancestral remains are without question Chitimacha,
documented as such by your museum.

Museums will argue that these remains need to be in their
possession because they may be of some 'scientific value' in
the future. It does not matter that our ancestors who are in
possession of the different institutions in England are older
than our mothers. They are still directly related to our people,
known and documented to be Chitimacha. They are our
ancestors. We need to put them to rest. Their spirits will not
be at peace until they are home, and safely placed back in the
earth where they belong, resting for eternity.

It is unconscionable that our ancestors have been placed
in boxes on shelves, put on display in cases, handled and
examined for research purposes, knowing that they remain
in a state of unrest. Mr Speaker, I ask each of the members of
the House of Commons to search your heart and understand
how we feel as people. I ask each member to put aside all logic
from the scientific point of view. Open your hearts as one

human being to another. For it comes down to a simple but
important fact; all human beings, regardless of race, origin or
creed deserve the right to be properly and respectfully buried
at the time of death, without fear of disturbance or treatment
as specimens. I ask the Honourable Members of the House
of Commons to honour our request for the return of our
ancestors.

To understand our present, said LeBlanc, 'we must look to our past'.

Most people search at some point in their lives for an
understanding of who they are, by performing genealogical
studies. This endeavour is undertaken so that the individual
and their families may establish a link with their past, to give
them a sense of who they are at present. This link to our past is
an integral part of who we are as Chitimachas.

In the summer of 2019, some months after my return, I watched,
by television, the return of the big winds to New Orleans: flooding
down Claiborne Avenue and the evacuation of Plaquemine, the
Mississippi about ready to burst its banks. And had guilty pangs of
nostalgia about sitting in that jazz bar in New Orleans, listening to
the man in the pork-pie hat play the song about the flood of 1927.
Even the most fleeting familiarity with a place facilitates a kind of
sympathetic feeling that pulses more strongly than it would in the
absence of that acquaintance.

The horrors inflicted by such events lie less in any malevolence
imputable to 'her', for a thing is just a thing, and more in the
very human injustices they expose, compound or instigate. By a
large margin, those impacted by Hurricane Katrina in 2005 were
black and living in poor districts like the Ninth Ward – swept
away by flooding. Further indignities were heaped upon them by
misreporting and fraudulent reporting of looting and lawlessness,
as if to suggest that the disaster was somehow deserved.

Many, especially black families, found that, because they lacked
title to properties possessed by and lived in by their families for

over a century, they were ineligible for compensation or insurance, and they drifted away from New Orleans because it had become too hard to stay. Now the money – artsy money, bohemian money, keen-to-culturally-integrate and Airbnb money – is coming into those neighbourhoods, a kind of reverse 'white flight', but not necessarily of any greater benefit to those communities.

It packs a lot of history, does this low-lying territory stretched between Texas and the Mississippi, named after an extravagant French king and bought from the Spanish for a paltry $15 million; and it struck me how hard it is to make sense of any totality of experience, given the quite unique strands: African, Native American, French, British… (and I haven't even mentioned the plight of the Vietnamese prawn fishermen bankrupted by the Deepwater Horizon oil spill). 'It's a hell of a state,' was the verdict of a man who told me about some of these things over a craft beer on Frenchman Street. 'But it's not a hellish state.'

16

The Lord Bless the Lords of Romnie Marsh

That works of draining are most antient and of divine institution we have the testimony of holy Scripture, 'In the beginning God said, "Let the waters be gathered together, and let the dry land appear, and it was: And the earth brought forth grass, and herb yielding seed, and the fruit tree yielding fruit after his kind and God saw that it was good."'

The History of Imbanking and Drayning of Divers Fenns and Marshes, both in forein parts and in this kingdom, and of the improvements thereby extracted from records, manuscripts and other authentick testimonies, William Dugdale, 1662

From April, Romney Marsh is coolly ablaze with the blossom of blackthorn bushes: thick white stripes, chalk white, signalling the end of the austere seasons and the beginning of the lambing. Blackthorn is the small shrubby tree from which sloes are picked and the Irish walking stick-cum-cudgel, the shillelagh, is carved. Its presence is more than a pleasure. From the fourteenth century onward, the penalty for unauthorised harvesting of blackthorn was the forfeiting of an ear. Blackthorn, marsh and law were a trinity, each a necessary condition of the others' existence.

It's all on account of the wall.

The wall runs from Dymchurch to Lydd and is almost four miles long. It is a bulwark against the sea, the merits of which Jim Pilcher and I discussed. Of itself, it's a construction that is concretely neutral to the point of joylessness. But it is walkable, and from it the view of the Marsh is good and stirring, affording vistas of pylons striding across the fields, and the mutable pallet of sea-tones, and the ships that roam upon it. At Lydd there is a kite-surfing centre. It's amusing, as you drive alongside the wall, to see the polychromatic oblongs jerking frenziedly above.

According to Jill Eddison's book, *Survival on a Frontier*, it became necessary to build some sort of a wall at Dymchurch in 1288, 'to plug a gap in the shingle'.

It isn't wholly understood how that was originally undertaken, but by the seventeenth century the system was well established, says Eddison, the land 'armed and fenced against the wash and the rage of the sea'.

The first step was to build a substructure, creating a woven lattice of thorn bushes and timber. Large bundles of thorn were laid together and stamped into the clay. These were secured by oak stakes called 'needles' on account of the 'eye' at the top.

'First,' writes Eddison, 'half the length of the needles was driven down through the faggots into the clay of the wall. Then long flexible rods or "edders" were woven round the projecting tops of the needles, and short wooden "keys" were driven through the eyes. Finally, the needles were driven down as close as possible to the clay without breaking the keys.'

The combination of clay and blackthorn, kilned in the summer sun, was supremely durable. But it demanded constant upkeep throughout the year, the Marshmen preparing the ground for repairs by pulling away old and damaged timber and beating the clay flat with heavy-headed implements called 'beetles'.

'In high summer,' says Eddison,

the clay was brought up from appointed fields on carts, which were traditionally 5 foot long, 3 foot wide and 14 inches deep,

each pulled by a horse led by a boy. In 1622 around 200
carts were in action, making two trips a day in a continuous
procession. While half were being loaded and going up the
wall, the other half were being unloaded and the clay was being
spread out, stamped down and the cart set to rights before
making the long return journey.

Along the way and on the wall, men equipped with goads stood,
guiding the horses, and ensuring that they didn't run out of control
or over the boys. If something happened to disrupt the steady
stream of clay-laden carts, the boys would shout, 'A coye, a coye, a
coye,' to attract their attention.

Running roughly perpendicular to the line of the wall were
groynes or 'knocks', in essence the same as those that still break the
force of the waves and prevent the overly enthusiastic and erratic
shifting of the shingle at Pett and Dungeness. Where now these are
wood, they were more laboriously constructed in the seventeenth
century and before, consisting of parallel rows of piles four feet
apart, filled with rocks that had been placed on 'a *carpet*'[1] of timber
and bushes.

The piles were driven into the shingle by use of an engine called
a 'ram', eighteen feet high, and supporting 'a great wheel', and
powered by the brute strength of up to thirty men.

'The operation,' writes Eddison,

was directed by the tenor man, who pulled the main rope.
Attached to that were 24 'ringing' ropes, each pulled by one
man. This brought the ram down on the pile, which was bound
fast to the middle post of the frame and was kept steady by
'levermen'. Each knock contained 500–600 piles, and if the
beach consisted of soft sand, it might be possible to drive 60
piles in a day, but if it was stony, only 20...

[1] A technical term, not poetic licence.

On 29 July 1622, 203 'fillers', each bringing a cart to the party, brought clay to the wall. Similar numbers of 'wallers' arranged the bushes and timber. The total cost of maintaining the wall in that year was £2,391 16s 8½d – the equivalent of around £300,000 today.

A physical barrier against the marauding sea had always been bolstered by a complex arrangement of statutes placing obligations on all those that lived on the Marsh 'to maintain the walls and sewers against the salt and fresh water, and as often as there shall be need, to repair and strengthen them, according to the Law of the Marsh'.

To William Dugdale, the author of the doughty *History of Imbanking*, the virtues of draining marshland were incontrovertible. By doing so, he said, 'veritable wastes' would be transformed for crops and livestock, and by broadening unnavigable creeks, channels could be created by which isolated communities 'can trade with the rest of the world and profit from their labours'. The improvement of such dismal landscapes would be most appreciable in winter, when, for want of proper drainage, the rivers burst their banks, and the ice is strong enough to hinder the passage of boats, but not take a person's weight, and the dwellers 'in those regions' face starvation, their children are deprived baptism, and women remain unaided in their 'travails'.

'And what expectation of health,' he asked,

> can there be to the bodies of men, where there is no element good? The Air being for the most part cloudy, gross, and full of rotten harrs. The Water putrid and muddy, yea full of loathsome insects, the Earth spungy and boggy, and the Fire noisome by the stink of smokey Hassocks...

Left undrained, he implied, the marsh was like an unlanced boil.

A lawyer at heart, Dugdale cites copious precedent in making his case for draining marshlands. The first half of his 'history' consists of a round-about tour of 'the most remarkable Bankings and Drainings in foreign parts, which by way of introduction [he] thought it proper to take notice of'.

He begins with Egypt, because 'that country is more marvellous than any other – and the works there more remarkable than the country', and describes with great admiration the imbanking [embankment] of cities, first performed by Sesostris, and then 'Sabacon² the Aethiopian, who employed therein all persons condemned to death' to prevent them from conveying the secrets of water drainage.

Of Babylon, he notes the reason given by Sir Walter Raleigh as to the scantiness of the material to be found on the successor of Nimrod, its mythical first monarch: '… that … he spent much of his time in draining the low lands … and drying and making firm ground of all those great fens and over-blown marshes which adjoined it.'

The Romans were also masters of the art of marsh-draining, and of the Pompeian Marshes ('which lie eastward of Rome between the river Tiber and Campania') there is lots to say:

> The maritime parts of this vale, for a great extent, are drowned,
> not so much through any inundations of the sea, whose tides
> are here but small [so much as because the rivers] having not
> their passage sufficiently open unto the sea, diffuse themselves
> over those spacious low grounds up towards Sulmo and Setia…

Turning to Belgium, he examines the claim that Baldwin the First, husband of Judith, daughter of Emperor Charles the Bald of France, 'did much in clearing of the woods and exsiccation of the marshes, for making the country more habitable and fruitful'. And he walks through similar histories of Friesland, Zeeland and Holstein, and even the New World, for as he reminds readers,

> Neither do we want [for] examples of this nature in America,
> for the city of Mexico, being situate in a great lake, frequently
> subject to inundations which had almost destroyed it, in the

²Though I can find no subsequent record of 'Sabacon the Aethiopian'.

year MDCXXXI, with mighty industry, secured that habitation
by turning the lake and so laying the city dry.

But these titillating gobbets of history are for Dugdale a mere
entrée preceding the main event, which is Romney Marsh,

more anciently secured from the inundations of the ocean than
any other part of this realm, as may be observed by the laws
and constitutions for regulating its repair, which have been
long ago made the rule and standard, to which all the other
marshes and fens in this nation ought to conform.

From 'time out of mind', Dugdale informs us, twenty-four
jurors, or 'jurats', locally elected in the communality, had been
responsible for the administration of the marsh, raising taxes from
landowners 'for the repairing of the banks and watercourses against
the violence and danger of the sea and upon all others who are
obliged and bound to the repair of the said banks'.

In the thirty-sixth year of the reign of Henry III, the jurats
approached their king to describe the kinds of issues that they
were having in raising the money needed to prevent the marsh
from slipping back into the sea. They begged his assistance, and
Henry obliged them, appointing a roving judge, Henry de Bathe,
who, aided by his sidekicks, Nicholas de Hanlou and Alured
de Dene, held annual sessions in the town of Romney, where
differences between the 'jurors and the Marshmen' might be aired,
and grievances addressed, and 'provisions might be made for the
security of the said Marsh'.

Henry, Nicholas, Alured, the jurats and the Marshmen so
convened 'on the Saturday after the Feast of the Nativity of the
Blessed Virgin', and having taken stock of everyone's complaints
and interests, issued a set of checks and balances to try to ensure
that everyone paid their due (or 'scot') and that the banks
and drains were regularly inspected (hence the origin of the
term, 'scot-free', to describe a person who has got away with
something).

It was a good system, but it could not wholly eradicate the grumbles. Dugdale says it would be too 'tedious' to give instances of all those that rubbed up against it – even were it possible! But he does describe, in excruciating detail, the particulars of the legal case commenced by Godfrey le Fauconer against Hamon Pitte, John Cobbe and others, who had taken it upon themselves to confiscate ten of Godfrey's cows, as they said they had a right to do, as some compensation for his failure to repair the ditches for which he was responsible. This was the 'ancient custom', and in keeping with the King's Charter.

Tedious, indeed, is the saga of Godfrey and Hamon, but its tortuous legalese exudes the spirit of its times, a muddy and harsh landscape always on the verge of giving way, neighbourly struggles and bureaucratic wrangling.

The Kentish historian Edward Hasted, whose prose is a little less arcane than Dugdale's, says that all the comings and goings with jurats and itinerant judges and ordinances, and sessions, and the painstaking record of the beef between Godfrey and Hamon, 'shews with what continual care and assiduity the several kings of this realm watched over the safety and preservation of this great and fertile marsh, and how highly they estimated the value of it'.

Edward IV, he points out, further fine-tuned the governance of the marsh, granting its inhabitants special dispensations,

that they should be one body in substance and name, and one commonaltie perpetually, consisting of one bailiff, twenty-four jurats, and the commonalty of Romney Marsh, having a continual succession, and impowering them to purchase lands and tenements, to have a common seal, and to hold a court every three weeks, and all pleas of action, real and personal, civil and criminal, and to chuse four justices of the peace of their own yearly, besides their bailiff, who should have the same authority, and to have the return of all writs, the benefit of all fines, forfeitures, the privileges of leet, lawday, and tourn, the exemption from toll and theam, and from so many other charges, that hardly any other place in England had the like…

All of which had the explicit objective of 'inviting men to inhabit the Marsh, which was then much deserted [and still recovering from the Black Death], on account of the danger they were subject to from foreign invasions, and the unwholesomeness of the soil and situation'.

In 1462 the creation of the Corporation of Romney Marsh afforded its officers, the Lords of the Level, presided over by the Leveller of the Marsh Scots, a near-unqualified grip on the lives of the ordinary Marshmen.

The Law of the Marsh extended beyond the regulation of water flows, chasing up debtors for unpaid scots or squabbling over cows. It was as picaresque and prosaic as people always are. And on the flat and not always colourful marsh, even the ghosts of those that fell foul of or gained by it add a touch of colour to its sometimes sallow-cheeked history.

The frontispiece of the *Poor Book of Broomhill*, a parish near Lydd, is written in a flourishing, Gothic hand, its rich embellishment at odds with both the title and the purpose of the document, which was to serve as a record of payments made to the poor, and reimbursements to traders for the services they've provided pertaining to the alleviation of poverty.

'Paid William Wraight for cloathing of Judith Jordan, a Poor Child belonging to this Parish…'

'Paid John Partridge for the board and lodging of two of the late Mark Moore's three children.'

'Paid Richard Bishop for Poisoning of 7 Ravens – 7 Shillings…'

'Paid John Pepper, Carpenter, for a coffin for the late Robert Rolfe deceased, a Pauper of This Parish…'

There is money for the upkeep of Bastard Children, for Relief during the Severe Winter, for nursing the sick and clothing paupers, and the provision of coal, barley and animal feed to those who would not otherwise have it. Mark Skinner is reimbursed for a load of wood given the Widow Brown and Henry Fidge; the Widow Brown is bought a new Woollen Wheel; Henry Brown 2 Bushells of Wheat; Richard Brown the Shoemaker has 18 shillings for 'shoes and mending of same' for Richard Moore and Susan, Poor Children belonging to this Parish, and there are various disbursements for Burying a Drowned Man and other sundries.

Perhaps a still more revealing insight into application of the law in local marsh lives lies in the church records belonging to the village of St Mary in the Marsh of the 1590s, which describe the crimes of John Suckling, a notorious ne'er-do-well, and 'not a man of good name or credit', whose antisocial behaviour was such that he was obliged to perform an ancient rite of penance, appearing in church, clothed in white, carrying a white rod and confessing before the assembled congregation.

Suckling's sins were petty but disruptive. He had composed unpleasant rhymes that had travelled contagiously through the village before reaching the ears of the authorities. The rhymes, of which unfortunately there is no record, had disrupted the equilibrium of a small community, which could only thrive if such balance that he had pushed out of kilter was generally maintained.

Suckling, it seemed, paid his dues only grudgingly, maintaining that the rhymes were justified for drawing attention to the beating, by a local woman, of her own mother. Had he not previously come to the attention of authorities, whether ecclesiastical or civil, the slander might have been allowed to pass, but he was known to have been mixed up, in ways unspecified, with a series of accusations and counter-accusations that divided the loyalties of the villagers along lines that reflected the degree of their affection for George Baker, a curate, whose reputation with his 'neighbowrs' was that he was quiet and sober and did liveth well among them, but who was reported by Richard Norton as being overly fond of the local 'tippling house'.

'Tippling' was not of itself a crime, but the gambling that took place in the house was. During the Christmas period preceding the accusations, Baker, it was known, had brawled with a visiting glover, the casus belli being the outcome of a game of dice – and his friends had had to restrain him to ensure injury didn't ensue.

In his defence, said his 'neighbowr', Richard Murrell, Baker only ever went to the alehouse because his friends would ask him along and he was easily led. And it was commonplace knowledge that Norton only made his accusations out of malice.

Ironically, Murrell's own wife Susan had a reputation in the village for bad-mouthing and making false accusations. She herself had slandered Norton, the finger-pointer, and on a separate, unrelated occasion, threatened to 'dashe out' Margaret Spurnell's 'tethe' when the two came across each other in Blackmanstone Field, and so she would have, had another neighbour, who declared herself 'ashamed to see Susan' behave the way that she had and so misbehaving and disordering herself, not put herself between the two of them.

Looking back on the thumping and shaming, the teeth-dashing and mud-flinging, weighing them in the balance, are they not mitigated by the nobler sentiments let loose in the fray, the instinct towards sympathy on the parts of some of those involved, and the instinctive sense of in/justice? And perhaps also, the law here speaks of a community that, though small, was concerned for itself as a singular entity, and for its constituents.

But the historian Paula Simpson thinks the record reveals something more than everyday conflict between neighbours, that it reflects, however muddily, the larger religious tensions playing out across the nation and the Christian world.

The church building itself, she points out, was in a miserable state. Loose stones, it is recorded, were 'very dangerously ready to falle down upon the peoples heads' as they attended services, and a pigsty had been built against the church wall. Pages were missing from the Bible, and for as long as anyone could remember, the parishioners had had to make do with a communion cup that was not even made of silver.

More tellingly still, Richard and Mrs Norton, Simpson discovers, repeatedly failed to receive communion from the established church, and were thus added to a list of recusant Catholics. John Suckling, likewise, was a recusant; both were chased for payment of tithes by the rector, Nicholas Monday.

Ordinarily, thinks Simpson (by which she means, when religious fault lines were less evident), allegations of rhyme-making, tooth-dashing, dice-throwing and glover-bashing would not even have made it to the ecclesiastical courts, but would have been resolved by less formal means. The fact that the record exists is symptomatic of a deeper malaise, unresolved tensions in Tudor Britain's religious identity, fed perhaps by other jealousies – of access to grazing and other forms of wealth, however they may have been come by.

17

The Last Roar

Tyger Tyger, burning bright,
In the forests of the night;
What immortal hand or eye,
Could frame thy fearful symmetry?

In what distant deeps or skies,
Burnt the fire of thine eyes?
On what wings dare he aspire?
What the hand, dare seize the fire?

And what shoulder, & what art,
Could twist the sinews of thy heart?
And when thy heart began to beat,
What dread hand? & what dread feet?

What the hammer? what the chain,
In what furnace was thy brain?
What the anvil? what dread grasp,
Dare its deadly terrors clasp!

'The Tyger', William Blake, 1794

Beside myself, the other passengers of the wooden-hulled ferry, nudged across the Gangetic currents of the silver river by its gnarled and dhoti-clad boatman, were women wrapped in saffron, emerald and amethyst saris, a legion of spotlessly uniformed schoolchildren, and porters, upright as pillars and unflinching beneath the sacks and boxes upon their heads and surely compressing their vertebrae. And Prasenjit Mandal.

It drew towards the jetty. I clambered out of it, onto Prasenjit's motorbike, and we rattled along for a while on the embanked brick roads above the paddy and other fields. In a shake, we stopped at a *chai* stall near what might have once had ambitions to be a building site, and Prasenjit introduced me to a man who had once been attacked by a tiger.

The ill-matched encounter had occurred seven years ago, and it was, said, Prasenjit, who is the executive director and chairman of the Sundarban Foundation, the 'usual story'.

The man had been fishing in the core reserve, the deepest part of the forest, only permissibly trod upon by those with a right to, inherited from forefathers who acquired it 'time out of mind', just as the Lords of Romney Marsh had inherited their rights. As he was packing up his nets and his fish, 'A tiger jumped at him!' said Prasenjit.

'My God!' I said, 'What did he do?'

'He pushed the tiger away, to save his life.'

'Just like that? He just pushed the tiger away?'

'Yes sir,' said Prasenjit.

I mimed what pushing a tiger away might look like.

Prasenjit and the man both nodded, seriously and affirmatively.

I was flattered to think my feeble simulacrum might be at all convincing.

'Yes sir,' said Prasenjit. 'To save his life.'

It wasn't clear to me, really, what he could have done to deter the tiger, given that they have the reputation for being both well practised and not easily deterred. 'Indeed,' writes the author of *The Mystery of the Sundarbans*, 'the Sundarban tigers are cunning and strategists par excellence in preying upon human beings.'

'What happened then?' I asked.

'He ran away,' said Prasenjit. 'And never went back to the *jangal* for fishing.'

The man was a ghost of a man. One eye was permanently closed, he showed scars on his face and legs, and he looked haggard in the way a habitual drinker (or perhaps a perfectly temperate tiger-attack victim) does. His clothes were ragged, at odds with the bright and clean and pressed shirts, trousers and lungi of other men on the island. Perhaps he now relied on charity. We bought him tea. He shrugged. The tiger hadn't killed him. Nor had it made him stronger.

As we made our way, Prasenjit sighed. 'Too many attacks by tiger. Too many widows also.' For the Sundarbans are almost as famous for their tiger widows as they are for their tigers.

But not, I probed, not wholly sure as to where Prasenjit's sentiments lay on the issue, *too many tigers?*

'Not at all! Tigers are good. Everyone loves tigers,' he said. Though it struck me that the man who had drunk his tea and sloped into the golden day might be permitted to feel, at the very least, a degree of ambivalence.

There are, I read in an article in the Kolkata[1] press, many kinds of ghosts (or *bhoott*) in Bengal. *Penchpenchi* look like owls and 'keep following people to the jungle to eat them up'. *Khondhokata* are headless ghosts, and they are ferocious. Mostly they are the ghosts of victims of train accidents.

There are 'beautiful lady ghosts', like *Shankchunni*, who were, in the temporal realm, unsatisfied 'with their married life' and on passing into the spirit world wait in trees for attractive young men upon whom they fall, and never leave.

Aleya is the name of the 'marsh gas apparitions', ghosts of drowned fishermen, which, curiously, can bode good or ill for the living members of their own profession, making them lose their bearings, or, depending on whim, helping them find their way. As anywhere, there are the ghosts of questions that no one ever properly answered. And everywhere there are the ghosts of those

---

[1] The name of the city that was called Calcutta was changed in 2001, to better reflect its pronunciation in Bengali.

carried away by *bagh*, the tiger, whose essence shapes not only mortal fears, but permeates the soul of the Sundarbans, a 2,300-ish-square-mile archipelago of forest-daubed islands, sitting within the Ganges-Brahmaputra delta, stretching across 300 miles of coast, shouldering the brunt of the cyclones and hurricanes, like Aila, which ripped apart villages in 2009, battering what was once the great, expansive, rich domain that is Bengal. And which still *is* that great and expansive domain, albeit that it is shared between the nations of India and Bangladesh.

The figurative bedrock of the Sundarbans is silt, washed through eight millennia down those thundering rivers to the sea, and into which has taken seed the sundari tree, but also hental, gewa, keora and golpata or mangrove palm, a staple for building the roofs of village houses. A total, apparently, of thirty-four species of 'true' mangrove plants, forty 'associated' and others beyond numeration.[2]

Among the winding roots, the little feline called the fishing cat fishes, and the terrapin does little. Fish spawn in the tidal shallows, and the Irrawaddy dolphin captivates those who will probably never see it, inspiring writers like Amitav Ghosh, whose novel *The Hungry Tide* pivots around a quest for the shy, blanched creature.

The tigers may be fewer in number than are the bears plodding about in the Dismal Swamp, but each individual beast casts a net further than its ursine counterpart. 'Tiger' is written into

---

[2] I learn in a scholarly article that they are 'true' in so much as they 1) occur only in mangrove forests and are not found in terrestrial communities; 2) play a major role in the structure of the mangrove community, sometimes forming pure stands; 3) have morphological specialisations to the mangrove environment; 4) have some mechanism for salt exclusion. Other notable specialisations of mangrove plants include: aerial roots to counteract the anaerobic sediments, support structures such as buttresses and above-ground roots, low water potentials and high intracellular salt concentrations, salt-excretion through leaves and buoyant, viviparous propagules.

the personal, political and godly scripts of this extraordinary wilderness, caught between the land and the open sea of the Bay of Bengal.

'None of this would have existed if it wasn't for *tiger*,' a Ph.D. researcher called Radhika told me. 'They would have cut it all down, and the islands would have been swept away.'

Swept away by the swift currents of the tributaries of the Ganga, by hurricanes and cyclones, and by indifference to the Sundarbans' beauty for their own sake.

An academic colleague of Radhika's wrote, a decade ago in the wake of a cyclone:

> People's needs in the Sundarbans are made to appear as if they are secondary to a grand protectionist imperative i.e., the conservation of the natural resources and the wildlife of the delta.
>
> The conservation drive is based upon an implicit assumption that the Sundarbans can grow as a natural habitat of non-humans like tigers, crocodiles, monkeys, deer etc. only if humans are kept at bay. In other words, the image of Sundarbans as a natural wilderness is based upon the recognition of tiger as the legitimate claimant to the land and people as only intruders or mere 'food' for the tiger…

Here, *bagh* has played two cards. For millennia, the forest was too deep to take much more than a stab at: despite this, and rather in the manner of the original members of the Great Dismal Swamp Company, bands of adventurers became convinced that in the Sundarbans lay the foundations of future riches. If it wasn't for all the insurmountable obstacles, tigers especially.

In 1665, François Bernier, author of *Travels in the Mogul Empire*, described how, among the islands, 'it is in many places dangerous to land and great care must be had that the boat, which during the night is fastened to a tree, be kept at some distance from the shore, for it constantly happens that some person or another falls prey to tigers', for 'these ferocious animals are very apt, it is said, to enter into the boat itself while people are asleep, and to carry away some victim who, if we are to believe the boatmen of the country, generally happen to be the stoutest and fattest of the party'.

'*Plus ça change, plus c'est la même chose*,' a contemporary Bernier or Sundarban fisherman might be heard to mutter.

The colonial powers, in their taming zeal, tried harder in the later nineteenth century, but were hampered by the 'predations' of what were invariably described as 'infestations' of 'man-eaters', who were always 'brazen'. A not untypical entry in the *Bengal District Gazetteer* describes 'a well authenticated instance where such a maneater charged into a line of some 6 or 8 men, working along a *bund* [embankment], at about 8 or 9 a.m. and carried off a man from their midst'.

Working parties of 'coolies' would set out, accompanied by local hunters or *shikaris*, tasked with seeing off the tigers. With the labour force increasingly devoured, disconsolate or deserted, plans for reclamation were set back. But not for want of resolve. In 1883 the British Indian government, bristling with pluck, made a concerted stand against the tiger, authorising rewards for their individual, and ultimately collective extermination. A fully grown beast brought fifty rupees, a cub ten. Presentation of skull and skin were required for the offer to be redeemed.

Like the swamps of Louisiana, or the fens of East Anglia, the Sundarbans' range is dwarfed by the memory of its former self. But it remains considerable, and, though not boundless, capable of giving the impression of being so.

In the 1870s an English magistrate tasked with reclaiming the Sundarbans for agriculture described the apparent futility of the endeavour, given the propensity of its 'evil fertility' to rewild itself without intervention.

Clearing the forest, he reported to his superiors, was a most arduous undertaking, the trees intertwining with each other 'to such an extent that each supports and upholds the others. Some of these trees too, are of immense size [and must be] taken piecemeal and cut into little pieces.'

The size of the trees, the impenetrable brushwood, and the malevolent fecundity, which means that 'deforested land springs back into jungle to become as bad as ever' is 'not the only difficulty,' he said, for 'there is no small danger from wild animals', and though crocodiles are seldom met with, tigers are encountered not infrequently and 'they occasionally attack the defenceless forest-clearers, if the latter approach their lair too closely'.

Sometimes, he said, 'a tiger takes possession of a tract of land and commits fearful havoc there', while the depredations of an unusually fierce tiger might force a family of forest-clearers to give up on land 'reclaimed after years of labour'.

The tigers couldn't be killed fast enough. By 1909, 500 people had been taken by tigers and the prize money had quadrupled. Inflated rewards spurred ingenuity: the forest was now aquiver with spring-loaded traps and poisoned arrows, though they didn't work well at the best of times, sometimes killing the self-same people that had set the traps, and were anyway destroyed when the tide came in. Nonetheless, between 1881 and 1912 at least 2,400 of the audacious animals, almost as many as are now thought to still be at large in the whole of India, had been 'dispatched'.

But if ferocity and brazenness had been the tiger's first, and only partially successful trump card, the winning second was its downright sex appeal. In 1973 India initiated a major undertaking, creating wildlife corridors and reserves and relocating human activity to prevent the snuffing-out of its iconic species. It was called 'Project Tiger' and was as much the outcome of global politics as a reflection of local conservation concerns.

Now tigers were to be revered, and where bagging one had once brought rewards, harsh penalties could be expected, not only against individuals, but also against whole communities shamed both for poaching and for what local people regarded as 'revenge killings' against the tigers that had taken one of their own.

I see that I've now made the Sundarbans sound a darker place than they are. Modern Kolkatans lyricise about the quality of light, and the clean air, and simplicity of life in the villages. 'It is poor but it's peaceful,' they say, 'and really, you can get there in a day from the city.'

Though it is a long day. By train, from sprawling, busy Sealdah station in north Kolkata and through the burgeoning suburbs, before arriving at the market town of Canning, named after the lord of that name, who had 'put it on the map', seeing in what was then little more than a bustling village the prospect of an entrepot and access point to the Bay of Bengal that could rival Calcutta.[3]

From Canning onward to the islands necessitates a succession of hops from rickshaw to ferry to rickshaw. There are cars and buses, but not so many, a good thing given the narrow, brick-lined roads, and the promise of a couple of yards' tumble into a ditch in the event, say, of a sharp swerve.

Prasenjit had met me at the place where the cars come to a halt and bought us coconuts to drink from with straws.

'I am too happy that you came here,' said Prasenjit.

And I was too happy to meet him too. He wore a light blue Puffa jacket and smiled broadly, and though he was thirty, I guessed he was forty, to flatter his sense of importance as the director of the Sundarban Foundation, an institution the exact nature of which I still couldn't quite discern.

The light breeze borne by the river, and the expanse of water and forests beyond, were immediately entrancing. Only a lack of humanity, imagination or spirit, could lead one to not love Kolkata. But even its inhabitants, in fact especially they, find the ceaseless energy, the competing semiotics of scooter horns and temple bells, hawker cries and clattering trams enervating, sometimes infuriating. And they crave peace, greater even than they can find on the recreation grounds of the Maidan at the south of the city,

---

[3]But not successfully. H. E. A. Cotton, author of *Calcutta Old and New*, described how the year 1864 'witnessed the speculative mania over an unlucky scheme for the reclamation of the Sunderbans, of which nothing remains but the deserted wharfs of Port Canning, but which resulted in the ruin to many.'

where tranquillity is sought in cricket, or watching the ships from the quiet banks of the Hooghly River.

We waited on the jetty steps as various boats came and went. None would win awards for safety. There are no guard rails. Passengers sit on the not-very-high gunwales, or stand or squat upon the decks, and the weatherbeaten, lungi-wearing ferryman, to whom a fare of ten rupees is paid, navigates by means of a steering oar, cajoling an antediluvian engine with a length of string tied to a bamboo pole somehow attached to the throttle.

Had there been an incident, most of us would have drowned. But that does little to dispel the enjoyment of the river and the fresh sky, and the jetty coming closer until the ferryman cuts the engine in such a way that the current brings the prow neatly alongside the wharf of an island, Bali,[4] which lies much closer to the Sundarbans *proper*. And to tiger.

I was decanted into another auto-rickshaw, the front of which was emblazoned with the image of the Goddess Kali, her eyes wide and wild, face as black as the cosmos and tongue lolling, red and lascivious. Prasenjit followed behind on his motorbike and we hummed, bumped and rumbled along the raised mud road that was paved with the yellowish bricks in a herringbone fashion. In a convoy of two we honked past dozing dogs and slumbering puppies, schoolchildren, spotless and bright, on bicycles or on foot, improbably small kids (bleating, not brattish), already sporting little beards, scattering chickens…

And amid all of this, it was easy to be drawn into a fantasy of a bucolic and sensual India, dignity incarnate in the easy smile and grace of a farmer's wife carrying, on her head, a polished steel pot of well-drawn water, in the careful stacking of straw, or in the attentive feeding of a kohl-eyed cow. The warm air was coloured with wood and dung smoke and cooled by the river, and, though what do I know, I couldn't help but think that this was a community at ease with itself.

---

[4]Just for the avoidance of any confusion – not *that* Bali.

The 'main roads', such as they are, spread across Bali like the veins of a leaf, dictating the placing of each small homestead, which, though it may be built from mud or timber or (less likely) brick, follows a pattern: a main house for living and a small outhouse; a beaten-earth yard; an adjacent pond in the pattern of a round-cornered rectangle around which grow some palms and banana trees; a small bamboo hut raised on stilts that houses, at night, the poultry that spend their days dirt-bathing, yard-pecking, and occasionally making way for rickshaws and motorbikes.

The paddy, in the fields close by or adjacent to the houses, had been harvested some weeks before. But in small, carefully tended patches, it had begun to spring up again, green, and as bright as newly spilt blood, striking against the saris, in all the spice colours, that were hanging out to dry in the sun.

The pond belonging to each house acts as a kind of anchor to the place it occupies. Dark, deep, anciently present, the pond is the sort which, for millennia, has borne mute witness to trysts and heartaches, ineffable pleasures and unspeakable sorrows, and served as the altar at which numberless necessary rituals, sacred and profane, sanitary, sanctifying and satisfying, have unfolded.

Strung from poles above the ponds are filaments, like loose cats' cradles, and here perch kingfishers in every possible shade and size, frowning with priestly purpose and piscatorial intent, and green and honey gold bee-eaters, perched lightly above the soft, knowing water.

It was at such a pond that Prasenjit's mother was washing dishes when we arrived at the Mandal home: I was sitting at a table on a porch to await my lunch. A baby (Prasenjit's) was produced to be inspected for its plumpness, and a younger brother brought forth unwillingly for introduction. Prasenjit's wife briefly and shyly said hello.

In the yard, under a woven-reed awning, a woman dressed in a flame-red sari stoked glowing charcoals in a mud-built oven, the kind that has a cavity for fuel and a disc-shaped aperture on which to place a shallow cooking pot or pan.

All these characteristics were shared with the other homes we'd passed on the forty-minute rickshaw ride from the jetty. But on one side of the yard, Prasenjit had built three adjoining one-room cabins for paying guests, with flushing loos and running water from a tap. Another cabin had been built, slightly apart, at right angles. Each had, set before it, a table laid with an oilcloth.

Next to the house, on the road, was a building that had not been constructed for domestic use. It was, perhaps forty feet in length and fifteen feet deep, its windows so small as to not serve any obvious function.

Prasenjit opened a door, revealing a dozen or so women, all wearing face masks, presumably to protect them from inhaling fragments of fibre. They looked up briefly, before reverting to the mindlessness of the task that would occupy them for perhaps another four hours, having, Prasenjit said, 'started early morning'.

On the walls, posters extolled the virtues of Khadi India, 'khadi' being a cotton-based fabric that the Indian government is promoting as a means of sustenance, and livelihood, and general benefit to the nation's manufacturers and consumers. It all looked rather dismal.

But Prasenjit implied, in so many words, that this, actually, was a thing of hope:

'These women sir, many of them are *tiger widows*,' he said, his voice dropping in octave and amplitude as he pronounced the last two words. 'We are helping the women. Without the jobs they have nothing. We give them work. So they can make money.'

I had found Prasenjit on the internet, and he'd expressed much pleasure at the prospect of showing me 'his' Sundarbans. And given that he'd been able to steer me as far from home as this, it was only fair that our first stop after lunch should be one of the foundation's flagship projects.

The foundation says on its website:

Our trustee has a key project on this matter [of tiger widows] to develops & transform the lifestyles of those tiger victim widow women's who the women already loses their husbands

due to sudden attack of Royal Bengal Tigers in the mangrove
forest area of Sundarbans, we the trustee works behind
and stand up to giving them support with skillful trainings
according to our capability and potentiality of trustee in an
honest manner as much as possible from different sources.

After I'd eaten *puri* and rice, and some vegetable curry that
Prasenjit's mother had cooked, we were on Prasenjit's motorbike
rumbling through villages, ponds and paddy, hammer-and-
sickle motifs painted on the sun-scoured walls of buildings and
booths: *chai* booths, booths selling mobile-phone cards, cigarettes
and all-sorts booths, medicine booths and cosmetic booths, and
arrived presently at a whitewashed and yet still dowdy school
building set amid litter-strewn 'grounds'. It wasn't prepossessing,
as seats of learning go.

'Come!' said Prasenjit, and I saw a subtle change in demeanour,
a sort of clustering of face lines intended to indicate Status and
Importance, and the fawning of a man we met on the staircase
suggested that, at least in this milieu, Prasenjit possessed both of
those capital qualities. Where he had before fairly bustled, his stride
now assumed gravitas, and we marched towards a classroom on the
first floor, where we found a man with a blackboard behind him and
thirty village women of all ages sitting on the floor in front of him.

We entered the room and Prasenjit loftily waved his hand as if
to say, 'Despite the awe that you undoubtedly feel in my presence,
there's really no need for you to stand.' And they didn't.

We had interrupted a class in making leather goods. The
lecturer had come from Kolkata to give it. I was shown a chair, and
Prasenjit addressed his class – in Bengali –and introduced me (I
heard 'writer') and everybody turned to look (it was all dreadfully
embarrassing), and he proceeded to talk at the women in a way that
might be described as an unequivocally one-sided exchange.

Unable to understand a word, I could only look closely at
their faces, the expressions upon which appeared to show respect
in various gradations, but also degrees of scepticism, and both
amusement and bemusement.

Some of them spoke, in response to questions that he posed, and I sensed less than unanimous agreement with everything he had 'explained' to them.

But also, was he flirting with them? Ribbing them? Cajoling?

'What are they saying?' I asked Prasenjit.

'Sir,' he said, 'they are saying that they are only too happy that you are here to visit us. They are saying that they are only too happy that they are learning important skills for empowerment of women. They are saying that they want to learn more so that they can improve their prospects and increase family income here on the island of Bali.'

'I'd love to ask them,' I said, hopefully and naively, 'about their lives here and, you know, challenges and what they hope for.'

'Sir,' he said, 'there is no need. They are saying all these things that I have told you that they are saying. This is what they are saying.'

I couldn't believe it for a moment. The conversation had clearly been more nuanced than his rough summation suggested. There was no pushing it, given the absence of anyone else to ask. But it all seemed so archaic – lots of women squatting on the floor being 'instructed' by men standing above them.

One of the younger women was sent out to find some samples of their handiwork, and returned with a crude facsimile of a wallet, fashioned out of plastic. Anything that might have been intended to have been at right angles was not. Its stitching was irregular and distracted. It was, in sum, schlocky. And yet, evidently, a source of great collective pride and portent of future things.

And then the same woman was asked to sing.

She wore a rich purple-and-black-striped sari, trimmed with gold, a felt jacket the colour of milk, embroidered at the edges, and a simple silver bangle on each wrist.

She stood, leaning bashfully against the classroom wall with her arms crossed, and introduced herself by saying that she was 'a housewife' and she lived on the island of Bali in West Bengal in the district of 24 Parganas.

The rest of her 'class' squatted on the floor around her patiently while she gathered the words and began, without any of the traditional accompanying instruments of sitar, tabla or harmonium, to sing a song which began, '*Jodi tor dak shune keu na ashe tobe ekla chalo re…*'

'Ekla Cholo Re', for such is the name of it, is one of the most often sung of the 2,323 that make up the *Gitaban*, 'Garden of Songs', written by Rabindranath Tagore, Bengal's revered genius writer, social reformer and so-so artist.

It is a song with a melody that is catchy and compelling, and which urges the objects of its lesson to follow their own path in life, heedless of any derision or disapproval, or even in the absence of approbation. 'If there is no one responding to your call, then go on all alone…'

It does, it's true, have some political, even nationalistic connotations, but as the balm at the end of what had felt like a long and rattling journey, from the symphony of sounds and smells of Kolkata to the very edge of the Sundarbans, it was sweet indeed.

Prasenjit says that each year fifty people from Bali alone are killed by tigers, which seems like a fantastical number. 'Tiger killed someone only a few weeks ago,' he said. 'Very sad.'

Of course, it was. As is the entire topic of 'tiger widows', which seems to have become as synonymous with the Sundarbans as the tigers themselves, attracting journalists and writers,[5] and Ph.D. candidates and public health officials, in, if not their droves, not inconsiderable numbers. And the issue has fundraising potential too, as various non-governmental organisations and well-meant or not-so-well-meant charitable initiatives are aware.

Some write that the tiger widows fare especially badly compared to those who have lost their husbands by other means, and that they assume a pariah status and the especial dislike of mothers-in-law, who, by some warped logic, blame them for incurring the wrath of the murderous tiger and hence the death of their spouses. Widowhood is always difficult, perhaps more in India than other places. But was this true? That it is worse to lose your husband to a tiger than to a snakebite, a passing car or cardiac arrest?

[5]Mea culpa.

'No sir. Not at all sir,' said Prasenjit. 'Nothing like that.' But I couldn't be sure.

An embankment runs along much of the southern edge of Bali, part of nearly 22,000 miles of it that are intended to protect the Sundarbans from freak tides and storms. Like Romney Marsh, many of the islands would be washed away if it weren't for their constant maintenance, and they are similarly political, especially when the embankment is neglected or parts of it are, and rumours emerge that the wall is maintained selectively; that corruption or favour-winning determines whose paddy or farms are best protected.

And yet, as the embankment demands continuous and vigilant upkeep, it does also provide a source of income to anyone prepared, in return for RS400 per day, to push barrows, dig trenches and fill gaps. It is safer work than collecting honey or fishing in the mangroves, and the income more constant than that derived from farming.

Only the fringe of mangrove around the shore of Bali betrays its swampy past, where women collect crabs by jigging a baited line, and the fishing boats, the fat-bellied freight boats and the little ferries wait out the changes in the tide, and the egrets and night herons dab in the mangrove mud.

'In the early days of the Mag[6] invasions it was the custom of the immigrants in the Ballaganj Sundarbans to seek out some little creek leading into the heart of the forest and … establish a settlement, clear the jungle and cultivate the land…' writes Ranjan Chakrabarti in the eminently helpful pamphlet I found called 'The Sundarbans and the Tiger'.

Bali was settled later, and perhaps not at sword-point, but the model must have been the same. No one has been tiger-taken on Bali *itself* for 'a long time', said Prasenjit. The deep forest is a mile's swim across the river – not impossible for a tiger, but

[6]'Magh', 'Mag', 'Mog' – same word with different spellings, is still a chilling one in Bengal. These were the people of Arakan, now the Rakhine State in Myanmar. In the seventeenth century they pushed westwards in sophisticated naval craft, taking prisoners whom they traded in the slave markets run as a racket by the Dutch East India Company.

a bother. And the Forest Department has placed nets around the 'tiger' islands. But the prospect of a transgression remains at least a possibility, and with it, the distinction between the tamed and civilised island of men, with its paddies, and village houses, Kali temples and *chai* stands, and the wild *jangal* across the river, palpably narrows.

The mangrove forest proper, which from the top of a watchtower sings with verdant boundlessness, is almost impossible to enter without possession of permits issued to government officials or scientific researchers, to fishermen and honey collectors, who, before slipping warily into the mangrove forest inlets in their slim-heeled craft, two or three at a time, also supply relevant prayers to 'Ma' Bonbibi or Banbibi, a local deity worshipped by both Muslims and Hindus. Banbibi is the arch-foe of the fearful Dakshin Rai, another local god, whose spirit, in McCavity-esque fashion, is somehow present when tiger goes snatching, and her good offices are thus worth courting, although, given the unpredictable nature of *bagh*, the weather, snakes and crocodiles, even the most assiduous supplications to Banbibi cannot be guaranteed to ward away the predations of Dakshin Rai and his stooges.

In the absence of the protective caul bestowed by either the Forestry Department or Ma Banbibi, the rest of us must be content with a cruise around the islands in one of the boats repurposed for the nascent but burgeoning tourist industry, such as it is, that sits oddly with the Sundarbans, but is inevitable, perhaps.

The craft chosen for the enterprise possess an almost lepidopteric charm. The hulls follow the contours of the other river boats, lithe and sleek, but support a two-storeyed, galleried superstructure, top-heavy in appearance, like a howdah built for mostly ceremonial purposes, the hull painted lightly and brightly, and suffixed with a single-person shed at the stern, the function of which, for the avoidance of doubt, is described by the single word carefully painted upon its door: 'Toilet'. Through an aperture in the floor, the river waters swirl and sway and a cool wind plays…

One morning, Prasenjit announced he had secured such a vessel to ourselves, the better to listen and watch and keep our own thoughts. We boarded at the quay, feeling a little self-conscious (or at least I did), that we should have, were we to want it, a whole deck to ourselves. And (were we to need it) sufficient latitude to navigate the holey stern-box without ridicule.

Not that other boats weren't always in view. Mostly tour parties, or family groups of visitors from Kolkata, and even Delhi – their conviviality danced across the water – we returned it with an occasional wave. But the chances of any of us seeing *bagh* were as thin as the slimmest shoot of sundari.

In any event, to clap eyes on the great feline would seem almost absurd, the poetry of the incident ('What dread hand? & what dread feet...') punctured by the realisation that 'tiger' is both more and less than a myth, is a real-life, overgrown and potentially dangerous cat.

It seemed sufficiently thrilling to be in the proximity of the brightly burning one's habitual haunts and know that in these muddy, tidal creeks, amid the dagger-like upward-protruding growths of the mangrove, and the gnarled and twisted roots and trunks, he/she/it/they prowled, growled, slaughtered and slept.

And there are other animals to see. Delicate and dappled chital deer which, in brief bursts of bipedality, stretch to the lowest hanging fruit of any obliging tree, black boar charging among the undergrowth, and shy monkeys picking for morsels on the foreshore with effete but determined connoisseurship, working their eyebrows in the way that monkeys have.

Nobody appears to be terribly bothered about seeing a tiger anyway. Tourism is at a stage in India where the point of being a tourist is still just to be a tourist: to be away from the alienating isolation of a commuter queue or computer terminal or helpdesk, at leisure amid the company of others with whom you feel familiar.

Young men like to travel in groups, laddishly joshing, unshackled from tyrannous aunts and uncles, bosses, mothers and sisters, all of whom seem to make up another group. And all of them will see a tiger: not any old tiger but a verified 'man-eater' by the name of Babu, who resides behind high barbed wire at a little reserve in Sonakhali.

I, too, have seen Babu. But it was the faintest of interactions. He was a long way off, asleep behind a wire mesh like a hardened crim. Prasenjit and I went to see him. He (Babu) has, Prasenjit says, killed 'many people' and is now awaiting relocation to somewhere where he's less able to strike again. Though given that tigerish appetites are attested as not being parochial, one might wonder how that might be achieved.

Failing *bagh*, there is another predator who is much more likely to make an appearance, the sighting of it eliciting the cry, '*Khoomi khoomi khoomi!*'[7] But to me, *khoomi* looks boorish and slothful. Like a tree trunk that can't even be bothered to stand.

But simply gliding between the islands in the subtly changing light – faint pinks and blues, and later hints of crepuscular violet – casts sufficient spell, watching the hawks, intriguing ripples and jumps in the river, sudden squawks from the forest…

The candy-coloured, waterborne howdah pushed deeper into the reserve as the tide ebbed, narrowing the channels, and lending the impression that the walls of the forest were slowly growing upward, more enclosing.

Now we were far from village life. Daylight had only shown the faintest inclination to purple; and in the guttering light, because they were now closer, we saw more of the sleek-keeled fishing boats.

Typically, a man would be standing close to the stern, forging the silhouette of a triangle: the slant of the steering oar, his legs and back and the upward-curving hull. The only shelter was canvas, covering hoops of bamboo. Aboard most boats, the complement appeared to be three, two men and a woman, or three men. Only by squatting could all the tasks of cooking, sorting fish, throwing nets, washing and boat-tending be achieved with such finesse. And only poverty would drive one to it.

Slightly larger boats possessed a sail or two, their plastic-sacking sailcloth doing nothing to disguise the ancient, lateen-esque cut.

[7]'Crocodile, crocodile, crocodile!'

The stares of the people on the boat are hard; not unkind, nor obviously envious. But wondering.

'Tonight, they sleep in the boat,' said Prasenjit. 'Maybe tiger will come! They must think about it every night.'

'Are all the tigers of the Sundarbans man-eaters?' asks Haraprasad Chattopadhyaya, retired professor, Department of History, University of Calcutta, in his comprehensive but generously slim *Mystery of the Sundarbans*. It is the question one might never oneself dare to pose.

His conclusion, based on careful reading of academic authorities such as A. B. Chaudhury and Kalyan Chakravorti, is, reassuringly, both for tiger and man, that 'all tigers of the Sundarbans are not so'. Perhaps only 25 per cent show such a proclivity, which leads one to the obvious sequitur: 'How to account for the Sundarban tigers turning man-eaters, even though their percentage be small?'

It is Chakravorti, he says, who has the best answers:

The major causes are the easy availability of human prey. With the forest such a draw to fishermen and honey collectors, they are as good as on tap, and easier to catch than chital, being less fleet of foot and more prone to sleep.

But the feline appetite, adds Chakravorti, is possibly sharpened by the brinish-ness of the water flowing through the creeks and upon which they must depend, which 'could probably have brought some change in the liver and urethra inducing man-eating propensity of the tiger'.

That the reserve is so closely monitored and mapped and logged, and the area generally so peopled, at least permits closer scrutiny of the tiger–man experience. The zoologist Dr Jagannath Chattopadhyay has collated data that suggests that, typically, the tigers' victims are male, between thirty-six and forty-six, and that the most 'kills' are made in April, 'because this is when the honey collectors enter the forest for the collection of honey'. Most attacks are between 6 a.m. and 8 a.m., and between 3 p.m. and 5 p.m.; in other words, when the woodcutters and the fish-catchers and the crab-netters and the honey-gatherers enter and leave the forest. But also 'at dead night' when everyone aboard the boat is in the spell of a fitful sleep.

Some days later, Prasenjit farmed me out to a friend of his to show me around, and we went up a watchtower from which one could look out on to as much of the core reserve as it's possible to take in. Here was a whole of many parts (though few wholes are not, but it seemed particularly true), mangrove being among the most extravagant of nature's clockwork creations. Briefly, everything came together and made a semblance of sense. Not intellectually, but poetically. But, without believing in any or all of them, how to take on board the gods: Ma Kali and her big red tongue, which lolled, two-dimensionally, from the breast of almost every road vehicle? And Ma Banbibi, jungle queen and nemesis of Dakshin Rai, the tiger god. And Tusu, the god of the tribal people who called themselves, as far as I could make out, Tusu.

Where did such an omnipresent pantheon sit, alongside the equally ubiquitous hammer-and-sickle motif? And whatever happened to my quest to find a tiger widow to speak to… had I been sold a cub?

The most circle to square was that, however lyrical I might wax about the beauty of the Sundarbans, the atemporal profundities of village life and the perfumed colours, almost all of those for whom the entirety of their lives were lived in such abundance would have given it up for a life in Kolkata if the right opportunity arose.

Possibly, in that dissonance, lies a clue as to why those of a socially improving bent are attracted, as they are, to the Sundarbans.

In Gosaba, which is as much of the Sundarbans many tourists will ever see, aside from the obligatory boat trip, there is, in a scruffy little park, a large statue of Tagore, whose bodily frame, it must be said, lent itself well to the form, being almost as statuesque in life as he is in stone.

Half a dozen paces away is a tumbledown villa, tinted by time to the tone of a well-used teabag, and almost invisible among encroaching and caressing palm fronds, which no one has ever seen fit to save from dilapidation.

Here Tagore stayed for a spell, and it was ironic in some ways that the great bard, an inveterate globe-trotter, especially after winning the Nobel Prize for Literature in 1913, was visiting at the invitation of a Scotsman, who had the cabin built especially.

Despite India's concerted efforts to repugn even the most benign aspects of the British legacy, some grudging acceptance is made of that part played by Sir Daniel Hamilton, a Scottish merchant, born on the Isle of Arran, and Indophile, who arrived in Gosaba a few years after the death of Victoria, determined to Make Things Better, and a person who, despite his previous years as a shipping magnate, showed a surprisingly communistic turn of mind, leaving, for a foreigner, 'an indelible impression of self-sacrifice and magnanimity on the mind of the people of the Sundarbans, and of Bengal in general'.

Hamilton bought leases and created a *zamindari*, or estate, on land that had remained largely uncultivated, and still very much prone to attacks by 'man-eaters' and crocodiles, and proceeded to invite migrants to clear it, not only guaranteeing employment, but taking steps to create a kind of cooperative or commonwealth, where distinctions of caste and religion were to be disregarded, and villagers weaned from the habit of borrowing from *mahajans*, the loan sharks who lent at exorbitant cost.

In 1915 Hamilton established the Gosaba Bank, which still exists, to provide what one might now call 'micro-finance' to those otherwise cut off from sources of reasonable credit. There followed cooperative stores selling basic supplies at cheap rates, a dispensary, and village schools set up with the active involvement of his wife, Lady Hamilton; he sunk wells, imported distillation equipment to ensure continuous supplies of drinking water, and arranged a system whereby each household contributed paddy to safeguard against cyclone or crop failure; he built 130 miles of dykes to protect his estate against flooding, started initiatives for making communal mustard oil and weaving, and brought affordable life insurance and lending libraries.

All of this was terribly Tagore, by which I mean in the improving spirit of the Bengali intellectuals whom Rabindranath inspired and encouraged, and the two professed to be hugely mutually admiring of their visions of what the country could and should become.

'I have not much faith in politicians when the problem is vast, needing a complete vision of the future of a country like India entangled in difficulties that are enormous,' Tagore wrote to Hamilton in 1930.

> These specialists have the habit of isolating politics from the large context of national life and the psychology of the people and of the period. They put all their emphasis upon law and order, something which is external and superficial, and ignore the vital needs of the spirit of the nation…

I'd like to know more about Tagore's visit, on 29 December 1932, to the Hamilton *zamindari*.

It was a return match. Tagore had invited Hamilton to a conference the year previously, but one can imagine the pair, who, born within a year of each other, had both recently turned seventy, taking a turn round Hamilton's projects, the Scot explaining and elaborating, Tagore nodding sagely and asking wise questions, and a great warmth and excitement between the two, before, perhaps, dining on the veranda of the freshly painted bungalow, a breeze snaking between its stilt legs, amid the song of frogs in the ponds and streams.

What happened after Hamilton's death in 1939, whether the estate flourished or went to seed, I'm not sure. I imagine that the project was set back by the dramas of the 1940s, first the war, and the Bengal famine, and, across the Sundarbans, agitation for land reform and greater equality between tenants and landowners. Then of course, in 1947, Britain's exit from its erstwhile empire, and the tragedy which, on account of its violent bloodiness, could as well be described as 'parturition' as it could Partition.

An episode in the 1970s, a confluence of environmental and other politics culminating painfully, reads like a blasted inversion of Hamilton's 'experiment'. The war that had been waged between East and West Pakistan had created a refugee crisis on a scale that hadn't been seen since Independence. While middle-class refugees with resources and connections were easily settled in Calcutta and elsewhere, a group of around 10,000 lower-caste Hindus or Dalits, who had been placed in a camp at a place called Dandakaranya, had attempted to settle on the Sundarban island of Marichjhapi, having made a voyage of several hundred miles to reach it. Marichjhapi, unpopulated and uncultivated, could, the would-be settlers thought, be a place where they might create a home for themselves.

But the island was protected under the Reserve Forest Act, and a part of the territory restricted under the Project Tiger initiative, and the Communist Party government of West Bengal, resolute in its determination not to allow the refugees to set a precedent, responded to their presence with scant regard for their rights.

The Dalits began arriving on the island in small boats in the middle of 1978 and set about not only clearing the land but setting up schools and clinics and workshops. Not necessarily mindful of the Hamilton spirit, he having been only one of so very many philanthropists in India, the initiative was very much in keeping with it and had the support and blessing of well-wishing patrons across the country, especially among the intellectual classes of Calcutta. They denied that they were causing any kind of environmental degradation. The island was only scrub, they pointed out.

In a book about the Marichjhapi episode called *Blood Island*, author Deep Halder interviews a survivor, Safal Halder,[8] who remembers

> … magical days. We slept in open fields under a sky full of stars. We lit fire around us to keep insects and animals away. During the day, we built huts from logs that we got from neighbouring islands. Golpata leaves were used to make thatched roofs. Residents of neighbouring villages got us food

[8] It isn't made clear whether he is a close relative.

and other essentials, and we pooled in money we had saved
during our Dandakaranya [refugee camp] years.

'Over time', the same survivor recalls,

the population of Marichjhapi swelled to 40,000 from
the initial 10,000. It had become a functional village with
three lanes, a bazaar, a school, a dispensary, a library, a boat
manufacturing unit, and a fisheries department even! Who
could have imagined that so much was possible in so little
time? Maybe all those wasted years in Dandakaranya had given
us superhuman will.

The government of West Bengal, led by the Communist Party,
gave the settlers short shrift, and the police blockaded the island
to prevent supplies being brought from the mainland. Soon they
resorted to terror tactics, Halder's reporting revealed: raping
women, and torturing and shooting at both sexes, despite a High
Court judgment ruling that the settlers could stay. The *coup de
grâce* came in the form of a bottle of poison, dropped into the
only well on the island, killing many, regardless of age or gender.

'On 14 June 1979, it was all over for us. The police came, set fire
to our huts and forced the remaining ones out of the island. It was
the end of the Marichjhapi dream. One year of dying by the dozens
yet carrying on with fire in our souls,' Halder told Halder.

The would-be 'utopia' was dispersed, its brief inhabitants scattered
across Bengal, but mostly to shanties in the neighbourhood of
Sealdah station, where they had disembarked from the train that
had left from Canning.

One afternoon, at early dusk, when I had just returned from Gosaba
with Prasenjit's friend Dani, we were milling around a tea stall
waiting for Prasenjit, who had some business to do, as he always
seemed to, and it was suggested we go to a cockfight. I shrugged
in noncommittal manner, but acquiescing, walked along the dusty
main drag to an open area close to a Kali temple.

I knew that cockfighting was a significant pastime on account of the not inconsiderable numbers of men, young men, not-quite men, old men and every other age of man that I saw, drawn as though by a single, inexorable pull, babying cocks beneath their arms, or holding canvas bags from which protruded dark glossy feathers and combs. The devotion squandered on these birds, considering what they were to be asked to undertake, seemed extravagant and peculiar.

The crowds gathered at the waste ground. There were perhaps 150 men, several dozen bearing a bird, coddling and crooning and encouraging. The cocks were shown to each other to get them in the mood. Some seemed flaccidly indifferent. Others crowed with pugilistic intent, rising up, squaring up and clucking. A man with a box of little spurs visited the owner of each combatant, who, with much deliberation, chose which weapon suited mood and opponent, before it was tied to the gamecock's leg. Not everyone had their own cock: for those that didn't, spectacle, and the brief thrill of a few rupees' worth of a flutter would suffice.

We, for I'm afraid I slightly fell under the spell of it too, gathered to make a cockpit, and watched as the first fighting pair was matched. A bookie quickly trotted around the perimeter taking bets.

The fight itself was intense and brief, like overdue lovemaking, the prelude to actual contact symmetrical and balletic. They sank low, tails in the air and beaks to the ground. They rose. They sank. The flew up at each other. All was feathers and the flash of spurs. Then a capitulatory shriek and one of the roosters ran away, scooped into the arms of his humiliated owner. And that was that. I had seen a cockfight. The evening was still a fine one. Soon all would be dark as pitch.

In May 2009 the Sundarbans were hit by a cyclone called Aila (Severe Cyclonic Storm Aila or 02B) and most of the area was flooded. Man and tiger alike were drowned, and their respective habitats ruined for what was feared would be years to come. Paddy was destroyed, *bunds* ripped and battered. Trees were plucked like mushrooms. Cows were killed, and ponds left stinking and contaminated. Surviving villagers crowded onto the slippery, weakened embankment, hoping that the floodwater wouldn't reach them, pleading for food and water and materials with which to create some form of shelter.

As soon as the area was navigable, conservationists headed out to the reserves with fresh water for the tigers, Aila having rendered the springs brackish. Not so many villagers were killed on Bali, but for many, and despite the aid efforts of government, living on the island became untenable. There were reports of families sending their children to Kolkata, having been persuaded by dubious 'agents' to do so. Or just upping sticks to try their luck on the city streets.

In November 2019 another cyclone, sobriquet Bulbul, hit West Bengal, and there were fears that it would be as bad as Aila.

It wasn't.

In places, the sea wall had been breached and needed urgent repairs. But by the time of my visit three months later, the only (visible) signs of Bulbul were storm-felled, uncleared trees – and, critically, after Aila, the government built a large storm shelter at Gosaba, where inhabitants could be at least sheltered and receive food.

But Prasenjit described how quickly the mud and brick roads wash away, the un-sturdiness of the prettily constructed houses revealed and the ponds spoilt by the cyclones.

In other words: it isn't always so lovely here. And anyway, he said, the Sundarbans will only be inhabitable for another two or three generations. 'Sir,' he said, 'climate change means each year the well is deeper and deeper. Now it must be fourteen hundred metres deep for fresh water. And if there are more floods, everyone will leave. No more tigers. No more people.'

He shrugged. For now, he said, he would do his bit. But he was under no illusion as to the permanence of the Sundarbans or their inhabitants. And he decanted me, with much sadness on my part, from motorbike to ferry, and for onward travel to Kolkata via Canning.

18

Living with Syn

On the way he met Doctor Syn, who was standing silhouetted
against the skyline with his telescope focused upon some
large vessel that was standing in off Dungeness.

'Ah, Mister Mipps,' said the cleric, handing his telescope to the
sexton, 'tell me what you make of that?'

Mipps adjusted the lens and looked. 'The Devil!' he ejaculated.

'I beg your pardon?' said the Doctor. 'What did you say?'

'Well, it looks to me … it – looks – to me – uncommonly like
a King's frigate. Can't you make out her guns on the port side?'

'Yes!' cried the sexton; 'I'll be hanged if you're not right, sir; it's
a damned King's Ship as ever was.'

From *Dr Syn: A Tale of Romney Marsh*,
Russell Thorndike, 1915

In time, I had the opportunity to visit New Hall, the ancient seat
of the Corporation of Romney Marsh, which is in Dymchurch, by
arrangement with Yvonne Wanstall, its chief clerk.

It isn't very new at all, but it replaced its predecessor, destroyed
in a storm in 1575 and no one has got around to giving it a more
imaginative title in almost half a millennium.[1]

---

[1] Nobody knows the name of the previous building. Surely not 'Old Hall'?

Nothing about New Hall stands out particularly: it is tucked into a little close, New Hall Close, the entrance to which is marked by a war memorial, built, reputedly, upon the site of the old town gallows. Opposite the hall is the churchyard, adjacent to it a primary school, and at just before nine o'clock and just after three o'clock on weekdays in term time, a murmuration of parents, children and cars gathers noisily and briefly before dispersing.

The modest buildings around New Hall share its brick-redness. They are all more recent, and the common hue disguises the fact that for so long New Hall was the epicentre of Romney Marsh's political and judicial life.

It is now rather on its uppers, almost literally, for the ground-floor offices have been let out to a local start-up IT company, whose young employees, no doubt, resent opening the door to the curious. Visiting the hall was only by appointment with Yvonne, for she it was who had the key.

Yvonne comes from a line of Lords of the Marsh, and though enjoying the title of chief clerk, said, 'In the past, the person who had my role was called the "chamberlain". I think I would have rather liked to have been a "chamberlain". It sounds grander than "chief clerk".'

But she bears that burden with fortitude.

Two sets of antlers, one once attached to a middling stag, the other cast in bronze, share, with an umbrella stand and little more, the task of adorning the otherwise quite frugal corridor that leads to the mysteries of New Hall's upper floor.

Ascending into the upper chamber, the walls are lined with rough cloth, like hessian. The roof is timber-beamed and plaster, in places, has fallen away to reveal the lath. The room is not particularly big, but exudes authority, not least by dint of the judicial bench that takes up one end of it, at which the dignitaries of the corporation sit, mostly now on ceremonial occasions. And below lies an ancient committee table, steeped in the solemnity of the decisions it has borne witness to, at which I took a seat.

It really resembles a sort of private museum, glass cases protecting from cobwebs and curious hands muskets, pistols, swords, seals, the coins that were a currency in a uniquely local Romney Marsh trading system, and photographs and porcelain. Maps and charters hang on the walls. And hessian.

It was good to hear the history from Yvonne, who was of retirement age, well-coiffed, and wearing a red gilet. Good indeed to hear it from a living human being, not just wrested from the dense pages of Dugdale and Hasted, or my copy of *The Level and Liberty of Romney Marsh*, signed by the author, Teichman Derville, a high sheriff of Kent and well acquainted during his time with New Hall.

The Corporation, she reminded me, was founded out of necessity as a response to the storms ravaging the marsh, 'not just because of the flooding from the sea, but because the rivers would burst their banks, carrying the run-off from the Weald,' and was more demographically representative than you might think it was, given the times, in that while the Lords of the Marsh were for the most part landowners, the jurats were often drawn from the ranks of ditch-clearers, bank-builders and others with the necessary understanding of how the forces of sea, land and the heavens acted upon each other.

After Henry III had restructured the corporation, she said, the Marshmen possessed a kind of unique impermeableness to the writ of the law of the rest of the Kingdom:

'Did you know,' she asked me, 'that the monarch still possesses the authority to oblige any man in his or her realm to marry the eldest royal daughter?'

'I didn't.'

'Well, of course Princess Anne is spoken for. But, theoretically speaking, that law remains unrepealed and yet...' she said, 'there exists an exemption. No Marshman may be made to marry against his will, even at the order of the sovereign.'

The Marsh, she said, was riven by rivalries, the cause of which may have lain in dynastic, economic or religious conflicts in London, Canterbury or well beyond.

What made it unique was that its local governance was almost wholly unaccountable to any higher power until shortly after the Second World War, said Yvonne, explaining, while emphasising the anecdotal and not wholly verified or verifiable nature of the claim, that in the course of golfing with the Lord Chancellor, the chairman of the corporation happened to mention that in so much as he had (unexercised) authority to execute criminals and personally appoint magistrates, and possessed all sorts of other arcane and draconian powers, he was a more significant personage within his own jurisdiction than the Chancellor was in his. The Chancellor took note.

'The Corporation really serves a ceremonial role now. All the decision-making about the management of the Marsh is now in the hands of the Internal Drainage Board and DEFRA. But it's still important, I think, because it's about identity, and history and memory.'

There, we paused. This being the end of September 2019, it was those very things that lay at the heart of a divisive and painful national conversation. And indeed, I was feeling even then a kind of ambivalence about my presence in a hessian-walled chamber full of pepperbox pistols, fearful, somehow, of complicity in wallowing in the past, when the present's needs seemed so much more urgent.

No, she said, the lords and the jurats no longer had any *actual* authority over anything, but that didn't mean to say that the appointments weren't political. There were factions, she said. Things could get quite difficult. Sometimes, she said, there was 'argy-bargy', not that she could elaborate, of course. It would scarcely be fitting for the chief clerk, once chamberlain, to do so.

We also talked about the writerly and arty people who had been and continue to be fond, less of the Marsh itself than its fringes. Siegfried Sassoon had lived in Port Lympne, home now to a safari-zoo. Rudyard Kipling would motor from Batemans near Robertsbridge to take lunch with Henry James at Lamb House in Rye… while the village of Aldington, where Yvonne lived, on the ragstone escarpment looking over the Marsh, had always attracted the 'literati', she said. Noël Coward moved there once he'd become successful. As did Ford Madox Ford, who collaborated with his near neighbour Joseph Conrad. And a well-known musician had bought the house of a television celebrity and was spending a fortune on its renovation...

We moved through to an adjoining room, where in 1803 William Pitt had met with the lords and the jurats of the Marsh and put to them his idea for a plan, the digging of a canal from Pett to Hythe, which might save Britain from invasion by the French.

Framed on the wall was a reproduction of a newspaper clipping from the *London Chronicle OR UNIVERSAL EVENING POST.*

'Canterbury, May 16, 1764' (it read).

R. Sparkes and Mr. Lakes, Riding Officers at Dymchurch, with a party of Sir John Mordaunt's dragoons being on duty in the parish of Rucking on Monday the 7th instant; met six horses loaded with 31 bags of tea which they seized with the horses and carried to his Majesty's Warehouse, New-Romney.

In an almost confessional whisper, Yvonne said that while the Lords of the Marsh possessed, as previously noted, the power of life and death and more over their fiefdom, they didn't greatly mind or attempt to hinder the smuggling trade.

Indeed, very few Marshmen were ever convicted of it. If any at all!

You had to understand, she pointed out, that people were terribly poor, and smuggling was a way of surviving.

More recent news headlines, slews of them, had concerned the smuggling of people across the Channel in scarcely seaworthy boats and dinghies that had either been apprehended at sea, and their 'passengers' taken aboard coastguard vessels, or had come ashore on Kentish beaches such as at Pett, Camber or Dungeness, in other words, using the same routes that had always been used for the illicit passage of people or other commodities between France and England.

A typical story on the BBC read thus:

Channel Migrants: Two boats found after 86 attempted crossing

11 September 2019

Two boats carrying 21 migrants have been intercepted off the
Kent coast after a record 86 made the crossing in one day.

One man was airlifted to hospital from a dinghy which was
carrying 13 people, including three children.

A second vessel carrying eight men was intercepted and
taken to Dover.

Eighty-six people were detained by Border Force on Tuesday.
It is thought to be the highest number of migrants to make the
crossing in one day.

In the late 1500s, Rye, which had always had Protestant sympathies, became a magnet for Protestant refugees from religious riots in France, the numbers growing from some dozens in the 1560s to very many more after the St Bartholomew's Day Massacre of 1572, a frenzied exercise in the killing of Huguenots, which spread from Paris outward and upward. Where many of the earlier refugees had been merchants, such as glovers, bookbinders or locksmiths, who set themselves up nicely in Rye, the early 1570s saw 'great numbers of the Frenche being very poore people, both men, wemen and children, to the great crye and grief of the inhabitants of the Ry and other places about the same'.

Whether the 'crye and grief' was in sympathy for their plight or horror at being 'overrun' is open to interpretation, but by a February 1574 edict from the Town Assembly, any freight vessel or fishing boat who 'shall bringe or suffer to be put on land any of the Frenche or Flemish nation [excepting merchants, gentry or messengers] could be suffered to pay a 40 shilling fine', a tool of dissuasion that anticipated the twenty-first-century imposition of fines on lorry drivers found to have even unwittingly conveyed stowaways.

Nonetheless, by the end of the 1580s, 1,300 such immigrants had come to settle in and around Rye, contributing to the local skill base and introducing new trades. But local people felt threatened by their success, and in 1578 the Rye Assembly decreed that French bakers should not be allowed to sell bread, even to other French people, on pain of imprisonment. Further ultimatums penalised shipwrights and drapers, and by 1600, things having settled down a little in the

'French and Flemish nations', most of the 'foreigners' had returned home, leaving the locals happily chewing their own, English loaves.

I mentioned the immigrant boat landings to Yvonne, conscious that it was an issue that was perceived quite differently across a political spectrum, and was, thus, a potentially sensitive topic.

She didn't say anything for a while. But then she said, 'An important mentor of mine, a rabbi who had escaped from Nazi Germany, always reminded me that persecution, wherever in the world it happens, is the same.'

This was an intriguingly personal turn for our conversation to take, amid the musty cobwebs of New Hall.

Yvonne explained that, though she was the daughter of a farmer, and her siblings had happily continued 'in that way of life', her interest had always really been with people. Her career, she said, had been in working with those with severe behavioural difficulties, trying, forensically, to understand the incidents and patterns in their family histories that had manifested themselves as they did. In this regard, she said, the rabbi had been instrumental in encouraging her to study and develop.

After working with a young man who had witnessed his father killing himself during an auto-erotic act, she decided to undertake master's-level research, with the rabbi's encouragement.

'Only by unpeeling the layers of his *father's* psychology, I realised, would it be possible to find the route to addressing the son's behaviours,' she said.

And Yvonne told me about other cases she'd worked with, looking at family histories behind muteness, and self-rejection, all of which was very much more than I'd expected to learn from the chief clerk of the Corporation of Romney Marsh.

Returning to the past, Yvonne repeated that, despite or because of the broad sweep of their authority over sewers and ditches and ponds and all points in between, the lords and jurats had not done a great deal to interrupt the free trade of the smugglers, and that those that took the rap tended to be outsiders.

What is it about the 'Golden Age' of smuggling – the term is somehow both wildly appropriate and inappropriate – that's so enthralling? Not least, I suspect, because the smugglers cocked a snook at a stultifying establishment that reinforced primacy of inherited wealth and privilege. And perhaps because violence, cloaked in a greatcoat or riding cape, topped with a tricorn and shod with a pair of spurs, inevitably exerts a kind of glamour, in the old gypsy sense of the word.

Every two years Dymchurch holds a sort of cultural festival. Unlike the one held in the Venice Giardini, this more modest biennale references Dr Syn, a fictional scholar-turned-smuggler, and the central character of the eponymous novels by Russell Thorndike, brother of the actress Sybil, and the plots of which unfold upon the mist-shrouded badlands of Romney Marsh.

The 'Day of Syn', invented in the 1960s to raise funds for a church roof, sees local people dress up as excise men, redcoats and more particularly smugglers, wearing that profession's disguise of choice, a sackcloth hood. There are parades, mock battles and quite a lot of drinking.

The Syn character is a former pirate, Captain Clegg, erroneously believed to have been hanged in Rye, but who washes up in Dymchurch, reinvented as a country parson, who hides his past behind a façade of avuncular bonhomie and godliness.

Clegg/Syn is lured back to his recidivist ways, but as the cover note on the back of my own copy of *Doctor Syn, a Smuggler Tale of Romney Marsh* reminds me,

> Although a criminal, Syn's appeal is almost Robin Hood-like. He uses his ill-gotten gains to help his parish and the King's Men sent to ferret out him and his men [*sic*] are hardly a sympathetic lot, even though they represent the forces of law. It's little wonder that *Doctor Syn* proved a hit among readers of its day!

The book was first published in 1915, and readers couldn't get enough of Syn, even – especially – after his author killed him off. Two decades later, Thorndike relented to his fans' clamouring with a series of prequels, refusing to commit the sin of resurrecting him, *pace* Holmes' Lazarus-like return.

In a sense, he represents a happy medium of virtue: not so good as to be dull or puritanical, and neither cruel nor vicious. Those qualities he leaves to the *bad* baddies and to the brutish representatives of the British State, between whose stars he must steer his own course, lining his own pockets, but doing the right thing by those that deserve it.

The dozen Marsh churches that remain standing possess a kind of Nordic, barebones spareness, the centuries alive in the faint smell of cedar and plaster and wax, in rafters, and the pews upon which the buttocks of so many generations of sinners have squirmed.

Of all of them, St Clement's church in Romney, built on the site of a Saxon longboat, sitting with quiet aplomb and casting a quizzical eye at the passing traffic on the A259, is no less apparently true to itself than the others.

But a good dollop of that 'trueness' comes courtesy of Disney.

Two films and a television series, all as hammy as their inspiration, have been made of the Syn books. The 1937 film stars George Arliss as Syn, and Margaret Lockwood as his daughter (and the love interest).

The second, a 1967 Disney production starring Patrick McGoohan, released as *Dr Syn, Alias the Scarecrow*, peers over the lip of the quasi-horror genre.

When Disney came to the Marsh to film it, the production team alighted on St Clement's as being the right church for Syn, and they badgered the parish council to be allowed to paint the interior pink, to make it, as they said, 'more authentic'. The plan wasn't greeted enthusiastically. But, promised the global entertainment corporation, they'd return the interior to its original colour and pay for the roof to be repaired.

And yet the pink took hold, the parish agreeing that it was a marked improvement on the dismal hues in which its pews and beams had previously been bedaubed, and it asked whether it might be left as Disney had made it.

Notwithstanding the pleasurable irony, it's easy to see how landscape and the narrative of smuggling are insinuated, manifest in each other.

At St Dunstan's church in the village of Snargate, the picture of a 'great ship', a graffito almost, was discovered beneath a layer of paint during refurbishment. The image is both primitive and sophisticated, drawn with the care that a precocious child might give it, its spars, decks and rigging represented with sufficient accuracy that experts can date it to around 1500, give or take twenty years.

It is also possible, they've suggested, that the ship served as a literal sign that the church was safe for keeping contraband, though they say that without disproving the theory that it may just be a nice drawing of a ship. (Surely, were it only a glorified hieroglyph, much of the detail is superfluous?)

The high bluff above Pett Level, where the remains of an anti-aircraft defence moulder forgetfully among their rolling, rabbity surroundings was, famously, a place where real-life smugglers would look out for the ships of the King's Men, just as Thorndike said they did.

Once landed, or on the way to export, consignments of tea and brandy and wool could be moved around the Marsh out of sight, pushed in shallow-drafted boats through the ditches, or under cover of twilight on tracks and unbeaten paths. And just as (mostly male) celebrants of the joys of naturism giddily wind their way through fern-banked paths to a secret beach below the cliffs with their daypacks, Panama hats and rolled-up copies of the *Daily Telegraph*, so once did the smugglers lead their pack-mules to rendezvous with profit, danger and romance...

There are Smugglers Inns, and Smugglers Arms, and 'The Smuggler's'. Even the pubs that aren't called the Smugglers Something almost certainly were, their true callings cunningly concealed by more innocuous names, such as the Bell Inn at Ivychurch, which, with the adjoining church of St George (the 'Cathedral on the Marsh'), served as a warehouse for contraband *en passage* to coast or capital.

The Bell was once sponsor of a unique Romney Marsh pastime, an annual competition that saw participants attempting to hurl a toilet brush out of a cubicle erected on the village green, while seated on a porcelain throne. The winner was he, or she, who threw it the furthest.

When I visited the pub for a Sunday lunch (a huge hock of ham, as long as a pig's arm), only one man at the bar could remember the last such event. 'Times have changed,' he said, shaking his head. 'No one's got time for such things any more...'

Smuggling, on the other hand, is likely to prove a more enduring pastime.

Depending on how you see the relationship between the law, the activities it prohibits, and vested interest, Edward I, aka 'Longshanks', and 'Hammer of the Scots', can in no small measure be blamed for what would become a violent scourge across the Marsh and beyond.

It was Edward who, in the late 1200s, imposed a duty on the export of wool: the tax was £3 a bag – around £2,000 in today's money, and it soon after doubled, immediately creating opportunities for anyone prepared to take the not very considerable risk of running it across the Channel without paying the requisite fee. Research is inconclusive as to whether Baa-Baa was himself a smuggler, but the original rhyme alludes to the fact that by the time church and state had taken their 'bagful', there was *nothing* left for the little boy that lived down the lane.

Predictably, the levy was a boon for poorly paid officials. In the ports from which exports were permitted, it was necessary to have a collector, and to watch over the collector, a controller, and over the controller, a surveyor. The system could have been prolonged to absurdity, and arguably was, as a highly informative pamphlet available for £5 from Rye Museum points out:

> Even with this number of officials, no more duty was collected than before, although the merchants had to pay more by way of bribes. In the small harbours around the coast, almost every individual was involved in assisting the smuggler and was appropriately rewarded for his labours. If a merchant was caught smuggling, therefore, the local jury, duly packed with smugglers itself, would acquit him...

The corollary of lax enforcement was stiffer sentences, and by the time of Elizabeth I's era, a two-strikes-and-you're-dead approach was taken to the smuggling of live sheep. It did little to prevent its continuation.

The name given to these smugglers was 'owlers', a word that some believe to be a corruption of 'woolers', in other words, a reference to people involved in the illegal trading of wool. Others attribute it to the owlers' reputation for hooting at each other, in the manner of owls, as a means of nocturnal signalling.

Then, as now, the fortunes of smugglers see-sawed in a way that reflected the state of the economy, fluctuating demands for exports on either side of the Channel, and the government's need for revenues. When domestic demand for wool was high, smuggling lost its sheen. When the siren call came from across the Channel, its attractions improved.

Actual, proactive resistance to the smuggling trade was more likely to come from private individuals than the state.

In the late 1600s a brave clothier, William Carter, set out on a crusade against its perpetration. On one occasion, Carter, armed with a warrant from King Charles II and accompanied by a self-assembled militia of citizenry, arrested the captain of a smuggling ship at Dover. By the time he had dragged him to the magistrate at Folkestone, the captain's wife had warned the captain's accomplices, and by the time the party arrived at the assizes, the townswomen launched a fusillade of pebbles from the beach which they 'flung about [Carter's] ears' until the captive was freed.

Undeterred, Carter went on to arrest ten owlers engaged in their business *en plein air* on the Marsh, dragging them to the mayor at Romney for committal. But the mayor declined the invitation.

Owling set a nice precedent for an arguably more interesting trade in sensual and intoxicating products, most of which were more likely to be imported *from* the Continent than exported *to* it.

But the moral calculus remained the same, and no less difficult in retrospect. The customs imposed by Edward Longshanks and his successors provided little, directly, to the inhabitants of Romney Marsh, whereas the disbursements liberally dispensed by smugglers across the supply chain, from electively myopic officials to publicans and parsons, fishermen and fieldhands, were a more effective form of poor relief than any provided by the government.

Discarded seamen and soldiers found more gainful employment in the service of the smugglers than they might find legitimately, because the profits were sufficiently astronomical to assuage any concerns that they may have had about the lawfulness of their activities: of a single tub of spirits, wrote John Banks, author of the slim but esteemed *Reminiscences of Smugglers and Smuggling*,

> Its cost in France was from ten shillings and sixpence to thirteen shillings – fourteen to sixteen shillings would be thought dear. A tub of spirits contained three and a half gallons of spirit so much over-proof that it would bear the addition of two and a half gallons of water, and the six gallons would sell easily for three or even four pounds or guineas. Here was a profit of from four to five hundred per cent! After paying out of this, the cost of transport wages of the lookout men, &c., the profits were so good … that if one cargo out of three was saved, there was a profit.

'Batmen', says Banks, armed with bats or eight-foot poles, and later firearms, employed to protect the transport of contraband, were paid upwards of twenty shillings per landing. Given that the chances of having to perform any batting were as slim as a proverbial reed, there was little shortage of takers. Smuggling even had intellectual supporters. The proponent of free market economics, Adam 'Hidden Hand' Smith, wrote, 'A smuggler would be an excellent citizen, had not the laws of his country made that a crime which nature never meant to be so,' which was essentially a libertarian argument, striking at government interventionism.

The reality was that, had the laws of his country not made that a crime which nature never meant to be so, the smuggler would have been out of a job. And the real beneficiaries were always higher up the tree: the magistrates, and merchants and mayors, not the dirt-poor ditch-digger or otherwise impecunious innkeeper, while the price of smuggling was that as long as the smugglers controlled trade, and notwithstanding the long arms of the Lords of the Marsh, the Marsh was in the hands of criminal gangs who were venal and quarrelsome, and for whom the threat or exercise of violence, with batmen, blackmail or other means, was a quotidian necessity.

Methodist John Wesley, who preached his last sermon in a chapel in Winchelsea overlooking the Marsh, abhorred smuggling. 'The duties appointed by law,' he thundered in a 1783 pamphlet entitled 'A Word to the Smuggler', 'are the King's right, as much as your coat is *your* right... Therefore you are as much a thief if you take his duties as man is that takes your coat...'

It was, as they say, personal for Wesley, who was terribly affected by the death of the son of a close friend: eighteen-year-old Captain John Haddock, precociously appointed commander of a revenue cutter called *The Scourge*, whose ship was blasted by the big guns of a smuggler's boat.

Some years later, Wesley noted that the man responsible for Haddock's death had been killed in a skirmish off the coast: his vessel boarded by a Captain Bray, the author of Haddock's demise pointed a pistol at the customs man, who 'hewed him to pieces with his cutlass'.

The website of the George Hotel, previously Inn, in Lydd, may reassure readers that it is 'in the process of refurbishment to bring it from an old, dated building to a more modern feel', but fails to mention that its premises were the location of one of the most notorious clashes between smuggler and state – the rescue of Jacob Walter and Thomas Bigg in 1721.

Walter and Bigg had been seized at Camber Point by the riding officers of Lydd, chained, and held in a room at the George guarded by six officers who were armed with '20 fire locks loaded with powder and ball'.

At 5 p.m. the following evening (it was March – the afternoon was clement for the season), nine men on good horses and well-armed

comes up to the house & dismounts from their horses & runs
up stairs fireing all the way up, & ye officers fired down on
them – wounded 3 officers & got between ye officers & their

Armes & carried away Walter and Bigg & if these 9 men had
not carried them off a 100 more was hard by ready to make
another attack.

Victory for the 'gang' was noisy but also pyrrhic. Bigg and
Walter were later recaptured. Walter, the record says, was 'about
40 years old, a tall man, sandy complexion, thin longish face, short
well made person',[2] and Bigg, a 'short little man with a black Wigg,
round visage'.

But frequently the law was humiliated by the smugglers' greater
resources and numbers, by nobbled juries, and by the supine
approach taken by the government towards the free trade.

Romney Marsh lends itself well to reimaginings of the scrape
of the hull of a midnight-landed craft pulled up onto shingle,
the near-silent pattering of a laden donkey through soft fields,
the crack of a pistol and the scattering of rooks. And the ever-
champing sheep only momentarily distracted by a rustling in the
reeds not occasioned by the breeze.

Places for concealment and silent, crepuscular or moonlit
conveyance abound, secreted in the banks of sewers, beneath the
big skies and the gaze of indifference.

One afternoon in the brightly lit and ever-so-modern Kent
archives in Maidstone I came across the handwritten transcript of
a testimony before the Court of Sessions, by a customs man, John
Love, from 1829, which read thus:

About midnight last night I saw a boat to northward of
mine and bore up and boarded her – I was nearly off Leaden
Spout. In bearing up I saw the boat letting go of tubs from
the starboard bow. On boarding her the boat smelt strongly
of liquor and she had two sinkers on deck ... for sinking
tubs. I took charge of the boat – the party now present [at

[2] I cannot account for the contradiction in terms: perhaps being 'short' and 'tall'
simultaneously was an eighteenth-century nonbinary status.

this juncture, a note in the transcript says, he points at the
defendant, Edward Taylor] was in the boat. I put off in my
own boat, and while rowing towards Leaden Spout I saw a
boat rowing off with two men toward a boat. The boat was the
'Olive Branch'. I asked the two men if they belonged to the
Olive Branch and they said they did.

I told them to go on board the Olive Branch & saw them
go on board. I had not seen them on board the Olive Branch
before that day. Their names are Thomas Baker and Edward
Abbot. I seized the boat & brought the three men to day to
Dover.

The court records being incomplete, it was impossible to say
what penalty, if any, was paid by Taylor, Baker and Abbot, or what
they forfeited, but the same bundle of documents reveals that the
quantity and quality of goods involved was staggering, regardless of
whether it was literally intoxicating.

And pity, or envy, poor Josephine Henry, arrested and prosecuted
in 1832 for handling goods which included:

> ... eleven brass buckles of the value of sixteen shillings and
> sixpence, twelve Buttons of the value of twelve shillings,
> thirty pairs of leather gloves of the value of two pounds five
> shillings, thirteen silk gauze handkerchiefs and six silk crape
> handkerchiefs of the value of two pounds ten shillings and
> sixpence, one silk gauze veil of the value of two shillings,
> two pieces containing seventy five yards of plain silk lace
> of the value of one pounds, and eighteen pieces containing
> two hundred and ten yards of silk gauze ribbon, and twenty
> four pieces containing three hundred yards of narrow silk
> ribbon of the value of four pounds five shillings, the said
> goods being all foreign manufacture, and amounting in
> the whole to the value of eleven pounds eleven shillings of
> lawful money...

Or Louise Desjardins, whose haul included:

one silk and velvet reticule, of the value of seven shillings,
and sixpence. Four cambric handkerchiefs of the value of
one pound and ten shillings, one cambric bag of the value of
five shillings, one worked net pelerine [a pelerine is a kind of
brocade fitted item that sits over the shoulders] of the value of
one pounds ten shillings, thirteen worked pelerines of the value
of seven pounds sixteen shillings, five worked net crowns for
caps, worked muslin, silk lace etc.

Smugglers were as fascinating to their law-abiding contemporaries
as they are to us, with our grandstand view of their times. Self-
mythologising gangs thrived on swagger and bragging, and would
pass their days in pubs, openly brandishing pistols, jeering and
threatening. And they had scary names like 'Nasty Face' and 'Towzer'.

That smugglers used the same psychology of fear and control that
characterises modern drug-gang violence is ghoulishly evident in
the sequences of events that led to the deaths of Daniel Chater and
William Galley, two more-or-less innocent men who were tortured
and killed with a Tarantino-esque degree of sadistic cruelty, which,
in the dying words of one of them (as he pleaded to be shot through
the head), represented nothing less than 'barbarous usage'.

The story lies, a little convolutedly, in a scheme hatched by two
gangs to 'rescue' a consignment of tea and spirits that had been
seized by revenue men from a boat in the Channel and taken to
Poole, way to the west of the Marsh, in Dorset.

The recovery being successfully accomplished, the gangs openly
made off with their booty, in broad daylight, even attracting
cheering and generally supportive crowds.

On their way to the caravan's final destination (the consignment
was to be broken up for onward sale), Daniel Chater, a shoemaker
who happened to be among onlookers, was spotted by one of the
gang members, John 'Dimer' Diamond, who knew him from field
labouring at harvest time, and threw him a small pack of tea in
friendly greeting.

After the authorities got wind of the apparent acquaintance
between Chater and Diamond, the cobbler was coerced into

becoming a key witness in the prosecution of the theft of two tons of tea and thirty casks of liquor, and on Valentine's Day 1748, he, accompanied by Galley, an elderly customs official and also a witness, set out for Chichester gaol, where Dimer was being held, with the intention that he should identify his former acquaintance.

On the way, the unlikely pair got lost, and sheltered at what one might today call a 'smuggler-friendly' pub,[3] the landlord of which alerted the Hawkhurst Gang – one of the outfits involved in the 'recovery scheme', some of whose members came to the pub and drank, seemingly amicably.

But when cobbler and customs man were asleep, the gang members decided to put paid to the threat of the evidence they might bring.

They abruptly woke the pair, who were spurred in face by the gang's leader, Jackson, before being dragged to a horse on which they were mounted, their legs tied beneath it, and continually whipped, all the time Jackson squeezing Galley's testicles.

After Galley had appeared to have died, he was shoved in a dug-out foxhole and buried in it, while Chater was chained for three days in a turf-house, continually whipped, his face slashed to the extent that his nose was severed, and his body thrown down a well.

Galley's corpse was discovered by a man walking his dog on the common; the body of Chater was found after one of the gang members turned King's evidence. Jackson died before he could be hanged. Five others ended up dead and gibbeted...

All of which is darkly chilling and of its time, but there are shops in Hastings from which, it is said, it's possible to buy a pack of Marlboro Lights on which the correct duty has yet to be paid. And on Dungeness (some do say), there are strange lights and signals seen, and small craft rolling up onto the shingle. And even, dare one say it, interior designers in Rye who might give a lift to a Friday night with a non-prescription dose of something tingly from far

[3] Then the White Hart Inn at Rowlands Castle. Now it is the Castle Inn, and dog-friendly. 'Bring your four-legged friends!' it exhorts.

away, blithely unconcerned by the Chaters and Galleys who may have been left in its wake.

Further, I read, in a comment piece produced by the University of Kent, 'While the UK orchid industry has, to a certain extent, been in decline even before Brexit reared its head, everything is now up in the air, with the potential to see an increase in smuggling.'

'It's tragically sad about the refugees,' said Yvonne, meaning the Iranians who had been picked up in the Channel the day before. It was, I agreed.

Some years ago, a photographer friend and I set out to document the razing, by the Mayor of Calais, of the 'Jungle', the unofficial migrant camp from where so many from across Africa, Asia and the Middle East set out to try to cross the Channel to make a life in the United Kingdom.

Our preparations had been cack-handed and the whole experience dust-strewn and deeply unsettling.

At the camp's outskirts, by the entrance, which was 'protected' by a seemingly endless line of police vans, we met a Canadian anarchist, who was, she said, an 'organiser', which made us feel naïve in the extreme for asking what it was that an anarchist organiser actually *organises* (By way of answer, she had shrugged way of answer, shrugged as if to say, 'What kind of planet are you people from?').

Close by, a farmer with a voice so lacking in hertz as to be almost subsonic, complained that all his tarpaulins, corrugated sheet and timber had been appropriated by those living 'over there', nodding to where, beyond an ineffectual barrier consisting of a three-foot-high earth wall, the camp lay.

As we walked over this dusty, dyke-like structure, a Spanish man wearing a vividly coloured Mohican crest screamed with rage. 'It makes me feel so FUCKING ASHAMED TO BE EUROPEAN', he said, tugging at his Mohican with frustration.

Nearby, a young Sudanese former medical student was sifting through the burnt wreckage of his tent, which, he said, had been set fire to by Afghans who accused the Sudanese of receiving favours from the authorities.

Around the camp, groups of young men, African and Middle Eastern, roamed in ill-fitting hand-me-down clothes, looking for any kind of escape. All of it was unspeakably, disconsolately, tragically sad.

'When I think of them,' said Yvonne, 'and the things that they must have experienced to put themselves through those journeys…'

And I thought of 'the great crye and grief of the inhabitants of the Ry and other places about the same', and I also thought that indeed, Yvonne deserves a very much more magnanimous title than chief clerk, or even chamberlain, for steering a course through dark and perilous swamplands of other people's souls.

19

Unwritten Chapters

On the slope of the desolate river among tall grasses I asked her, 'Maiden, where do you go shading your lamp with your mantle? My house is all dark and lonesome – lend me your light!' She raised her dark eyes for a moment and looked at my face through the dusk. 'I have come to the river,' she said, 'to float my lamp on the stream when the daylight wanes in the west.' I stood alone among tall grasses and watched the timid flame of her lamp uselessly drifting in the tide.

Gitanjali, Rabindranath Tagore, 1912

My experiences in West Bengal were coloured by the Indian government's attempts to introduce new laws that granted citizenship to anyone from a neighbouring country, unless they were Muslim. Prime Minister Narendra Modi had touted the law as a 'landmark day' for India. But it had caused great consternation among most of those that do not share his Hindu nationalist ideals.

Even friends I had met, whom in every other respect I found enviably intelligent, insightful and humane, supported the new law, which in Kolkata is seen by its proponents as an attempt to stop undocumented workers from Bangladesh claiming benefits that they 'shouldn't' be entitled to.

Those affronted by the law are not only Muslims who feel relegated by the 2019 Citizenship Amendment Act (CAA) to a lesser status than their compatriots, but also 'the Left', and others who regard the changes as a sideswipe at the rights and equalities enshrined in the constitution, hard fought for in their various ways by leaders such as Mahatma Gandhi, Jawaharlal Nehru and Subhas Chandra Bose.

And there's concern for the ethnic tribes in north-eastern areas such as Assam or Darjeeling, who have traditionally lived easily across borders and may not possess the now required proof of 'registration'.

Except where it is impassable in the Himalayas, there's an intrinsic fluidity to India's boundaries. As Radhika the Ph.D. candidate pointed out to me, in the Sundarbans 'the "border" runs through a shifting river. That means that there are islands that are sometimes in India, and sometimes in Bangladesh. There are houses that enjoy joint sovereignty!'

The notion of borders is a painful one because before 1947 there was only one Bengal, and, albeit that it was always religiously and ethnically and topographically diverse, there was a notion of, as Radhika describes it, 'brotherhood', transcending the fractures and shared agonies.

'On one day during the ten-day Durga Puja festival in September, the government of West Bengal blows a horn, and it is legal to cross the border. Technically, everyone is supposed to return to "their" side of the border by the evening, but they don't always,' she said.

On the day before I was due to fly back home there was a strike against the law called by the Chief Minister of West Bengal, Mamata Banerjee. I had no advance notice of it, but was awoken by the glaring absence of noise on College Street: it was as though perpetual motion had been brought to a halt. The dogs looked bored. The booksellers' booths were shuttered and the roads empty of rickshaws, bicycles and bicycle carts, scooters and lorries.

'Holiday?' I asked a man selling tea.

'Not holiday. *Hartal.*'

Soon a procession of demonstrators turned out with placards, loudspeakers and pamphlets to wage war against a slew of abbreviations, not all of which I'd caught up with.

'Say no to CAA.'

'No to NRI.'

'Down with CAB.'

But mostly they themselves were their only audience, everyone else catching up on sleep.

In England, the rich memories of Indian colours (parakeet greens, turmeric yellows, kingfisher blues and the ineffably deep, crepuscular violets of dying days) slowly subsiding, it was grim to hear about the violence that the CAA had elicited, with armed thugs rampaging, first through Delhi university campuses, singling out opponents of the law, threatening to trigger an age-old pattern of violence and reprisal.

On the plane I read an article in my (complimentary) *Economist* about a Chinese doctor arrested for 'startling' those around him with claims that a new virus had taken hold in his hospital – and within weeks the coronavirus had become the lead story, its corollaries and consequences usurping any other world event from the front, second, third and back pages of newspapers and websites and old-fashioned gossip mills.

National politics had been wholly eclipsed by a global emergency spawned and escaped from the cells of a bat, or a pangolin, or, it had been rumoured, a laboratory in Wuhan.

On 1 April 2020 I sent a message to Prasenjit, wondering how he and his family were doing.

'Sir we not now well at all … our India is lockdown due to Corona virus,' he said.

In the United States (the capital city of which is no less a swamp than it ever was), New Orleans was preparing for (non-meteorological) disaster. Cyprus had as good as closed its borders, both maritime and air. Adrian in Tulcea reported that he, and his gingerbread dachshund/Labrador cross, Schnapps, had barricaded themselves into their apartment. At this time of year, the Delta villages, Mila 23 and Letea, would be effectively blockaded by the out-of-season ferry services, I supposed.

And of course, my own marsh wings had perforce been clipped. Not before time, my publisher might say.

Had they not, I would have liked to have spent Easter in the company of Tollund Man, residing, since he was dug from a bog in 1950, at the museum at Silkeborg in Jutland. As I mentioned, some ninety-odd thousand words ago, Tollund's dark calm, and a kind of ageless wistfulness, had been among my favourite treasures found in my father's books, and the star attraction of P. V. Glob's *The Bog People*. (Elling Woman made me sad. And copper-haired Grauballe Man scared me.)

The poet Seamus Heaney, I think, felt the same draw in his own cast: 'Some day,' he wrote,

I will go to Aarhus
To see his peat-brown head,
The mild pods of his eye-lids
His pointed skin cap

In the flat country nearby
Where they dug him out,
His last gruel of winter seeds
Caked in his stomach

Naked except for
The cap, noose and girdle,
I will stand a long time
Bridegroom to the goddess...

I might have made that strange connection between childhood memory, and the present and a deeper past. I wonder what might have happened, and whether, as the prospect of a tiger sighting promised to, it would have disappointed. (What was his name? What were the last words he uttered? Why, despite cord tightly twisted around his neck, does he look as though he died at peace with himself? These were the questions that I remembered half forming as I'd tried to look beyond those 'mild pods'.)

Had I, as another schoolchild's 'favourite' poet wrote, world enough and time, I might have trotted from bog to bog in search of bodies, such as those in Heaney's Ireland, like Cashel Man, *twice* as old as Tollund, reputedly an Irish king killed because he failed to stop the failure of the crops. And darker stains on a nearer conscience, the border bodies, sacrifices to the Northern Irish Troubles.

Once sated on the mummified flesh of god-gobbled ancients, the Devil's Swamp of Florida beckoned, and the Sudanese Sudd, last known whereabouts of more Nile explorers than you could shake a paddle at, and the eerie forest marshes at the borders of Belarus and Ukraine. The Po Delta of Italy. The Camargue of France. And – were I brave enough – I might pay homage to Thesiger and Maxwell in the now mine-ridden (but thankfully rehydrating) marshes of southern Iraq. And what of the wetlands of Ethiopia – a directory of which I recently stumbled upon? And how much would I give to revisit all 'my' swamps and marshes and bogs again… The Finnish mires in cloudberry season, the Delta in February when the lakes and streams are frozen. The bayou in high, buggy summer when the alligators are hot and frisky…

And I'd like to check in on the Andreis in Sulina, especially the smaller Andrei with the west London accent, though I imagine that by now, only the slightest trace of it will remain. Indeed, I can assure you that I will.

As I mulled the book's denouement, it was clear that I'd be going nowhere soon, for here was the rub. On account of an ague of the first order, a week spent in the remnants of the Fens of East Anglia, or the British Library, was no more realistic a prospect than were the Hanging Gardens of Babylon to William Dugdale. Even a tramp across Romney Marsh, where the lambs were now gambolling and frogs are strengthening their tonsils for the next month's choral extravaganzas, might have ended with a police warning and a fine. (I know that Jim Pilcher has not survived my writing this book, by the way.)

All that remained for me to explore are Hollis's (or more rightly, my own) *Swamplands of the Soul*, around which all the while I've been skirting, and which make, in any event, for harder, darker excursions.

'To the Depths of the Cupboard and Back, a Journey of Shelf-Discovery', may be the final unwritten chapter of this book.

Don't mean to swamp you, but...

GENERAL

Books

Ash, Eric H., *The Draining of the Fens: Projectors, Popular Politics, and State Building in Early Modern England*, Baltimore, Maryland, Johns Hopkins University Press, 2017

Giblett, R., *Cities and Wetlands*, London, Bloomsbury Academic, 2016

Glob, P. V., *The Bog People: Iron Age Man Preserved*, London, Faber & Faber, 1969

Hollis, J., *Swamplands of the Soul: New life in Dismal Places*, Toronto, Canada, Inner City Books, 1996

Maxwell, Gavin, *A Reed Shaken by the Wind*, London, Longman, 1957

Thesiger, Wilfred, *The Marsh Arabs*, London, Longman, 1964

Articles and websites

Bonaccorsi, Luca, 'The Miracle of the Iraqi Marshlands', 2017 (accessed at: https://www.birdlife.org/middle-east/news/miracle-iraqi-marshlands)

Frost, Ruth Sterling, 'The Reclamation of the Pontine Marshes', *Geographical Review*, vol. 24, no. 4, 1934

Ramsar Convention, www.ramsar.org. The website of the Ramsar Convention, the mission of which is 'the conservation and wise use of all wetlands through local and national actions and international cooperation, as a contribution towards achieving sustainable development throughout the world', is a vast repository of information about the characteristics of wetlands recognised by the United Nations as being 'of international importance'.

Widmer, Ted, 'Draining the Swamp', *The New Yorker*, 19 January 2017 (accessed at: https://www.newyorker.com/news/news-desk/drain ing-the-swamp)

ROMNEY MARSH

Books

Carpenter, Edward, *Romney Marsh at War*, Stroud, Sutton Publishing Ltd, 1999

Clark, Kenneth Michael, *Smuggling in Rye and District*, Rye, Rye Museum, 1997

Derville, Max Teichman, *The Level and the Liberty of Romney Marsh in the County of Kent*, Ashford, Headley Bros Invicta Press, 1936

Dugdale, Sir William, *The History of Imbanking and Drayning of Divers Fenns and Marshes, both in forein parts and in this kingdom, and of the improvements thereby extracted from records, manuscripts, and other authentick testimonies*, printed by Alice Warren, London, 1662. Note: It is a shame that there does not exist an accessibly priced, nicely published edition of this classic – or, at least, not one that I can find. But digital versions can be accessed, such as the University of Michigan version: https://quod.lib.umich.edu/e/eebo/A36 795.0001.001?view=toc

Eddison, Jill, *Romney Marsh, Survival on a Frontier*, Stroud, Tempus, 2000

Finlayson, Iain, *The Sixth Continent – a Literary History of Romney Marsh*, New York, Atheneum, 1986

Ingoldsby, Thomas, *The Ingoldsby Legends*, London, R. Bentley & Son, 1881

Kaye-Smith, Sheila, *Joanna Godden*, London, Cassell & Co., 1921

Mayhew, Graham, *Tudor Rye*, Falmer Centre for Continuing Education, University of Sussex, 1987

Purseglove, Jeremy, *Taming the Flood*, London, William Collins, 2015

Websites, articles and online documents

Chin, T. and P. D. Welsby, 'Malaria in the UK: past, present, and future', *Postgraduate Medical Journal*, vol. 80, 2004, pp. 663–6

Dobson, Mary J., 'History of Malaria in England', *Journal of the Royal Society of Medicine*, Supplement No. 17, vol. 82, 1989

—, 'Contours of death: disease, mortality and the environment in early modern England', *Health Transition Review*, vol. 2, 1992

—, 'Death and Disease in the Romney Marsh Area in the 17th to 19th Centuries', OUCA Monograph 46, 1998

Romney Marsh Historic Churches Trust, https://romneymarshchurches. org.uk/. For anyone interested in the churches of Romney Marsh, this is a must.

Romney Marsh Internal Drainage Board, http://www.rmaidb.co.uk/. This website is quite a good source of historical and technical information about the Marsh.

'Romney Marsh Landscape Character Assessment Final Report 2016', Fiona Fyfe Associates (accessed at: https://www.folkestone-hythe. gov.uk/media/366/Romney-Marsh-Local-Character-Assessment/pdf/ Romney_Marsh_LCA_low_res._complete_final_report_April_2016. pdf?m=637001790067930000)

Romney Marsh Research Trust, http://rmrt.org.uk/. There is an embarrassment of riches (historical, archaeological, geological, geographical and more) to be found on this website. While the website is no longer updated, its trustees have allowed the research to remain freely available for posterity.

Siegel, Rudolph E. and F. N. L. Poynter, 'Robert Talbor, Charles II, and cinchona: a contemporary document', *Medical History*, vol. 6, no. 1, January 1962

Museums

Brenzett Aeronautical Museum, Ivychurch Rd, Brenzett, Romney Marsh, Kent, TN29 0EE

Dungeness Power Station Visitor Centre, EDF Dungeness B power station, Romney Marsh, Kent, TN29 9PX

Rye Museum and Rye Castle Museum, 3 East Street, Rye, East Sussex, TN31 7JY

THE DISMAL SWAMP

Beecher Stowe, Harriet, *Dred: A Tale of the Great Dismal Swamp, in Two Volumes*, Boston, Phillips, Sampson and Co., 1856

Berland, Kevin (ed.), *The Dividing Line Histories of William Byrd II of Westover*, University of North Carolina Press, 2016

Grandy, Moses, *The Narrative of the Life of Moses Grandy; Late a Slave in the United States of America*, London, C. Gilpin, 5, Bishopsgate-street, 1843 (available online at https://docsouth.unc.edu/fpn/grandy/grandy.html)

Library of Congress, https://www.loc.gov/resource/lhbcb.22884/?st=gall ery. William Byrd's plan to drain the Dismal Swamp can be found here.

Royster, Charles, *The Fabulous History of the Great Dismal Swamp*, New York, Knopf Doubleday Publishing Group, 2010

Sayers, Daniel O., *A Desolate Place for a Defiant People: The Archaeology of Maroons, Indigenous Americans, and Enslaved Laborers in the Great Dismal Swamp*, University Press of Florida, 2014

Simpson, Bland, *The Great Dismal: A Carolinian's Swamp Memoir*, University of North Carolina Press, 1990

Strother, David Hunter, 'The Dismal Swamp', *Harpers New Magazine*, 1856

Wilson, Robert Forest, *Crusader in Crinoline: The Life of Harriet Beecher Stowe*, University of Michigan, 1941

Wright, Louis B. and Marion Tinling (eds), *The Secret Diary of William Byrd of Westover, 1709–1712*, Richmond, Virginia, The Dietz Press, 1941

THE DANUBE DELTA

Useful resources in English on the Danube Delta appear to be thin on the ground. There is very much of interest in Tulcea in the Ethnography and Folklore Museum (Strada 9 Mai 2) and the Delta Aquarium (Strada 14 Noiembrie 1). But also see the following:

Bart, Jean (Eugeniu Botez), *Europolis* (as translated into French and published by Gabrielle Danoux, 2016)

Conybeare, Frederick C., *The Russian Dissenters*, Harvard University Press/Oxford University Press, 1921

Krehbiel, Edward, 'The European Commission of the Danube: An Experiment in International Administration', *Political Science Quarterly*, vol. 33, no. 1, 1918

Kozlovsky, Mirela, *A Study Of The Dobrogean Lipovan Russian Wedding Repertoire*, The Ovidius University of Constanta, 2004 (available at: http://icc-online.arte-ct.ro/vol_01/10.pdf)

Marin, Constantin, 'A Fishermen's Village: On the Lipovan Belongingness to the Danube Delta in Jurilovca (Northern Dobroudja)', *Sociologie Românească*, vol. 13, no. 1, 2015

Ramsar Convention, overview of the Danube Delta at: https://rsis.ramsar.org/ris/521

Van Assche, K. et al., 'Forgetting and remembering in the margins: Constructing past and future in the Romanian Danube Delta', *Memory Studies*, vol. 2, no. 2, 2009, pp. 211–34

LAPLAND

Eriksen, Thomas Hylland, Sanna Valkonen and Jarno Valkonen (eds), *Knowing From the Indigenous North, Sámi Approaches to History, Politics and Belonging*, London, Routledge, 2018. The essays in this book, to which Paivi Magga has contributed, constitute a wonderful introduction to the difference between Sámi and non-Sámi perception and ways of seeing the world.

Lönnrot, Elias, *Kalevala: The Epic of the Finnish People*, translated by Eino Friberg, London, Penguin Classics, 2021. Essential reading, or at least dipping into, for any trip to Lapland (unless you're a Finnish speaker, it's best to find a translation into your language of choice).

Luhta, Vesa, *Nature Guide to Inari Lapland and its Bird Sites*, Pohjoi-Lapin Matkailu Oy, 1998. When we were in Lapland, Ludo and I came within a hair's breadth of meeting the very well regarded Vesa Luhta.

University of Texas, https://www.laits.utexas.edu/sami/dieda/hist/sami-west.htm. This website, a project of the University of Texas, has some interesting information.

CYPRUS

Durrell, Lawrence, *Bitter Lemons*, London, Faber & Faber, 1957. While not extensively cited in this book, Lawrence Durrell's *Bitter Lemons* remains the classic work in English on the last days of British rule in Cyprus.

Morgan, Tabitha, *Sweet and Bitter Island: A History of the British in Cyprus*, London, IB Tauris, 2010

Salt lakes: on this subject, the following websites are helpful: http://www.orokliniproject.org/en/web-pages/oroklini-lake/13; http://www.akrotirimarsh.org/en/web-pages/akrotiri-marsh/1

State Archives of Cyprus, http://www.mjpo.gov.cy/mjpo/statearchive.nsf/index_en/index_en?OpenDocument. This is a good and edifying way of staying out of the sun.

ICELAND

Agricultural Museum of Iceland (of which Ragnhildur is now director), http://www.landbunadarsafn.is/frodleikur

Auden, W. H. and Louis MacNeice, *Letters from Iceland*, London, Faber & Faber, 2002. This is a 'must-read'.

Laxness, Halldor, *Under the Glacier*, Non Basic Stock Line, 2005

—, *The Atom Station*, Vintage Publishing, 2004

Ramsar Convention, https://rsis.ramsar.org/ris/2129. There is little literature on the subject of the hay meadows but this gives some information.

Smiley, Jane (ed.), *The Saga of the Icelanders*, London, Penguin, 2005. This is an example of the Icelandic sagas and there are many others.

CAJUN COUNTRY/CHITIMACHA

Books

There are many books about Cajun/Louisiana history – a visit to any bookshop in New Orleans or elsewhere in the state yields a profusion of local history books. Here are some resources that helped me.

Barry, John M., *Rising Tide: The Great Mississippi Flood of 1927 and How It Changed America*, New York, Simon & Schuster, 1997

Blackbird, Leila K., *Entwined Threads of Red and Black: The Hidden History of Indigenous Enslavement in Louisiana, 1699–1824*, University of New Orleans, 2018

Choyce, Lesley, *Nova Scotia: Shaped by the Sea*, London, Penguin, 1997

Longfellow, H. W., *Evangeline, A Tale of Acadie*, CreateSpace Independent Publishing Platform, 2014

Richard, Zachary, *The History of the Acadians of Louisiana*, University of Louisiana, illustrated edition, 2013

Rushton, William Faulkner, *The Cajuns: from Acadia to Louisiana*, New York, Farrar Straus & Giroux, 1970

Swanton, John R., *Indian Tribes of the Lower Mississippi Valley*, Dover, 2013 (first published 1911)

Websites, articles and museums

Cajun music: YouTube is a fantastic source of leads for Cajun music and zydeco. My favourite remains 'La Valse De Riceville', Nathan Abshire and The Rayne-Bo Ramblers, 1935.

Chitimacha People, http://www.chitimacha.gov (and of course, if you're visiting, its museum)

Tabasco Museum, https://www.tabasco.com/visit-avery-island/. This is a small but interesting museum at Avery Island, home of tabasco pepper sauce. The gardens are quite beautiful, but the surfeit of merchandising and underwhelming canteen let down the tone.

Treme, TV series, https://www.hbo.com/treme. This gives a great sense of the vitality of New Orleans as it struggled to recover from Hurricane Katrina.

Usner, Daniel H., Jr., ' "They Don't Like Indian Around Here": Chitimacha Struggles and Strategies for Survival in the Jim Crow South', *Native South*, vol. 9, 2016, pp. 89–124, https://muse.jhu.edu/article/628230

SUNDARBANS

On account of the uniqueness and importance of the Sundarban mangrove, the Sundarbans have been extensively studied and there is copious literature in scientific journals, as a search in such publications will quickly reveal. Also see the following:

Bhargava, M., 'Forests, Wild Beasts and Supernatural Powers: A Folk Tale from Sundarbans', *Indian Folklore*, Serial no. 8, January 2008

Chattopadhyaya, Haraprasad, *The Mystery of the Sundarbans*, Calcutta, A. Mukherjee, 1999.

Chowdhury, Arabinda et al., 'Stigma of Tiger Attack: Study of tiger-widows from Sundarban Delta', *Indian Journal of Psychiatry*, vol. 58, no. 1, 2016

Ghosh, Amitav, *The Hungry Tide*, London, Borough Press, 2016. This novel marvellously captures issues relating to recent history and the sense of place.

Halder, Deep, *Blood Island: An Oral History of the Marichjhapi Massacre*, HarperCollins India, 2019

Hamilton, Sir Daniel, *The Soul of India*, paper read by Sir Daniel Hamilton at an All-India Co-operative Conference held in Calcutta on 28 December 1934

—, *Federation and Co-operation*, paper read by Sir Daniel Hamilton at the Co-operative Conference held in Gosaba on 4 and 5 February 1939

Mukhopadhyay, Amites, *Cyclone Aila and the Sundarbans: An Enquiry into the Disaster and Politics of Aid and Relief*, eSocialSciences, 2015

Scottish Centre of Tagore Studies, https://scotstagore.org/. This website gives more information on Sir Daniel Hamilton, and Rabindranath Tagore, of course.

Tagore, Rabindranath, and William Radice (editor, translator), *Rabindranath Tagore, Selected Poems*, Penguin, London, 2005

—, *Rabindranath Tagore, Selected Short Stories*, Penguin, London, 2005. As regards the works of Rabindranath Tagore, they're so voluminous that it's difficult to suggest where to start, but perhaps the two books listed above would be a good route.

Tagore's songs (Rabindra Sangeet) are widely recorded. Amongst those considered 'truest' to their author's intent are the interpretations by Iman Chakraborty. For a male voice, those sung by Rupankar Bagchi, known as Rupankar, are more soulful but less saccharine than others.

Acknowledgements

This book is really about people, alive and once living, the worlds that they inhabit or inhabited, have had thrust upon them and made the best of, or created for themselves. So, first I'd like to thank and acknowledge all those upon whose lives this book is built, whether on Romney Marsh, the swamps of Louisiana, in the delta of the Danube, the marshes and salt lakes of Cyprus, and all the other places the writing of *Swamp Songs* took me over the course of the years it took me to complete.

I'd like also to extend some special thanks:

On Romney Marsh, to Rob Monje, Dave, Les Ramsden and the late Jim Pilcher; in Iceland, to Ragnhildur Jónsdóttir; in Finland, to *Päivi Magga*, and in Louisiana, to Dean Wilson, 'the Basin Keeper', and Kimberly Walden, Cultural Director for the Chitimacha Nation.

The chapters on the Danube Delta could not have been written without the companionship, cheer and insight of the indomitable Adrian Cnezivici. In Cyprus, it was great fun as ever hanging out with Jimmy Roussounis (and Isabel, Alexia, Denis and Marina); in the Sundarbans, I think I would have got approximately nowhere without the assistance of Prasenjit Mandal – while the trip to West Bengal was enhanced in significance beyond measure by the accidental friendship made with Kousik and Sonali Bose – and with Ayanangsha Maitra.

Thank yous also to Tim Bates, my agent at Peters, Fraser and Dunlop, for, as ever, his impeccable judgement; to Michael Fishwick, for the timely insertion of a flea (in the ear); to Lauren Whybrow for all her help, to Kate Quarry for her excellent and much needed editing, and to Isabella Steer for early encouraging words…

On the home front, thank you Marie, for indulging me my absences; and Mark Cusick for bearing with me. (And Ludo, for putting me right on a few things…)

A Note on the Type

The text of this book is set Adobe Garamond. It is one of several versions of Garamond based on the designs of Claude Garamond. It is thought that Garamond based his font on Bembo, cut in 1495 by Francesco Griffo in collaboration with the Italian printer Aldus Manutius. Garamond types were first used in books printed in Paris around 1532. Many of the present-day versions of this type are based on the *Typi Academiae* of Jean Jannon cut in Sedan in 1615.

Claude Garamond was born in Paris in 1480. He learned how to cut type from his father and by the age of fifteen he was able to fashion steel punches the size of a pica with great precision. At the age of sixty he was commissioned by King Francis I to design a Greek alphabet, and for this he was given the honourable title of royal type founder. He died in 1561.

A Note on the Type